Madison Jones'
GARDEN OF INNOCENCE

For SHAILAH

Madison Jones'
GARDEN OF

Edited by
Jan Nordby Gretlund

University Press of Southern Denmark 2005

INNOCENCE

© The Authors and the University Press of Southern Denmark 2005
Printed by Narayana Press
Cover design by Anne Charlotte Mouret, UniSats
ISBN 87-7674-001-3

University Press of Southern Denmark
Campusvej 55
5230 Odense M
Denmark

www.universitypress.dk

Costumers in the United States and Canada please contact:

International Specialized Book Services
920 NE 58th Ave. Suite 300
Portland, OR 97213
Phone 503-287-3093 or 1-800-944-6190
Fax 503-280-8832

www.isbs.com

CONTENTS

Madison Jones's Vision of Innocence and Experience
by the editor 7

A Return to the Garden of Innocence:
Upon Receiving the T. S. Eliot Award for Creative Writing
by Madison Jones 24

The Uncanny World of *The Innocent*
by Lewis A. Lawson 32

A Declaration of Independence: *Forest of the Night*
by George Garrett 61

Cleansing the House: Race and Culture in *A Cry of Absence*
by Jewel Spears Brooker 71

Nobody Is Innocent:
Season of the Strangler and the Short Story Sequence
by Hans H. Skei 93

Country Innocence: *To the Winds*
by Jan Nordby Gretlund 110

The Innocent Stare at the Civil War:
Nashville 1864: The Dying of the Light
by David Madden 125

A Response to David Madden's Essay
by Madison Jones 140

Sympathy for the Devil: A Reading of *Herod's Wife*
by Richard Gray *143*

'Out of the Garden, forever':
Interviews with Madison Jones *158*

A Madison Jones Bibliography
by Jan Nordby Gretlund and Thomas Ærvold Bjerre *184*

Contributors *197*

Index *201*

Acknowledgements *207*

MADISON JONES'S VISION OF INNOCENCE AND EXPERIENCE

Madison Percy Jones (1925 –) is the only writer of the Nashville Agrarian movement still alive today. He is a product of Vanderbilt's conservative environmentalism, which he in his youth combined with a good deal of T.S. Eliot's thinking and made his mental heritage. He is a central figure in American literature, but paradoxically not very well-known. He remained transfixed in the shadow of the success of William Faulkner, Robert Penn Warren, William Styron, and the many other literary giants of his youth. Neither his eleven novels nor John Frankenheimer's movie of Jones' *An Exile* have brought him much popular recognition in his own country. Jones also remains almost unknown abroad, in spite of several excellent translations of individual novels.

Jones is *not* a deeply religious writer like his friends Flannery O'Connor and Marion Montgomery, but in all his fiction Jones has in realistic terms written about the presence of good and evil in man, in a classic Greek sense. Like his fellow-writers George Garrett and David Madden, who both have contributed to this volume, Jones has been preoccupied with the presence of the past in our present and its influence on our modern 'vacua' lives.

It has been for his lasting topics and preoccupations that Jones has been singled out for praise by literary critics, such as Monroe K. Spears, Lewis P. Simpson, and Ashley Brown, who tend to see Jones as the most important transitional figure between the generation born at the turn of the century and the Southern writers of today. Jones succeeded in finding his own language, characters, and images to create and recreate his existence, time, and experience. According to testimonies by contemporary writers, his achievement has become an example and a lesson in the possibility of the immediate. This is especially true for Madison Smartt Bell, Larry Brown, William Hoffman, and Lee Smith.

As the bibliography in this volume demonstrates, *not* sufficiently many have realized Jones' importance for the development of our society and its reflection in literature. There have been numerous fine essays and dissertations, but no book of criticism has so far been published in the United States or elsewhere on Madison Jones' achievement. We are proud to remedy this with our collection and invite readers to read Madison Jones' fiction.

★ ★ ★

Madison Jones has spent most of his life in the South and his fiction is set there. When Jones was thirteen, his father bought a farm twenty-five miles north of Nashville, and the boy spent every summer there until he was grown. At eighteen he worked on the farm for almost two years before enrolling at Vanderbilt University. There he studied under poet and critic Donald Davidson, whose lectures have had a lasting influence on him. It was in 1948 at Vanderbilt that Jones broke into print in the *Gad-Fly* with a story called "The Red Bird." After graduating with a B.A., Jones returned to the farm in Cheatham County, where for nearly a year he considered becoming a farmer. When he writes about "setting, topping or suckering" plants in the tobacco patch, it is based on his experience of tobacco growing, and the passages about horses in his novels are based on experience as a trainer of Tennessee walking horses.

Returning to school, this time to the University of Florida in Gainesville, Jones was taught by Andrew Lytle, novelist and critic. Under his guidance he specialized in creative writing and received his M.A. (1951) and stayed in Florida to do further graduate work. During the early fifties his stories in *Perspective* and the *Sewanee Review* began to win Jones notice. While serving his apprenticeship, he maintained himself by teaching first at Miami University, Ohio (1953-54), and then at the University of Tennessee, Knoxville (1955-56). Between these assignments, he received a *Sewanee Review* Fellowship and spent a year in Florida writing most of his first novel. After 1956 he taught at Auburn, Alabama, where he became writer in residence.

Jones's literary heritage has been the Agrarian movement. He has absorbed fully and somewhat pessimistically the Agrarian concerns of

Donald Davidson, Andrew Lytle, Allen Tate, John Crowe Ransom, and Robert Penn Warren. In the present generation of writers, Jones is the most notable proponent of their traditional ideals. He depends largely on established conflicts between the native and the alien, the old and the new, tradition and "progress," good and evil, and he is an Agrarian in practice as well as theory. On a piece of land twenty miles north of his home at Auburn, Jones keeps a herd of Hereford cattle. At times he writes there in a rock-and-log cabin that he built with his sons.

The split life of farming and teaching is reflected in his fiction. His eleven books are not attempts at creating a Tennessee Yoknapatawpha, but they do constitute an extensive chronicle of the South, and homogeneity of theme makes them cohere as a body of fiction. While Jones is concerned about the encroachment of the New South on old values, he is even more concerned with the concepts of innocence and guilt. His protagonists come to grief because they follow the optimistic philosophies of idealists such as Jean Jacques Rousseau or Thomas Jefferson. Jones believes that evil has an absolute existence and that man needs God's grace to be delivered from evil. About the general nature of his work he has said, "On a more obvious level, my fiction is concerned with the drama of collision between past and present, with emphasis upon the destructive elements involved. More deeply, it deals with the failure, or refusal, of individuals to recognize and submit themselves to inevitable limits of the human condition."

In Jones's first novel, *The Innocent* (1957), Duncan Welsh returns to his father's farm in Tennessee after seven years in the North. Profoundly dissatisfied with the materialistic nature of life in the North, where he has had an unsuccessful newspaper career and equally unsuccessful marriage, he settles on his inherited land, trying to rediscover the uncomplicated life he remembers from his childhood. But the forces of "progress" have also reached his native area, and they confront Duncan from the moment he returns. In a wrestling match at a fair, he sees a farm boy killed by Tiger Sloan, a professional wrestler. The incident, in which the boy dies because Sloan employs a new style of wrestling, prefigures Duncan's defeat in his battle against the encroachment on the old ways of specialization and mechanization. Nature is rapidly retreating in the Tennessee of the novel; and with the "renewing" occasioned by industry, there is little space for independent men. Lewis A. Lawson's contribution to this volume, "The Uncanny World of *The Innocent*," offers a detailed psychoanalytic reading of Jones's first novel. The Freudian interpretation deepens our understanding of the controlling role of the uncanny in the life and death of the protagonist.

Change has come to the South, and Duncan cannot stop it. He tries to uphold ideals that the past had held untouchable, so he will not be perverted into casting off his own nature. He devotes himself to the restoration of the large but worn-out farm, and above all, he works to save from extinction the once famous Mountain Slasher breed of Tennessee walking horse. It is a breed of horse that has been replaced by the more elegant Allen breed, which is preferred by the *nouveaux riches* of the area. His attempt to preserve the Mountain Slasher bloodline is also an attempt to preserve his own past. All his values are summed up in the colt Chief, which gives him hope, but the colt grows to be a stallion that belongs in the virgin wilderness. The horse is uncontrollable and is shot by Dickie Jordan, who is of a family of Allen horse breeders. Duncan's monomaniacal work with horses has isolated him from the community. When he allies himself with Aaron McCool, a depraved moonshiner, Duncan knows that he has lost his fight. His doom is inevitable and like his stallion he seems to belong to "a vanishing bloodline." Jones's first novel is finally deeply pessimistic, for the old ways prove irrecoverable.

The Innocent is a disturbing novel even today, almost fifty years after its publication, and it is still good reading because it is an expression of good craftsmanship. Few first novels are as soundly constructed, and the evocation of woods and fields, and horses and men, is perfect. The novel is full of powerful images, convincing characters, and dramatic scenes. While Jones was criticized for cluttering his novel with scenes and characters and for attempting to do too much, these remain minor flaws in a moving affirmation of Agrarian values. *The Innocent* is a first novel that made it plain that a major talent was on the scene. In a review of the novel Robert Penn Warren wrote: "Madison Jones has written an intensely interesting story, and one that clearly declares his talent."

In his second novel, *Forest of the Night* (1960), Jones goes back to the early 1800s and follows a young man into the Tennessee wilderness and down the Natchez Trace. Jonathan Cannon, who seems to personify American innocence, wants to establish a school in order to bring "light" into the forest of the frontier. The novel rejects the New Eden myth, and it also rejects the notion of man's innate moral nature. Ignorant of the ways of wild animals, Indians, outlaws, and pioneers, Jonathan discovers that his idealized virgin forest, during the progress of "civilization," has become a forest of the night. In the climate of hopelessness he succumbs to his desire for a girl who lives in the forest. He does not know that she has been the lover of the notorious Harpe brothers, outlaws who operate along the Natchez Trace. Because Jonathan bears an uncanny resemblance to the younger Harpe brother, he is finally pursued by the people he has set out to help and educate.

Novelist George Garrett's essay on Jones's second novel, "A Declaration of Independence," (included in this volume) deals with it from a writer's point of view and in the context of Jones's other novels. And he sees *Forest of the Night* as "a dark story set in a dark world," but with an ending "not without some solace." As in his first novel, Jones describes the shock of an idealist who is faced with the reality of innate human depravity. There is no room for innocent visionaries in this world, and there is little comfort in the fact that the pioneers endure. *Forest of the Night* seems to have been too pessimistic in its portrayal of mankind's degradation to become popular. Yet, as John M. Bradbury said of the novel, "Jones's linguistic power and ability to evoke the concrete image of living reality raises his allegory far above the common run of historically based fiction." There is not a more revealing exposé in American literature of the truly unromantic nature of pioneer life. It is perhaps Jones's best novel.

Jones's third novel, *A Buried Land* (1963), is set in the valley of the Tennessee River at the time when the Tennessee Valley Authority flooded the lowlands of Tennessee and northern Alabama. The destruction by water of a community plays a central role in the novel, which protests the loss of identity and memory through the inundation. Jones rages against the betrayers of the past who allowed the flooding of the valleys; he sees it as the last outrage against ancient modesty. The main character is the callous Percy Youngblood, who works for the TVA even though his family is to lose their ancestral farm to the waters. As in his first two novels, Jones is concerned with the integrity of individuals and communities in the face of change. The Youngblood family breaks up when industry comes to Tennessee. But this does not worry Percy, who concentrates on his seduction of Cora Kincaid. The young woman dies at the hands of a Nashville abortionist, and she is buried secretly in the old cemetery, which is soon to be flooded. The end of the ballad-type plot is that Percy leaves, makes a career for himself as a lawyer, and returns to the area convinced that his past is buried.

Fowler Kincaid is the dead girl's brother and the most interesting character in the novel. Like Aaron McCool in the first novel, Fowler believes in freedom without obligations and will defend that right with savage brutality, if necessary. It seems that every novel by Jones has at least one character that displays the naked visceral hatred of any authority. Fowler tries to discover what happened to his sister. Percy is haunted by his conscience, attempts to escape the responsibility for his past, and turns against his family and friends. He panics, kills Fowler, breaks down, and confesses to his mother. Percy realizes that the destruction of his ancestral home parallels his own spiritual bankruptcy. It is obvious that Jones is furious with outsiders who destroyed his native area and with local people who would not even help with the removal of the remains of their ancestors, but Percy's existential rebellion against "the impossible lack of proportion in things" is rendered with calmness and subtlety. After she had finished reading *A Buried Land,* Flannery O'Connor told Jones that, although she liked all his books, this one impressed her the most. She also told him that she had read the story carefully, wishing she could write with such "conciseness and force."

In the mid-sixties Jones wrote a picaresque comedy, "Tales of Dixie," which borders on farce. With the exception of two sections, "Home Is Where the Heart Is" and "A Modern Case," the manuscript has not been published.[1] One of the unpublished episodes deals with a young novelist who has been hired by a Northern newspaper to report on civil rights demonstrations in Mississippi. It is primarily a satire on Northern ideas of what was happening in the South at the time. The published fragments show what Jones can do in a humorous vein and look forward to the comedy of the first chapters of *To The Winds*.

An Exile (1967) has been Jones's greatest popular success to date. John Frankenheimer made it into a film called *I Walk the Line*. Columbia Pictures decided to use the title of the country song, which lends atmosphere to the film. Mèrimèe's *Carmen* was the inspiration for the short novel, and the plot has a similar classical simplicity. Sheriff Hank Tawes is torn between loyalty to his office and his passion for a bootlegger's daughter. He ought to arrest bootleggers, but he is looking for a way to change his life and believes for a short time that he has found it in Flint McCain's bootlegger camp. Although he is unhappily married and bored with his life, there seems to be no good reason why Sheriff Tawes should strip himself of all the virtues he has defended for years. Yet, this "good man" abandons honor and duty to cover for the liquor traffic.

Sheriff Tawes is a believable person; he displays the frailties of mankind, and there is tragedy in his fate. His motives are not sexual, but he sees the woman as a chance to escape from a world which has lost all sense of moral innocence. Tawes is modern man who, faced with evil, decides to seek the peace that follows self-destruction. As in earlier Jones novels, the protagonist is caught in a web spun partly by his own actions, but he is primarily the victim of his human heritage. The low-keyed psychological portrait of human weakness deserves its success, and the problems of the physical passion and moral disintegration of an aging man are expressed with great skill, and *An Exile* is an exciting novel on the ambiguities of life. Jones is supposed to have declared that he himself should have acted the part of Sheriff Tawes in the film. This is said to have been upon seeing his friend James Dickey act the part of Sheriff Bullard in the film version of *Deliverance*. As it was, the part of Sheriff Tawes was played by Gregory Peck.

Jones considers his fifth novel, *A Cry of Absence* (1971), his best book. It is set in a Southern town during the civil rights struggle and is an attempt at providing an objective statement on the South and its main problem. In his review of the novel, Monroe K. Spears called the action "austere, powerful, and inexorable as any in Greek drama, and as evocative of both pity and terror." It depicts the old conflict between family affection and duty to the law. The dilemma is that for one kind of right to be achieved, much of value must be destroyed. Ames Glenn and his mother Hester Cameron Glenn are at the center of the plot: the body of a black civil rights agitator is found in Cameron Springs, and Ames discovers that his brother Cam is one of the killers. When their mother learns of the murder, she is quick to blame the killing on "white trash." She has always romanticized the past and idealized her aristocratic family. And this is the special Southern innocence regarding the historical past that Jewel Spears Brooker writes about in "The House of Innocence," her contribution to this volume. It is an essay devoted to *A Cry of Absence* and Hester's attempt to cleanse her ancient Southern edifice that is contaminated by moral pollution. She does not fully succeed in purifying "the house" due to the presence of evil incarnate and triumphant. But, as Brooker points out, Hester's only surviving son will rent "the house" for now, for Ames has a vague idea that "since a spirit that had lived once could live again" – much more than this was perhaps recoverable.

The Cameron Glenns is one of the old families in town, and there is tension between them and newcomers. Among the newcomers are the Delmores, a family of industrialists, who intend to make the town over, and they do not see anything worth preserving. In the name of "equality" they want to break all links to the past of Cameron Springs, even "the tenuous threads of common memory." When she finally accepts Cam's guilt, Hester hints that it would be better for him to commit suicide. It has shocked her to discover that her own son believed she would consider murder to be within "moral" bounds in the present situation. In the final part of the novel, Hester realizes that it was her uncritical identification with the past that her son had totally misinterpreted, and she accepts her responsibility for his evil deed.

The triumph of the novel is that Jones manages to make the reader understand why Hester reacts as she does. Her fatal flaw is that she has been blind to the moral ills of the past and therefore can only be partially aware of ills in her own time. She does not fully realize that blind racism, here personified by Hollis Handley, is also a part of the tradition she passed on. Handley seems closely related to Aaron Mc-Cool, Fowler Kincaid, and Flint McCain of the earlier novels; and it is with Pike Handley, a representative of sinister poor whites, that Cam commits the murder. Ames does what he has to do, although it leads to the deaths of his mother and brother. His loyalties are divided, but he does not repudiate his heritage, he accepts full knowledge of the past, so he can avoid contributing to the evil of his own time. *A Cry of Absence* was well received by the critics.

The discovery of the existence of evil by an "innocent" young man is also the theme of *Passage through Gehenna* (1978). But in this novel Jones writes with a greater compassion, and with the savage ironic humor usually associated with Flannery O'Connor. *A Buried Land* and *A Cry of Absence* are topical novels. *Passage* is, however, a timeless allegory; of the earlier novels it is akin to *Forest of the Night*. The novel is set in the small river town of Hallsboro, Tennessee. Although Jones creates an Old-Testament world, the rural characters smoke as much pot as their cosmopolitan neighbors do. The scene is set for a clash between modern ways and traditional values. The novel focuses on the testing of Jud Rivers, who is brought up in the Church of Christ, one of the fundamentalist churches in the Tennessee hills. The stern religion of Jud's childhood emphasized rectitude at the expense of love, and the novel traces his struggle to liberate himself from his early training in order to be capable of loving.

Jud must also come to terms with evil in the form of Lily Nunn, a modern witch doing the devil's work. She hopes to prove to Jud that all Christians of Hallsboro are hypocrites. Ultimately, Lily's efforts cost the lives of Salter, a fundamentalist preacher, and Hannah Rice, who is in love with Jud. The uneasy relationship between fundamentalism and sexuality leads to a good deal of comedy when Jud tries to stare down his libido. He discovers that his impulses run counter to the morality he has been taught and seeks refuge in the world of the flesh. Yet, through Hannah's self-sacrifice, Jud makes it through his Gehenna. Like other Jones protagonists, he is caught in a trap only partly of his own making, but unlike the situations in earlier novels, the hero is here offered a chance to recognize his condition before it is too late. Repentant, he is allowed to tell his story as a memory, and Jud is finally at least capable of love.

Season of the Strangler (1982) depicts both continuity and change in the South. It is a short story cycle with the effect of a novel, in the manner of Sherwood Anderson's *Winesburg, Ohio;* William Faulkner's *Go Down, Moses;* and Eudora Welty's *The Golden Apples.* There are twelve interrelated stories; together they make up the tale of the long hot summer of 1969 in the fictive town of Okaloosa, Alabama. In spite of the title, the stranglings are relatively unimportant and may be read as symbolic incidents that frame the everyday life in town. The central motif of the strangler links the twelve portraits of black and white, old and young, men and women, and Jones makes it clear that nobody is innocent and above all that we "strangle" ourselves. There are the old men who realize they are not wanted in their families; young men who do not live up to their parents' expectations; frustrated wives who attempt to live double lives; and panicky middle-aged men and women who realize they have wasted most of their lives. When the summer is over, the murders stop, Okaloosa is dropped from the headlines, and no evidence that might have led to the strangler's identity ever appears.

The stories detail individual roads to spiritual bankruptcy. Mr. Cecil Peck, in "Break," is the owner of the local shoe store and a henpecked husband. But one day as he is holding a woman's foot, he has a vision and it changes his life. Like another Francis Macomber, he rebels against his domestic role and his short yappy wife. At first he satisfies himself by frightening her into believing that he might be the strangler. This is a sadistic enjoyment of the ability to terrify that he shares with others in town. (The cycle can be read as a study of fear.) Finally he liberates himself by moving out of his home. The fate of Mr. Cecil Peck is rendered with an irony worthy of Sherwood Anderson, and Jones's compassion for the shoe-store owner is unmistakable. "Familiar Spirit," the last story in the book, is about young people, the War Between the States, and the difficulty of preserving a commitment to the past. The skirmish that Douglas Bragg witnesses is between his mother and grandfather over integration. In a comic scene, he sends his bugle-blowing grandfather into a meeting of the local "Interracial Dialogue Group." The story ends as Douglas tries to invoke the scene of the Okaloosa Creek skirmish and fails: "There was something missing, something needed to focus things the way a memory did." This is Jones's only War story before *Nashville 1864: The Dying of the Light* (1997), which is surprising as he grew up with a grandfather who loved to tell him about the War.

There is a noticeable development in Jones's narrative technique over the years. In *Season of the Strangler* tension is still a primary consideration, yet he is willing to risk the "loose moment" in several stories. And they gain from the willingness to leave the reader time for the individual imagination to cooperate through a moment's relief. Hans H. Skei's essay, "Nobody Is Innocent," deals with Jones's book as a short story sequel. Skei points out just "how creative and productive the tension is between individual stories and the whole." He sees the darkness in the book as pervasive, but not as impenetrable, as the story is finally "a product of the human spirit." There is also a noteworthy development in Jones's attitude toward his fellow man from the pessimism of *The Innocent,* through a growing optimism in *Passage through Gehenna,* to the nuanced, complex, and compassionate vision of *Season of the Strangler.*

Wendell Corbin's existential situation is the subject of *Last Things* (1989). He is desperately looking for relief from his vexation with the "clowns, fools, self-deceivers, serviceable knaves" about him in graduate school. The novel starts in a comic vein with a convincing satire on life at a university, but the tone gradually darkens. Wendell rejects his poor-white family as luckless morons; not one of his ancestors had ever amounted to anything, so there is no Edenic Southern past, no garden of innocence, for him to build on when he contemplates his future. When he finally takes an interest in somebody else, it is his neighbor's wife. He studies Tricia Harker because he is writing a domestic comedy about her aristocratic mother-in-law. What fascinates him, besides her sexual appeal, is that she reads Nietzsche for pleasure. As he sees it, she "befuddles herself" with "the oracles of that old vapor-wit Zarathustra." Wendell consciously rejects Nietzsche's ideas, but he comes to embody them. It is hilarious when he seduces Tricia by quoting Nietzsche in a husky voice accompanied by Wagner's "Liebestod." But the serious issue is the battle between pride and humility, and the critical moment for his soul occurs when he imagines with pleasure that Mrs. Harker is listening to the seduction of her daughter-in-law. It is one of the virtues of the novel that Jones remains aware of the tragicomedy of most situations.

In his attempt to leave his background behind, Wendell tries to become the first *rich* Corbin. He turns to Jason Farrow, the local Pontiac dealer, who traps him into working in big-time drug trafficking. Farrow, who controls the town, is described as toadlike and is no doubt evil personified. Jones insists on the physical presence of the devil himself. His fellows in crime constitute "a true cross-section of the Genus Americanus" and corruption and evil pervade all levels of society. There are forces around him that could possibly save the young man from doing the devil's work: traces of feeling for his father, the fundamentalist faith of an "oversized God-crazy" revivalist, and a slow realization of the moral magnitude of Mrs. Harker. Wendell is ordered by Farrow "to put a hush on that old bitch," and he does so by having her murdered. The revivalist advises Wendell to repent, and he ends up confessing his darkest secret. Towards the end of the novel we see him, vision impaired, passing out handbills announcing the tent-revival. When he visits his father, Wendell begins to regain his sight. By giving him a sign of recognition the old man seems to forgive his son, but the sign is ambiguously in the shape of a hand that wants to hold a reefer. Drugs, for which Wendell has caused two deaths, invade the relationship between father and son.

It is no surprise that Wendell snaps out of his moral paralysis and purges himself of evil. But how did he come to be the right hand of the devil? *Last Things* details the growth of a mind from innocence to evil experience. This is what is so unusual about the book, it focuses on how an ordinary boy's mind deteriorates from a measure of lust, greed, and misogyny, through sadism, to the point where he has a craving for another's death. In this development drugs are the instrument of the devil. But drugs are only incidental to what happens to Wendell; the cocain is new (and topical), but the existential curse and spiritual emptiness are age-old last things. Focus is on life lived by a hollow man, a man who seems trapped in a game of which he does not know the rules. In a psychological portrait in the Edgar Allan Poe tradition, Jones masterfully describes Wendell's downfall by staying exclusively in his mind, and with this theme Jones is in the mainstream of the best literature. The novel ends, as it must, with searing pain, guilt, and remorse.

Though he has found himself "unable to believe with the absoluteness of the Christian," Jones has always been profoundly interested in ideas of innocence and evil. Evil is an ever-present characteristic of life in his fiction, and so is the violence that its presence often leads to. And the discovery of the existence of inexplicable evil is one of the hard lessons for most of his characters. *To the Winds* (1996) is a novel narrated in a Huck-Finn voice of innocence, in which Jones expresses the facts through a country boy's vision so that they reflect *his* perspective both then and now. This is a new narrative technique for Jones, which offers an opportunity to invent a changing psychology and show the process of realization. In its account of "what-all-happened" to a family, his story goes beyond childhood joys and worries. When he is faced with the reality of innate depravity, the youngest of the Moss brothers loses his moral innocence. But first he has to become aware of evil, accept its existence, and realize its absoluteness in his immediate environment.

Jones's theme of a farming community superseded by an industrialized society is brought out, and again the deprived farmers prove no match for the pushy intruders; so traditional lives, minds, and relationships disintegrate in the face of the "world of progress." In the essay below on this novel the editor of the collection writes about "Country Innocence" and the clash between the farming family's traditional way of life and the increasingly cityfied life-style in Clayton County. The failure of the farmers to recognize and accept the limits imposed on their present existence speeds up the disintegration of their family. In this way *To the Winds* becomes an expression of an Agrarian mode of thinking. With the final days of the Moss family as an illustration, the novel details the outrage committed against the ancient life of the farmer. Rejected by the town and pursued by the law, they find themselves isolated and bankrupt, also emotionally. The way they had thought, acted, and lived in the family through the generations is now obsolete and thrown to the winds. Although the new world that has come to surround them seems insubstantial, the changes are real enough, as they learn, for the new world proves a frightening place for country people who do not fit in. Finally the novel reads as Jones's moving elegy for a way of life.

Are politically correct opinions necessary to create great art? Or, can you sport awfully incorrect ideas, politically, historically, and morally, and still write fiction of the highest grade? Jones's acclaimed novel *Nashville 1864: The Dying of the Light* (1997) has been severely criticized for a passage of provocative interpretation of history, which questions the South's role as flawed exemplar in the national imagination. Novelist David Madden's essay, "The Innocent Stare at the Civil War," makes it clear that he dislikes the novel, not only for its political ideas but also as stylistically flawed fiction. Provocatively, David Madden critcizes Jones for his conservative view of Southern history. With Madden's permission Jones has read the essay and written "A Response to David Madden," which is also included in this collection.

In the novel Jones tells us how twelve-year-old Steven Moore and his slave-boy companion Dink become participants in the Battle of Nashville, one of the fiercest engagements of the Civil War. Driven by desperate conditions at home, Steven and Dink have set out to find Steven's father, a captain in J. B. Hood's Army of Tennessee. The story of their walk across the field of battle encapsulates in miniature some of the greatest themes of American history and literature, including the burden of slavery and the loss of old values, and integrity. The memoir was supposedly completed in the year 1900, and only recently discovered by a grandson, who, provoked by modern histories, had it published. Steven Moore was a Southerner of his century and *not* of our time. But the victors' history of the war is now the established version, so can modern critics accept a man with Steven's opinions on the war and its origin? The apology for the Confederacy takes up less than 3 of the novel's 129 pages. The book is really more about "the dying of the light" – the vanishing of a civilization and the focus is on the human concerns of all classical fiction. It has complex human dimensions and is about insight, recognition, and truth.

Nashville 1864 is about man's inhumanity to man, a boy's comprehension of it, and his loss of all romantic notions of class and race. The central passage of the novel has Dink and Steven witness the Rebels ambush a regiment of Yankee troops. The result of the ambush is that the ground is littered with wounded and dead black soldiers. From the moment that Dink meets a black Union soldier, who is also the first free black man he has seen, to the moment when the slave boy identifies with the dead black soldiers, Steven is feeling uncertain and troubled. He is slowly coming to recognize Dink's humanity, his race, his pride in it, and his certainty in his newfound allegiance. In Steven's rejection of slavery and acceptance of Dink's identity the parallel to Huck's recognition of Jim's humanity is unmistakable. Steven's loss of innocence, sense of frustration, failure and defeat, and his sudden awareness of limitation, responsibility, and guilt transcend the Battle of Nashville, December 15-16, 1864. As the history of Southern literature documents: to apprehend the South, and be nourished and sustained by it imaginatively, is not enough to be able to truly see it and to see beyond the region. In order to gain the necessary perspective and vision, a journey of self-discovery is required. Jones's *Nashville 1864* constitutes such a journey from one boy's discovery of his racism to the reader's self-questioning on the issue.

In *Herod's Wife,* Jones's latest novel, the people of Lakepoint seem burdened by anxiety. It is as if the Lakepoint community, in the place that used to be the town of Lorreta, has become estranged from itself and experienced a shift in values. The inhabitants of the modern town have come from everywhere, do not share a past history, have no religious inheritance in common, and as a community the town is without moral coherence. There are deliberate parallels to the estrangement of Nora and Hugh Helton, and other obvious parallels between community conflicts and domestic strains. Nora was first married to Hugh's brother and has a daughter with her first husband. If the town of Lakepoint, as the main character, Nora Helton, suggests, deserves to be destroyed – by fire, the marriage of the Heltons seems just as deserving of termination.

Jones brings up alluring potential themes throughout the novel, such as a new abortion clinic and the violent disagreement about it, but the topic is dropped again. Equally briefly and convincingly the racial tension in town rears its head. Cap Waters, the black spokesman, and young Qualls, who becomes a victim of prejudice, are some of the most convincing characters in the novel. Although it must have been tempting to dwell on racial issues, they come to life for a few pages and then disappear out of the novel. A third and potentially major theme is the clash of two organized fundamentalist religions, personified by

Father Riley and Reverend Stark. But as with the issues of abortion and race, fundamentalism is not allowed to stand as a main theme. Abortion, race, and fundamentalism are sample issues brought up primarily to show the "general moral incoherence" of the community and its individuals. Jones chooses to focus on moral incoherence and lack of faith, therefore the novel is mainly the story of Herod's wife and, once again, the presence of evil among us.

It is tempting to feel some compassion and pity for Nora. She seems to be a victim of basic human curiosity about the sinful and forbidden. Many share Nora's doubts about Christian faith, Jones even has Bishop Wells, a Catholic, declare "'nothing' is the word. Our Word." If he is right, the people of Lakepoint and many others are living in a state of useless and pointless faith. This is one of the topics of Richard Gray's essay in this collection, "Sympathy for the Devil: A Reading of *Herod's Wife*." Nora accepts modern nihilism completely and wants the degradation and destruction of the priest with a chilling absoluteness. Through Nora and the presence of her unidentified friend, evil is introduced into the community. There is no doubt that the devil visits Lakepoint and that Nora is totally possessed by him. It could be argued that if Jones shows absolute evil at work, he is perhaps also implying the existence of an absolute good, which seems to be gaining a footing in the town at the end of the novel when the Helton brothers find, as Richard Gray puts it, "something among the rubble, the devastation to enable them to survive and go on." Nora disappears from Lakepoint at the end of the novel and Jones is a bit diabolical in allowing Herod's wife to slip away, as easily as she sheds "her old skin."

Fortunately, it is too early to sum up Madison Jones's career, but certain merits are conspicuous. Jones is a consummate stylist and writes with the order and restraint of great art. Whether he uses rural dialogue, country preaching, or the whisper of a local whore, the language is convincingly authentic. He is an experienced storyteller in the best Southern tradition and does not let us off until the story has been told. A great tension is maintained also between climactic scenes, for Jones works hard at reducing "the elocution." His texts move on at exactly the right moment, and his transitions are unrivaled in smoothness. The economy is praiseworthy and every detail is essential in relation to the whole, but the austerity of the form does not diminish the richness of the texture. The detail is fully dramatized, and entire scenes are brought to life with a few specifics. As an expert craftsman, Jones avoids coincidence, but accepts the unavoidable. People kill, have abortions, and commit suicide also in his fiction, but the events are not shock effects, and the violence appears organic and unavoidable.

Madison Jones has a dark view of the human condition, but he also has self-knowledge, humility, and real compassion for his characters. In his fiction they are often caught by irresistible forces and hurled to an inescapable doom. But even when their world is changed beyond recognition, his characters retain their pride, courage, and dignity. The Southern concerns of place, community, and history figure prominently in his fiction. He shares the traditional regret at the loss of inherited values, and in this respect he is, perhaps, the last Agrarian. But his fictional universe goes beyond Agrarian thought, for Jones is true to his time and his South. He has created an emphatically moral world that transcends its particulars and reflects the universal.

NOTES:

1 The two published sections are: "Home Is Where the Heart Is," *The Arlington Quarterly,* 1 *(Spring* 1968), 12-69; and "A Modern Case," *Delta Review* 6 (July-August, 1969), 42-52, 72-75.

A RETURN TO THE GARDEN OF INNOCENCE:

UPON RECEIVING THE T.S. ELIOT AWARD FOR CREATIVE WRITING

Madison Jones

This is a great honor, and I am duly grateful to the Ingersoll Foundation, to the judges who bravely chose me, and to all concerned. Indeed I am not a little astonished that I am standing here today [Nov. 1, 1998] especially in consideration of the fact that this award bears the eminent name of T. S. Eliot, and also that my predecessors here may be said to range on a scale from most distinguished to illustrious. So, again, my humble thanks.

Let me begin by observing that now and then, looking back, I am also somewhat astonished at the fact that I became a writer at all. Reflecting on my youthful years, I would bet that my friends and acquaintances, had they ever thought about it, would have ranked me near the bottom of a long list of possible writers-to-be. The same may be said of my family, including my extended family, among whom, as far as I know, there has never been any writer or artist or even any intellectual. Unless, perhaps, one were to except a grandmother who wrote perishable verse and a Prussian great-grandfather who sang beautifully in German and crafted equally beautiful furniture.

My parents were genteel, responsible people, fairly stern old-time Presbyterians to whom, not untypically "bid'ness was bid'ness." Story-writing might be all right for idle hands or for ladies, but it certainly was no part of the serious work of the world. In fact, to them, it rather smacked of the effeminate, with, perhaps, something dishonest about it. At least this squares with the fact that my mother's term for "telling a lie" was "telling a story." And for my father, lying was very nearly the chief of sins. Woe to my brother and me if caught in the act. Today, an account of our upbringing would cause Freudians to shudder, and the law would put my just father in the penitentiary. And poetry, the handmaid of fiction? No male worth the name would be caught reading it, much less writing it. No use to point out that the famous poet and playwright, Christopher Marlowe, died in a saloon brawl (a very masculine thing to do), or that Aeschylus was also a distinguished soldier, or that Sir Walter Raleigh was a daring explorer. No use at all. Nor did it help that the Bible, the only much-read book in our house, is full of poetry. After all, Bible verse doesn't rhyme, so they didn't have to recognize it as poetry. I think, then, that I can safely discount my family background as a cause moving me in the direction I finally took... Or can I?

Except for the Bible, I think I can also safely discount most of my early reading. There was not a great deal of it and the greater part of that was such as *The Rover Boys* and *Tarzan* and Zane Gray's works. Of course in high school I was required to read some serious literature (and imbibe a considerable amount of Latin, taught by our rigorous old headmaster) but I was never really interested and remained an undistinguished student. My real interests (though I must not omit the fact that I was a religious boy) were in the physical domain. I loved hunting and fishing and wandering in the woods, to an extent, sports, and, very much though innocently, girls. But most of all, I think, I loved a large farm my father bought (I was in my early 'teens) in the then sparsely populated hill country twenty-five miles north of Nashville, my hometown. We soon acquired livestock and a couple of families to operate the place and, eventually, Tennessee Walking Horses. For years I never missed a chance to spend time there: week-ends and summers and, the first when I was eighteen and had dropped out of college, two stretches of time amounting to two years and more. Up to this point in my life I had never, I believe, had serious thoughts about a profession. Now I began to think more and more about becoming a farmer.

By now you may see why, when reflecting on my early years, I am sometimes astonished at the fact that my destiny, a large word, was to be a writer. But there are other times, more times, when I am able, or think I am able, to perceive in my life a sort of narrative of events, circumstances, and personal qualities at work, moving me toward my final choice. Contrary to the critical opinion now fashionable, I believe that at bottom life is built around a narrative and that, in consequence, so must fiction be. Without it we get the kind of disjointedness, or essential formlessness, apparent in the work of our more "advanced" fiction writers.

My long experience with that farm was certainly one of the great formative experiences of my life. This was so, I have concluded, because of earlier experience that was preparatory. Neither I nor my parents were born in rural environments, but two of my grandparents were, and so were a number of my kinfolks and old friends of the family. By reason of much talk at home and elsewhere, and often lengthy visits to kin and friends in the country, I early began to feel that I, we, had missed something: a life more interesting and more humane than the one we were living. Romantic, perhaps, but real to me. The pleasure I took in the nearby woods and wild things, in hunting and fishing, were, I suppose, reflections of, or contributors to, that romantic feeling. In this connection, the Romantic poet Wordsworth often comes to my mind. When in college I first experienced his poetry, I immediately knew exactly what he was talking about.

There was other relevant, preparatory experience with people close to me. From the time I was six until I was nineteen, my family and I lived in my maternal grandfather's house. My grandfather was a very old man, born several years before the Civil War, and he had little to do with his days. So he often entertained me and himself by reading aloud stories from the Old Testament, of Noah's Ark, and Joseph in Egypt. This memory has caused me to answer, when asked about early influences on me as a writer, that the greatest influence was the work of Moses. But he also read to me passages from Civil War history and, better, told me things he remembered from his early childhood before and during the War (or the "Waugh," as he called it). It was these memories that most firmly planted in me my feelings for that sad history and most potently made it my own. Till this day thoughts of that war are painful to me, though they partly furnished the basis for the short Civil War novel I recently published.

One other such preparatory experience was with our black, long-time maid, called Birdie. Mainly on ironing days when she was free to talk she told me wonderful country stories, many of them about snakes. She seemed to have had a wide experience of snakes and to have spent a considerable part of her childhood fleeing from them. There was the hoopsnake that would put its tail in its mouth and roll in pursuit of its victims. There was the fleet black racer and the jointed snake that, upon being struck, would break into pieces and later re-unite. There were also many tales that I later discovered were identical with tales from the Brothers Grimm and Hans Christian Andersen. Birdie was practically illiterate and I have often wondered where she got them.

I call these and other like experience "preparatory," exciting in me a sense of history, tragic and otherwise, and of nature with its wonders and mysteries. And so that farm my father bought was like a new world for my imagination. Sycamore Creek, then a clear-blue virgin stream, wound through and partly bounded the place, running for much of its distance beneath towering shear-rock bluff. It half-encircled bottom land that rose slowly to hills all in timber, from whose crests the farm buildings in the valley suggested the work of dwarfs. The hollows between the hills had names like Julie and Campbellite and Sodic, and in the central pasture was an old graveyard with nameless markers of rude fieldstone. I think Sycamore farm was one of the last places where, when people stopped talking, true silence would come down. I cannot say that I was not often lonely there. But it was a kind of loneliness whose memory I cherish. I think that loneliness had something to do with the development of my imagination, perhaps by nourishing my long-time habit of conversation with my alter ego. In any case I will never forget the ghostly night mist in the valley around my little house, or the voices of hoot owls, a whole contending congress of owls, from the steep bluffs and wooded hillsides along the creek.

It was not only the beauty and mystery of that place that inspired my love for it: there were the farm people. Besides the house I occupied, there were at some distance dwellings that housed one white and one black family. I came to know the men of these families about as deeply as I have known anyone, and I also came to respect them. The country around there in the thirties and early forties was still not much more than a generation removed from the frontier, and these people were in many respects its children. They were honest, simple people for whom a ten-or eleven-hour working day was merely the stuff of life. They had long memories and knowledge of every person and thing in that part of the country. They had due respect for us, my family, but they also had a proper and demanding pride in themselves.

In the tobacco field I learned what work was. I think I had never considered what it would be like to bend down hundreds of times in the blazing summer sun, with gum accumulating on my hands and arms and sometimes getting into my eyes like fire. But I could never see that Nell, the white man, or Arthur, the black one, were in much need of rest. It is astonishing what a man can get accustomed to.

Because my father wanted more pastureland, we were often in the woods with axe and brush hook. Most often there were only Arthur and I and the sounds we made of hacking and chopping and talking to one another. But I best remember one curious occasion when I suddenly heard, or deemed to hear, an alien voice dimly calling from somewhere deep in the woods. I asked Arthur, who was close by, if he heard it. He turned a grave black face to me. He had heard such voices, himself, in the woods. They frightened him.

When I ask myself why this particular small incident, and others equally small, have stuck in my mind as they have, I can give no certain answer. But I have thought this: that even then, without any clear intention, my mind was gathering, storing up, dramatic moments from which somehow, some day, they might be of use to me. An intuition, maybe, that some day they would make stories. Certainly I carefully listened to stories when I could. When Nell's father-in-law, old man Tom McCool came home after a life of wandering, I listened to him, drank with him, pumped him for his stories. And Red Ford, the moonshiner who lived alone on the ridge just west of our place, who spent about one of every three months in jail, was himself a story. Indeed I was to make fictional use of him eventually.

We had mules and a tractor and, by and by, several Walking Horses that, at expense of a good deal of physical suffering I learned to break and in some measure train in their gaits. But the high point of my experience with horses came when my father bought, from Lem Motlow of Tennessee whiskey fame, a very large and magnificent stallion. He was a former champion show horse and well trained except in one respect. A part of my job was breeding him to the mares, and here I ran into trouble. It turned out that he was immensely "sexually active." The first time I led him out of his stall for the purpose mentioned, I found myself instantly airborne at the end of his lead rope. He not so much mounted the poor hobbled mare as crashed into her at a dead run. It couldn't have been much pleasure and certainly was extremely dangerous to the mare. After several tries with the same dangerous results, I finally came up with a solution. It was to tie the mare just around the corner of the barn where the horse could not see her when I led him out. He came forth prancing and searching the landscape for his victim, but she being nowhere in sight he did not know in which direction to charge. So I tricked him. When he finally saw her rump just around the corner, there was no room for him to practice his accustomed form of rape.

By this time, though, I was back in college, at Vanderbilt, where I had re-started as a third-term freshman. I was soon to encounter a teacher who was exactly the right man for me. He was Donald Davidson, a poet, critic, historian, and important participant in that earlier movement, which, in defense of the South's agrarian heritage, had produced the distinguished collection of essays called *I'll Take My Stand*. He was a powerful man and teacher and I valued immensely his praise of my writing. But it was not his praise only that was of value. What he gave me also, though not yet adequately understood by me, was a rationale for my feelings and inclinations. A couple of years later, while doing graduate work at the University of Florida (where I also met my beautiful wife-to-be) I took writing classes under Andrew Lytle, another powerful Agrarian. Here I began publishing stories, a few, but it was a couple of years more before I undertook a novel.

As may have been anticipated, the novel was based on my life at Sycamore farm, and of my novels is the one that comes nearest to depending on my own actual story. Not very near, however. Duncan Welsh, my protagonist, and his story are related to me and my own only in tangential and accidental ways. I did, on purpose or not, give to Duncan certain of my own mental and psychological characteristics. The locale, pretty faithfully transcribed, was the farm and surrounding country. Most of the important characters were, though superficially, based on certain of the farm people and others who lived nearby. I derived the horse from the stallion described and had him die prematurely, though not in the way his prototype had died.

The story goes that Duncan, after some years of absence, returns in disillusionment to the home place, the simple world of his childhood. Living alone in the house of his now dead parents, he sets out to restore for himself an order of life that has essentially passed away. He breeds a colt from an old and nearly extinct bloodline, the animal being for him the symbol of restoration and becomes the immediate object of virtually all his love and hope. More and more he finds himself shut off from the world outside. His enmity with that world leads to the destruction of his horse and to his falling, now completely, into the hands of a thoroughly isolated and vicious moonshiner, who in a way represents the dark side of himself. Their alliance leads finally to the destruction of them both.

My idea for the novel began as one thing and ended as something else, changing shape as I proceeded. In the beginning I did not conceive of Duncan as possessed of any especially marked human flaw. I saw him mainly as victim, a man whose temperament and rearing made him intensely conscious of an emptiness in modern life, who very naturally sought to go home again but who would find in the end, to his own ruin, that the world would not let him be. So I proceeded without much of anything in mind more than developing the circumstances which the original idea had offered, in the faith that new plot elements would grow out of the old ones.

It was quite by surprise that the moonshiner (suggested by Red Ford and named Tom McCool after the old father-in law mentioned) intruded into the story. This was one of those "lucky" accidents that fiction writers learn to count on, and indicated to me, in terms of plot and idea at the same time, the direction my story must take. It seems clear now that the appearance of the sinister McCool was not mere luck but an image emerging by a dramatic logic from character and circumstance. He was a second self, a product of Duncan's moral flaw, and this was what gave McCool power over him. Duncan was a victim all right, but in the most important way he was a victim of himself.

In light of what has preceded this description one might detect a seeming irony here. The author, myself, might appear to be working at least partly in contradiction to his own agrarian views and those of his mentors: namely the implicit dictum that we in the South should, or at least should have rejected the industrial way of life and gone home again. But I will point to the novel's title, *The Innocent*, a title that I finally chose by something like intuition. It was some time after I had finished the novel before I understood the true relevance of the title. Then it said to me what is clearly the real heart of the story. It amounts to a Christian paradigm, not a contradiction. Duncan's flaw was a determined rejection of the inescapable evils of life, with consequent deliberate return to the garden of innocence. Adam ate of the tree of the knowledge of good and evil and was cast out forever, and we all share his condition. Evil is a prime fact of our existence: we may be forgiven for it but we cannot escape it. The "innocent" who re-enters the garden is destined to find that it is not God but the Prince of Darkness who walks there now. Duncan's flaw leads him into the hands of the Enemy, who destroys him.

The ideas of those old Agrarians are now probably beyond all hope of practical application. But they remain valid and valuable ground for criticism of modern industrial society. They can be valuable also to writers of fiction who still espouse them. For me, at least, they will continue to be among the ideas I hold closest to my heart.

THE UNCANNY WORLD OF *THE INNOCENT*

Lewis A. Lawson

In her very perceptive study of Madison Jones's novel *The Innocent* (1957), Simone Vauthier acknowledges that critical attention to "the socio-cultural aspects of the novel" (191) has deepened the reader's understanding of its concerns and appreciation of its craftsmanship. But she then suggests "that a reversal of emphasis is needed if one is to comprehend the total meaning and design of the novel. A closer scrutiny of the religious and metaphysical issues of *The Innocent* helps clear up some of the uncertainties and inconsistencies which have puzzled a number of critics." With characteristic probity, she continues, "Certainly, it would be presumptuous to claim that a reading of *The Innocent* as spiritual allegory eliminates all of the uncertainties pointed out by earlier critics or that it does not raise questions of its own, but at any rate it does bring out the secret unity of the novel" (192). Persuaded by her call for a reversal of emphasis, I shall offer, with the same proviso, a psychoanalytic reading of *The Innocent*, relying primarily on Freud's 1919 essay "The Uncanny." I do not argue that *The Innocent* reveals that the author was influenced by Freud's essay.

In "The Uncanny" (originally in German, *Das Unheimliche*), Freud spends the first seven pages teasing meanings out of *heimlich*, a word whose rich connotations are not satisfactorily conveyed in English by *canny* or *homely*, for example. He notes that *heimlich* has two separate meanings to the German, first, "belonging to the house, not strange, familiar, tame, intimate, friendly, etc.," and second, "concealed, kept from sight, so that others do not get to know of or about it, withheld from others" ("Uncanny" 222-23). He discovers that "among its different shades of meaning the word *heimlich* exhibits one which is identical with its opposite, *unheimlich*. What is *heimlich* thus comes to be *unheimlich*." Then he acknowledges that Schelling's aphorism, *"'UnHeimlich' is the name for everything that ought to have remained... secret and hidden but has come to light"* ("Uncanny" 224, original ellipsis, italics), was seminal to his investigation. Freud examines "individual instances of uncanniness" before offering a conclusion for his conception of the uncanny: "an uncanny experience occurs either when infantile complexes which have been repressed are once more revived by some impression, or when primitive beliefs which have been surmounted seem once more to be confirmed" ("Uncanny" 249). – Freud's method of exposition is to create a psychoanalytic tool from an etymological insight (the *unheimlich* is that which should have remained *heimlich*), then to apply the tool to "individual instances of uncanniness," and finally to conclude that such instances are symptomatic of the return to consciousness of formerly repressed ideas originating in early life. Freud's method is suitable to investigate what he regards as a universal mental function, repressed consciousness. But since I am investigating the unique repressed consciousness of Duncan Welsh, I will reverse the order of Freud's method, first to offer a provisional reconstruction of Welsh's early mental life, then to sift his mental life throughout the course of *The Innocent* for "individual instances of uncanniness," and finally to conclude that the cumulative pattern of his life is dominated by the return of the repressed, specifically the "infantile complexes" and "primitive beliefs" that had their origin in his relation with his mother.

The "Prologue" to the four "Parts" of *The Innocent* must be considered before Duncan Welsh's early psychological development is reconstructed. Certainly deepened by the dictum "the past is prologue," the "Prologue" announces that Duncan is to confront his home past in Tennessee after a seven-year stay in the North. In effect, the "Prologue" is similar to an operatic overture, setting the atmosphere of the work to follow, uncanniness, by featuring motifs of the uncanny that will be woven into the theme of the work. In the second paragraph Duncan looks at the past, but with, literally, a blind eye. The homecoming introduction is not just the convention that it often is in fiction, but becomes, for the reader of Freud's essay, extremely significant to the entire novel to follow. In the second paragraph, also, Duncan betrays his anticipation of homecoming by performing a ritual act, thus revealing the deference he pays to the efficacy of repetition. Freud "traces back to infantile psychology the uncanny effect" of "'the compulsion to repeat'," to engage in ritual behavior ("Uncanny" 238). Ritualism thus becomes an effort to prevent the emergence of forbidden thoughts (Rycroft 42), the *unheimlich*. Having paused to drink from a "branch," as small streams are known in Tennessee, Duncan washes his feet, shakes the dust out of his socks and from his shoes (2-3). A Biblical commentary on Matt. 10.14 explains: "The gesture of 'shaking the dust from the feet' is exclusively Jewish, practised on return to the Holy Land after journeys on the 'impure' soil of paganism" (A. Jones 870). Wishing to return to the land of *Heim*, Duncan performs an act to keep the *unheimlich* repressed. Then he jumps across the branch, which ought to be named "Jordan."

Then follows a description of the landscape through which Duncan must pass. We are told that he could have chosen an easier route, but prefers this one because it is unpopulated, even though he must walk. Trusting the tale rather than the teller, we discover that the chosen route is all too populated, if invisibly so. And there is a second reason, which must be quoted at some length:

> This stretch of country had kept in his imagination an undying strangeness. As a little boy he had been half afraid of it and dreamed it was a haunted land, a land where nothing, animal or man ever really died; where creatures out of the past lived a silent spirit-life, and showed themselves sometimes on rainy nights as wandering fires along the border of their little kingdom. On one side of the river was Bradysboro; its lights freckled the evening darkness of the river bottom, and hymns from tent meetings rose on the air and echoed across the quiet water. The other side was bluff, rising like a wall of shadow out of a narrow strip of bank and reaching many times higher than the tallest cottonwood. The hymns and sometimes muted shouts reached this wall, then bounded back, as though the Word Itself could not penetrate into the silence of that country....

Once or twice when he was older he had come over here hunting. It had been winter. He remembered clearly his impression that it was somehow much colder here than on the other side of the river.... He had started at the low barren north end where Little Pone Creek emptied into the river. He worked south, across the flat where piles of rock marked the Indian burying ground, up chert-covered bluffs which made him dig for a foothold, through sparse and twisted and rotting timber that could not tempt even the dollar-eyed lumbermen. Once a catamount screamed like a witch in the broad daylight; tales that wolves still survived over here came vividly back to him. He remembered the sense of warmth and sharp relief that came over him when he had mounted onto the thicket-covered ridge at the south end. Even now this stretch of country touched his body with a chill only different in its intensity. (4-5)

Why is Duncan drawn to this landscape, "a haunted land, a land where nothing... ever really died; where creatures out of the past lived a silent spirit-life," though it clearly evokes a sense of the uncanny, the *unheimlich*? Freud offers two comments that explain Duncan's response. In *The Interpretation of Dreams*, he writes: "There are dreams of landscapes and localities in which emphasis is always laid upon the assurance: 'I have been here before.' But this *'Déjà vu'* has a special significance in dreams. In this case the locality is always the genitals of the mother; of no other place can it be asserted with such certainty that one 'has been here before'" (*SE* 5 399). In "The Uncanny" he writes: "It often happens that neurotic men declare that they feel there is something uncanny about the female genital organs. This *unheimlich* place, however, is the entrance to the former *Heim* of all human beings, to the place where each one of us lived once upon a time and in the beginning. There is a joking saying that 'Love is home-sickness'; and whenever a man dreams of a place or a country and says to himself, while he is still dreaming: this place is familiar to me, I've been here before', we may interpret the place as being his mother's genitals or her body" ("Uncanny" 245). The excerpt reveals that Duncan had created a symbol of the river in early childhood, a symbol of the maternal source, bordered on both sides by a supernatural world, institutionalized (and therefore denatured) on the Bradysboro side and existential (and therefore terrifyingly natural) on the other side. Duncan will return to this place that was originally *heimlich* but became *unheimlich* as a result of a childhood complex.

As he walks along, still "vaguely troubled [in] his mind," Duncan is overtaken by a wagon with two occupants: the two figures sat, "like coachmen on a chariot. One was taller, like a bigger twin. Both wore bright straw hats which threw their faces in shadow. Each one carried his hands in fists upon his lap, as though the tall one too were driving, and held invisible reins. They moved like images drawn along by the little shuffling mule, their heads, their bodies, their hands all frozen into place" (6). In this scene there are two aspects of the uncanny cited by Freud. Regarding the frozenness of the two figures, Freud cites with approval a paper by Jentsch which states that "doubts whether an apparently animate being is really alive or conversely, whether a lifeless object might not be in fact animate" evoke an experience of the uncanny ("Uncanny" 226). Such doubts slyly hint that both animate and inanimate objects are manipulated by a supernatural agent, thus awakening a feeling of the uncanny. Regarding the "twinship" of the two figures, Freud cites with approval Rank's 1914 paper "Der Doppelgänger," which describes "the connections which the 'double' has with reflections in mirrors, with shadows, with guardian spirits, with the belief in the soul and with the fear of death… [and] also lets in a flood of light on the surprising evolution of the idea" ("Uncanny" 234-35). After amplifying Rank's investigation, Freud provides a summary: "When all is said and done, the quality of uncanniness [in this instance] can only come from the fact of the 'double' being a creation dating back to a very early mental stage, long since surmounted – a stage, incidentally, at which it wore a more friendly aspect. The 'double' has become a thing of terror, just as, after the collapse of their religion, the gods turned into demons" ("Uncanny" 236).

The remainder of the "Prologue" – fourteen pages – is an illustration of how "the 'double' reverses its aspect. From having been an assurance of immortality, it becomes "the uncanny harbinger of death" ("Uncanny" 235). The "twins" are an old man, Ezra Pack, and his nearly grown grandson, Dory. The old man is partially blind and, at first, his grandson appears to be similarly afflicted. Their sightless condition should evoke a sense of the uncanny in Duncan, for Freud is most emphatic that the phenomenon of blindness causes a special sense of the uncanny for males: "We know from psycho-analytic experience... that the fear of damaging or losing one's eyes is a terrible one in children. Many adults retain their apprehensiveness in this respect, and no physical injury is so much dreaded by them as an injury to the eye.... A study of dreams, phantasies and myths has taught us that anxiety about one's eyes, the fear of going blind, is often enough a substitute for the dread of being castrated" ("Uncanny" 231). Thus, when the text earlier describes Duncan looking at the past with a blind eye (3), the implication is that his vision of the past is distorted by his anxiety about blindness (or castration). For the "castration complex" teaches that if we can lose one organ, we can lose other organs, indeed life itself.

As he rides along in the rear of the wagon, Duncan begins to recall what he knows about Pack and his grandson. Living among virgin timber on a small holding inherited from his grandfather, the elder Pack had been for decades the most magnificent athlete in the community. Although now weakened by age, he had passed on his physique and his virility to his grandson, whose mother is dead and whose father is a "runaway" (8). The textual account of the grandson's parentage may be *unheimlich*, hiding a family secret. Dory's close resemblance to his "grandfather" may indicate his real paternity. Duncan is reassured to see that the grandson has good vision, after all. – When the wagon arrives in town there is a carnival, with the usual rides, games of chance, and "a girlie show, revealing the wonders of the female body, and a house of freaks with a real hermaphrodite and aborted monsters in bottles" (11). The association of the girlie show with the "aborted monsters" suggests that the female genital produces "aborted monsters," hence evokes the uncanny.

Duncan finds Pack and his grandson in front of the girlie show, with the grandson keenly watching a cootch dancer. The boy quickly looks away, as if to preserve his manliness. But for all his manliness, Dory may be, if another theory of Freud's is valid, exhibiting a curiosity that originated in very early childhood. According to Freud, the male child first assumes that all humans have a penis, hence "he begins to display an intense desire to look, as an erotic instinctual activity." Erotically attracted to his mother, he conceives "a longing for her genital organ, which he takes to be a penis. With the discovery, which is not made till later, that women do not have a penis, this longing often turns into its opposite and gives place to a feeling of disgust which in the years of puberty can become the cause of psychical impotence, misogyny and permanent homosexuality. But the fixation on the object that was once strongly desired, the woman's penis, leaves indelible traces on the mental life of the child, who has pursued that portion of his infantile sexual researches with particular thoroughness" ("Leonardo" 96). That Dory first looks for the mother with the penis is suggested by the textual association of the cootch dancer with "a real hermaphrodite," whose enlarged clitoris resembles a penis (Thomas 653). Thus the uncanny is present in the maternal aspect, first in the hermaphrodite, the mother with the penis, second, the hermaphrodite's double, the mother without the penis, who bears freaks and who, to the infantile mind, is a victim of castration and thus inspires anxiety about castration.[1]

Grandfather Pack has always defeated the carnival wrestler; now he brings his grandson to take his place. Duncan has been joined by Logan, a black man who works on the Welsh farm. Logan understands what is occurring: "And now he's done raised up that boy like him as a pea, and come down out of them hills. Like old times… living over again" (13). The carnival wrestler, Tiger Sloan, seems to use a technique for which the grandfather's coaching had not prepared his successor, more like jujitsu than traditional wrestling. From the beginning of the match, Pack and his grandson keep eye contact, as if the elder were projecting manliness and the younger were appealing for it ("Uncanny" 231). Finally, in desperation, the boy lunges at Sloan, flies over him, striking the canvas headfirst, dying almost instantly of a broken neck. All the while the jaunty calliope plays "Over the Waves" (19). The calliope reminds us of the Muse Kalliope, whose son Orpheus hated women, who avenged themselves by tearing him to pieces (Rose 254-55). The recession of the wagon, still carrying "twins" – one alive, one so recently dead – surely provides a repetition of their procession into town that evokes the uncanny. The "doubling" that the "twins" now represent is profoundly uncanny, for, according to Freud, "… the 'double' was originally an insurance against the destruction of the ego, and 'energetic denial of the power of death', as Rank says; and probably the 'immortal' soul was the first 'double' of the body. This invention of doubling as a preservation against extinction has its counterpart in the language of dreams…" ("Uncanny" 235).

As the novel proper begins, Duncan is in a wagon, being driven by Logan, a mentor of sorts, from Bradysboro out to his home. There is no indication that he senses his likeness to Dory Pack or experiences the uncanny that results from a repetition. Rather he uses the opportunity to review his life from 1928, when he was twenty-two, beginning with his sudden "decision of that summer seven years ago to quit school and go north to work" (22). The suddenness of his decision suggests that he fled in a fugue state, an inference supported by his thinking of the seven years as "a gap out of his life" and further supported by his realization that "he had been two persons – the one fixed in a changeless scene; the other drifting, never still but in moments of inertia" (see Rycroft 123). Having fled the *unheimlich* to become a "drifting" person, he is still fixed "in a changeless scene" of the *unheimlich*. "He went north, to Chicago, with his sense of freedom renewed." But he soon despises his fellow newspapermen, for they exemplify "the outrageous absence of proper order, of purity, of that which was either one thing or another" (24). Obsessed with repressing the *unheimlich* he is compelled to believe that somewhere there is *Heim*.

Along the way, Duncan had entered into a marriage that lasted less than a year (114). He now thinks "that it was nothing more than loneliness which had led him into his greatest single blunder – his marriage" (25). Duncan may be included in that subtype of people described by Freud: "Where they love they do not desire and where they desire they cannot love" ("Universal" 183). This condition is popularly known as the "Madonna-whore" complex. If Duncan had envisioned the girl as the incarnation of the virgin good mother (the *heimlich*), he might have soon discovered in the bridal bower that, because of the incest taboo, he suffered from lack of desire or "psychical impotence" ("Universal" 182). Sexual activity would invite the return of the repressed, the *unheimlich*, with its origins in a mother-complex. He later remembers that he did not often feel desire for his wife (192), as if her genitals aroused his sense of the *unheimlich*. The narrator thus summarizes Duncan's response to this episode in his life: "More than all the rest this failure had caused him, not by nature solitary, to assume an indifference that finally had become almost real" (25). Given the context, the "indifference" must be sexual.

One paragraph later, the narrator, having traced Duncan's drift from Chicago to Pittsburgh, describes his arrival in Philadelphia. While Duncan had fled the *unheimlich* in Tennessee, he had all the while remained obsessed with "the changeless scene" of *Heim*: "the image of his home, of the life he had left, thoughts of his father and his sister had been much in his mind for a long time. Now they came to him with increasing familiarity. The simplest thing – a smell, the tone of a voice, a leaf falling – was liable to call them up. He began to think seriously of going back" (25). As Duncan leaves the train station on his arrival in Philadelphia, "a cinder from a passing locomotive flew into his eye. The eye became infected, and he lost the sight in it." Following, as it does, Duncan's memory of his loss of desire, psychic castration, Duncan's memory of the blinding of one of his eyes (read "castration") strongly implies that he experienced an occurrence of the *unheimlich* violent enough to put him into flight again, for he "abruptly" leaves for home (26).

Duncan returns to the present, in the wagon with Logan. As the wagon goes through a village, Duncan observes: "Someone stood at the common well, waist-deep in lantern light. It was a girl – or woman. Her skirt was short and her long legs beneath it looked as pale as candles. When they went by in the wagon, the blot of her face turned and followed them. Logan muttered under his breath. The girl was still motionless, watching them, when Duncan glanced back at her" (27). Innocently, Duncan does not pursue the significance of Logan's muttering, which must concern the second definition of *heimlich*. What Duncan actually sees is indistinct, so that while his eyes register a typical well in Tennessee his mind pictures a well in the Old Testament, in which "the first step to a marriage is often a meeting at a well" (Power 164e, 209), as in the case of the virgin Rebekah, of Genesis 24, who is destined to be Isaac's wife. Back in the *heimlich* (first definition), the Holy Land, the Bible-cultured Duncan should expect to meet a virgin at the well.

When Duncan reaches his home, he is welcomed by his father, now grown old like Ezra Pack, and his sister Margaret Mary, thirty-four, five years older than he, and her sister's suitor, Reverend Garner, for whom Duncan voices an instant contempt, since Garner is a Methodist, therefore theologically liberal. (Such is the fear that he represses of his theologically conservative mother that is dominated by her beliefs.) Like the Prodigal Son's brother, Margaret Mary is none too happy to see Duncan: "'Where have you been languishing all these years? You've been loyal, haven't you?' She was almost panting. Even through his anger and through the shadows between them the flash of her rage was like a blade drawn suddenly. He wanted to retreat" (33). Duncan, having had his castration complex awakened by her sharp words, experiences the uncanny and wants to flee. But his father and Margaret Mary flee to their bedrooms, leaving him alone to confront the house of his mother. When he first re-enters the parlor, Duncan looks immediately to the picture of his mother that sits on a mahogany desk in the parlor: "Without approaching he envisioned her face, bound in a taut-lipped severity somewhat in excess of what was natural to her. He understood well the kind of integrity that had caused her unawares to exaggerate her expression. It was in this room that her body had lain, and the air embalmed so heavy with the scent of flowers that it had almost made him sick…. He went to the window and opened it" (35). Freud, seemingly with the conviction that he is addressing a universal condition, remarks that "man's attitude to death" is one of the factors which turns "something frightening into something uncanny" ("Uncanny" 243).

Sitting down on a sofa, Duncan pictures the past. He liked fishing and hunting and riding his pony. He had paternalistic feelings for the blacks who worked his father's farm. He remembers his sister sternly reprimanding him, "aping her mother," then further remembers that his sister was "for the most part" ineffectual, "because of her voice." (Duncan's sister is the surrogate for the repressed *unheimlich* mother-figure.) Margaret Mary's voice lacked

> her mother's tone of dignity, of tranquil authority,… his mother's voice was not to be imitated. The vividness with which he could still recall it was remarkable. She used to read to him a great deal, mostly from

the Bible. She liked the Old Testament best.... The woes of Israel, the strength and agony of Samson; these were things that echoed still in unforgettable syllables down certain channels of his mind. She did not neglect the life of Jesus. But all this was less clear to him now; here his image of her voice blurred uncertainly. He had been nearly a man before it had impressed him that the Beatitudes promised blessings for virtue, that they offered to the pure in heart another answer than sheer muscular resistance to the enemies of purity. It was not that she was ungentle, in voice or in act; but only that her gentleness seemed to him now less eloquent than her strength. (36)

His mother's voice (luring him home) he had heard before he left Philadelphia and as he crossed the creek approaching his home. It is fitting that Duncan remembers his mother's voice saying "I am the Lord thy God…," for she is quoting Exodus 20.2, following which God dictates the Ten Commandments to Moses. Thus his mother had implanted in her son's mind the transcendent rule of absolute submission not only to her God but also to herself. It is fitting, too, that Duncan then recalls the story of Samson. For although Samson was strong and clever, he had an eye for the ladies, one of whom, Delilah, saw that he got his eyes put out by the Philistines. Here is the source of Duncan's castration complex, an awakening of the process by which Duncan's mother ceased to be *heimlich*, becoming *unheimlich*, retaining that aspect after her death as an internalized figure.

Duncan remembers more about his mother: "In all but the very coldest weather she had mocked him when on winter mornings he came downstairs to dress by the fire. Nor would she tolerate his crying out when she thrashed him. Not even the time she whipped him so mercilessly with the horse crop, because she had caught him in a deliberate lie. He never doubted her affection toward him. Yet he could not remember her ever displaying it in terms of an embrace. He thought of her always as above such demonstrations. The time he had seen a friend of his embrace and kiss his mother had left him with a sense of childish disgust" (36-37). What this memory suggests is that Duncan's mother had been unable or unwilling to offer unconditional, mother love. But so strong had been Duncan's need to love her that, despite his experience, he remembers her as lovable. He does not consciously connect her coldness with his lifelong sensitivity to the cold, especially to the chilly landscape across the river from Bradysboro. Thus he never acknowledges that, having been beaten like a horse because he had been found guilty of lying, he returns home to breed a stallion which can freely act out what he unconsciously regards as his guilty desires. Noting that Chief is, for Duncan, "an extension of his self and a power symbol," Vauthier adds that Duncan's "love for the animal is another instance of the narcissism and excessive self-regard" in his character (Vauthier 205). Duncan never acknowledges that his having been denied maternal embraces and kisses causes him to find embraces and kisses repugnant.

In the text of the novel proper, on his first morning home, Duncan wakes to a streaming sun and the sound of a rooster crowing (42). Feeling roosterish himself, he enters the kitchen; seeing his sister at the well outside, he takes up the knife to slice the breakfast bacon. But, significantly, his sister immediately takes over the slicing, once again projecting the image of the castrator. That knife might as well be the "flaming sword" (Genesis 3.24) that kept Adam from returning to Eden. Not surprisingly, Margaret Mary's face reminds Duncan of his mother's face, as he starts for the door (43). After breakfast Duncan steps into a landscape dominated by sheep and pigeons, a pastoral that again tempts him to think that he has returned to Eden, the *heimlich* motherland. Saddling an old mare, all that is left of the family stable, he rides out to view the farm. Discovering that she is blind in one eye, Duncan thinks, "We're alike,... that much" (48). It is appropriate that one aspect of the uncanny carries him to another, Wesley, a black farm worker, who has an absent twin, Herman (nicknamed Bantam). Wesley is a man of "uncorrupted and spotless good will," but Herman had fought with Duncan when they were boys, and when the incendiary twin returns from Harlem, will, by his lack of servility and carelessness with fire, threaten Duncan's attempt to recreate Eden.

Leaving the horse to graze, Duncan continues his inspection afoot. Reaching a creek, "where the air had the feel of a cave," he comes to a place deep enough for swimming. Removing his clothes and diving into water, he reveals his yearning to return to the womb: "He liked it in this soundless world, turning and rolling, feeling the water bathe him, hair and feet and body, in its cold purity." But when he emerges, his next thought is decidedly post-parturitional: "he felt the way he used to feel when he had been very dirty and his mother had washed him clean" (50). "Dirty" and "clean" usually constitute, of course, the first distinction that mother applies to our skin, at a time when the child must rely on the appearance of his skin to form his earliest self-conception, his skin-ego (Kirschner 543-46). So powerful is the distinction between "dirty" and "clean" that the adult never outgrows it, rather extends it metaphorically to every aspect of thought and behavior.[2] Thus Duncan's adult mind is haunted by the rigid dualism that he absorbed from his mother's preachments and practices.

With his mother on his mind, Duncan continues his journey. Entering Sodic Hollow, perhaps so named by the earliest settlers because it contained a salt lick, Duncan climbs a steep bluff for a vantage point from which he can see whence he has come: "The whole farm lay spread out down there, as though at some obscure time it had as a single piece sunk beneath the plane of the long curving plateau and the range of hills that faced it across the valley. It looked as serene, as sun-drenched, as empty of life as a land below the level of the sea" (50). Whereas he had earlier envisioned the farm as Eden, he now envisions it as the plain of Jordan surrounding the Dead Sea, for the textual geological history of the farm valley is identical with that of the Dead Sea area in Hastings' venerable *Dictionary of the Bible* (Grant 204). Once again the *heimlich* becomes the *unheimlich*.

Continuing his journey, Duncan must crawl under a "tight-leafed roof" of laurel (50). In effect his crawl is a fetal regression, for his goal is the cabin of an elderly black woman, Aunt Virgy, who is, to him, a surrogate for the *heimlich* mother-figure in the earliest phase, the mother as Madonna. Hence Aunt Virgy's name. But it becomes apparent very quickly that Aunt Virgy is, to a less innocent observer, an *unheimlich* mother-figure, a witch, who delights in telling tales "about witches, and animals" (52), that is, animals as they appear to a mind believing in animism.[3] Probably Aunt Virgy is locally known as a conjure woman like Aunt Mehitable Green in Ellen Glasgow's *Barren Ground* (1925). Although, as a black person, she had been

Duncan's grandfather's slave, she is a devotee of the Welsh family mores and is contemptuous of her fellow blacks, probably because of her white, possibly Welsh family blood, indicated by her shoulder-length white hair. Her devotion to the Welsh family is illustrated by her story that she killed her brother Cole when he burglarized their house during the Civil War (60). Her uncanniness is conveyed by her near-blindness, the needle she habitually holds in her hand, and by her doll-like appearance, "her dried-up body, like a mummy almost." For her fellow blacks her uncanniness is reinforced by the fact that she consorts with crows and always keeps one as a familiar spirit (see Evans 412): "One she had always with her inside the house. She talked to it, and it could answer her. More than one Negro had heard them beyond the door" (51). The blacks believe that she commands the crows: "... God help the man who had displeased her. She would send them in swarms, sometimes even after dark, it was said, to pluck up his tender corn shoots, and peck great holes in his melons" (52). Their melon-pecking is a reminder that Corvidae, as the Bible notes (Prov. 30.17), peck out the eyes of their victims (Grant 834). Interestingly, though nearly blind, Aunt Virgy, after her inspection of Duncan's face, discerns that he has been blinded in one eye. At that point, her familiar-spirit crow – named "Cole" after her thieving brother – flutters up "onto the doorsill," then walks over to join her (56). Since this same crow had "pecked him cruelly on the hand" when he was a boy, his unconscious must regard Aunt Virgy and her crow as caretakers of the castration complex imposed on him by his mother.

Soon enough Duncan's father dies and his sister marries and leaves the house. Duncan works the land, roams the woods, and miraculously finds a Tennessee stud for his ancient mare. In short, the landscape seems Edenic, *heimlich*. With the house empty, Duncan frequently visits Aunt Virgy, but the text does not dramatize those visits, except to note that at his approach the crow flees in panic – though the panic must be Parthian. On the morning that his mare drops her foal, however, Duncan is so excited that he again visits Aunt Virgy, to recount for her the birth in great detail. Given her clairvoyance, she already knows that Duncan will visit, that the birth has occurred, that the foal is a "stud," and that the "stud" represents Duncan's yearning to throw off his castration complex (137-39). And she also knows that Duncan has dated a girl once or twice, a girl that she thinks of as "trash." But she knows that the girl has left town and hopes that she is gone for good.

Having willed into existence an animal anciently symbolic of masculine potency, Duncan feels a resurgence of sexuality in himself. At home after his visit to Aunt Virgy, he falls asleep, to dream of "something illicit." Apparently the dream caused an ejaculation, for he feels "a momentary sense of guilt, as when in childhood he had waked up out of such dreams" (144). As Duncan fully awakens, he remembers a recent incident. While crossing the creek that bounds his farm, he had happened on a young female who must be the woman lately seen at the well. Reclining on a rock, she musingly laves her feet in a pool. He wants to see her face, but it is averted. When she looks up, realizing that he has put the gaze on her, she offers the fleeting Mona Lisa smile that many females use when encountering an unknown male. This is Duncan's reaction: "At first glance he thought that her face was not pretty. Then he thought that it was, in an antique sort of way; very solemn once the smile had faded. It reminded him of a type of looks which was out of fashion, like that of Madonnas he had seen…" (145). Onto the face Duncan projects the image of the virgin mother, just as, conversely, Leonardo, so Freud thinks, projected the image of his mother on Mona Lisa and the Madonna ("Leonardo" 111-15). Duncan and the girl talk awkwardly. Again she averts her face, then gracefully elevates. This is Duncan's reaction: "On a little area of round-topped stone, perilously little for standing, she stood quite naturally, as though newly risen out of the water. All of a sudden she looked more mature than he had thought. Her body was the body of a woman. Her breast was full…" (147). Here the female poses both as Venus di Milo and as in Botticelli's Birth of Venus. Duncan is sufficiently aroused to ask her name, which she blushingly reveals, "Nettie Roundtree." Still struck by her "antique" face, Duncan probably does not ponder her name, but in time he might, for it conjoins the image of entrapment with the ancient identification of the tree with feminine sexual knowledge and enthusiasm (Dijkstra 93-97). In this encounter, then, dualistic Duncan sees her first as an object of veneration and then as an object of desire, but always as an object. Seeing her two weeks later in town, Duncan learns that she is going to visit her sister in Nashville for the summer, perhaps even longer.

Duncan immerses himself in his environment. He loafs on the town square, goes, once, to church, and he is bored. The one bright spot in Duncan's life at this time is his conscious delight in the colt. But Duncan unconsciously reveals his infantile sexual fixation through his behavior toward the colt. One of his first acts is to give the colt his thumb to suck, as if recognizing in the colt's need his own. Freud notes that the phase of sensual sucking precedes that of masturbation (*Three* 180). Soon, "every day more than once Duncan caught the colt and stroked it. He fed it bits of sugar, and laughed under his breath at the moist tickling of the lips and tongue in the palm of his hand" (148). By stroking the colt he indulges his own infantile auto-erotism, defined by Freud as "the instinct [that] is not directed towards other people, but obtains satisfaction from the subject's own body" (*Three* 181). Offering sugar, he seduces the colt into responding with a tickling of the palm, that ancient invitation to sexual activity.

Although the maternal landscape has more than once revealed that within the *heimlich* is the *unheimlich*, Duncan persists in thinking of the woods as irenic, finally, like Faulkner's Isaac McCaslin in "The Bear," renouncing his "gun" (153), accepting his castration, when he enters them.[4] Returning to Sodic Hollow, he encounters first a dog, then the dog's master, who does have a gun. Confronted by the man's moonshining paraphernalia, Duncan orders that it be gone by the next night. Then he weakens, saying that the man can continue his operation. At that the man "leaned the gun against the tree and stepped down the slope toward the still. He stopped at one of the barrels. He looked down at the whitish froth that floated thick over the mash. Still looking down at it, he said to Duncan: 'Do you like this beer?'" (157). The man has apparently sized up Duncan, sensing that he will not need his gun, for Duncan has not fully developed a genital character, but is still an oral character, needing the "whitish froth," mother's milk. Duncan drinks so much that he gets drunk; then he asks for a jarful to take home with him; when the man comes close to him, Duncan notices that "the odor of mash was stronger than ever; it seemed to exude from his body" (161). Since the smell had first reminded Duncan of "a perfumed woman," something womanly attaches to the mash, thence to the man. And since his name is Aaron McCool, something maternal attaches to him, evoking in Duncan nostalgia for the earliest maternal image, the mother with a penis ("Leonardo" 98).

As Aaron McCool becomes known to Duncan, he displays many aspects of the uncanny, for example, his indifference to the cold (184), his ability to forgo sleep (240), his epileptic movements (160-61), his always remarkable eyes (276-77), his unrestrained violence (272-73). But Duncan is so taken with Aaron that he does not scrutinize him, not even when Chief becomes "restless" in Aaron's presence. An observation by Freud is appropriate here: "We can also speak of a living person as uncanny, and we do so when we ascribe evil intentions to him. But that is not all; in addition to this we must feel that his intentions to harm us are going to be carried out with the help of special powers" ("Uncanny" 243). So deep is Duncan's need for Aaron that he is, as it were, blind in both eyes.

Since Sodic Hollow was earlier likened to the Dead Sea, it should be remembered that Sodom was one of the cities near its southern periphery. Perhaps Duncan has just met a Sodomite? The sequence of Duncan's display of susceptibility to homosexuality in consequence of his continued susceptibility to the castration complex is validated by Freud:

> Sadger emphasizes the fact that the mothers of his homosexual patients were frequently masculine women, women with energetic traits of character, who were able to push the father out of his proper place.... After this preliminary stage a transformation sets in whose mechanism is known to us but whose motive forces we do not yet understand. The child's love for his mother cannot continue to develop consciously any further; it succumbs to repression. The boy represses his love for his mother: he puts himself in her place, identifies himself with her, and takes his own person as a model in whose likeness he chooses the new objects of his love. In this way he has become a homosexual. What he has in fact done is to slip back to auto-erotism: for the boys whom he now loves as he grows up are after all only substitutive figures and

revivals of himself in childhood-boys whom he loves in the way in which his mother loved him when he was a child. He finds the objects of his love along the path of narcissism.... Psychological considerations of a deeper kind justify the assertion that a man who has become a homosexual in this way remains unconsciously fixated to the mnemonic image of his mother. By repressing his love for his mother he preserves it in his unconscious and from now on remains faithful to her. While he seems to pursue boys and to be their love, he is in reality running away from the other women, who might cause him to be unfaithful. ("Leonardo" 99-100)

The text of *The Innocent* reveals Duncan's perception of his father as a weak man and his mother as a strong woman. It also reveals Duncan's desire to put himself in the place of the mother, as when he allows the colt to nurse his finger, habitually croons to the colt, and tells it, "poor little Chief, I'm your new mammy" (177). But the text does not reveal that Duncan, in either the past or the present, has engaged in homosexual activities or even consciously experienced homosexual desire. All that is argued here is the proposition that Duncan's relationship with Aaron McCool is dictated by forces of which he is unconscious, as, for example, his sudden reversal of his decision to force McCool off his land.

After a time, Nettie Roundtree returns from Nashville, becoming once again an attraction for Duncan. Again he accidentally encounters Nettie. Picking her up on the road, he takes her over to pet his colt. The setting of the scene, a barn, suggests that Duncan still thinks of her as the Madonna, but when she leans forward to kiss the colt, he – the colt, not Duncan – bites her blouse and rips it off. Duncan runs to get a clean tow sack to cover her, feeling "a kind of excitement to which he had grown unused" (166). It could be that the colt senses that he now has a competitor for Duncan's love, or it could be that the colt, bred to be the symbol of Duncan's masculinity, reveals a hostility to the female-as-temptress that has dogged Duncan since early childhood. The explanations are not mutually exclusive, the former being animalistic, the latter animistic. Duncan takes her into his parlor and goes to get a blouse of Margaret Mary's that she can wear home. Still steamed up by "her naked flesh, her round breasts swelling the flimsy brassière" (168), he thinks of his mother and sister, a thought which promptly cools him off. He feels "a wave of disgust" at his "prurience." Apparently sensing that her rival is the *unheimlich* mother, Nettie asks Duncan if he believes in ghosts. Although he says he does not, the ghost wins the day.

Duncan does not pursue Nettie; he is apparently attempting to sublimate his desire by hard physical work (172). But his sexual excitement remains, for the text suggests that he attempts to discharge it with masturbation. There is a detailed scene in which he builds "a great fire… in the parlor." That he is controlled by narcissism is indicated by his close observation of himself in his bedroom mirror. He hunts up his old guitar: "The strings were intact. They did not break when he drew them taut. While he was tuning it he picked the strings so gently that the truth of the sounds was barely audible even to himself. Something on the air seemed too delicate to withstand even the least discordance. With scrupulous care he fingered out many silent notes until he began to feel them again" (174). Then, after playing through his entire repertoire, he stretches out with a pillow "in front of the hearth." There he considers a name for his colt, and then thinks of Nettie by name – completing a sequence of focusing on himself, then on his surrogate, then on the self to complete himself. He sees scenes of the past, even the wife he divorced and his seven-year loneliness; now, though, he feels that the present moment offers hope. But the scene ends with "something else – the sense that these moments would last only as long as his mother delayed in calling him up to bed" (176).

Duncan begins to take Nettie out, but makes no sexual advances, even as he continues to visit Aaron. After a spring snowfall, Nettie comes over to invite him to go sledding with her. They frolic until they are nearly frozen. Then, after Duncan has built a roaring fire in the parlor, she flashes her "come hither" smile. As he embraces her he does not look at her or talk to her, instead lets his fingers do the talking, all the while thinking that their coupling is "like the intercourse of animals" (188), which he has indeed made it, by his thoughts and actions.[5] Of course, since she was able to arouse his desire, then she is, ipso facto, a whore. With his body's detumefaction, his conscience returns, for, after taking her home, he looks for hymeneal blood before the hearth: the complex fantasy that controls his thinking requires that she had been a virgin. Although he finds no proof, he is burdened by guilt, and marries her three weeks later. – Duncan is astonished to discover how strong his desire for his wife is. But since she is an object, he still cannot talk to her during their moments of intimacy. Soon enough Nettie tells him that he had impregnated her on their first encounter. Duncan's response is significant: "He was annoyed simply because this new turn of events must curtail and modify the pleasures that the last two months had brought him" (194). Though his narcissism has been weakened, it has not surrendered. But gradually Duncan begins to change, sees Nettie as a subject, not an object, talks to her in both intimate and ordinary moments, and starts to fall slightly in love with her. Thus he seems to be escaping the "Madonna-whore" complex. The part of him expressed by his colt thinks otherwise, for it kicks Nettie. Duncan starts to whip the colt, but then refrains. His lack of action does not reveal a conscious scruple – for he strikes the colt on other occasions – but an unconscious value judgment.

Then, feeling guilty for neglecting Aunt Virgy, he goes to see her. She is still mummy-like, clairvoyant, and tells Duncan that the baby Nettie carries is not his, that Nettie had had carnal relations with the aptly named Dicky Jordan, that she had aborted a fetus that he had sired (203). Surely Aunt Virgy's lurid allegation that Nettie had been insatiably lascivious with Dicky: "And when he get through with her she keep right on begging him do it to her again. And he get mad and say he ain't no goat," transforms Duncan's view of her genitals from *heimlich* to *unheimlich* (206). As if motivated by one of Freud's "special powers," a solicitous Aaron approaches Duncan on his way home, as if offering himself as a replacement for the treacherous Daughter of Eve. Nettie confesses that she had been Dicky's mistress and that she had had an abortion, but asserts that she now carries her husband's seed. Again betraying a value judgment, Duncan strikes her once before she staggers away (212). That night she begins to miscarry, and the fetus is stillborn. Duncan offers a "faithless act of contrition," but Nettie must realize, once again, that a ghost haunts Duncan's house. – Nettie and Duncan coexist for six weeks, then Nettie leaves, leaving Duncan almost conscious of the uncanniness caused by repetition: "… in every phase of it he saw with a certain bitter ennui the repetition, or at least the familiar counterpart of what had happened before [i.e., in his first marriage]. It made him reflect how life in one guise or another was forever inescapably turning back on itself" (218). The next day Mary Margaret makes her first visit since the death of her father. The timing of her visit suggests that she comes at the bidding of "special powers" to be her mother's surrogate in repossessing the house.

With the idea of heterosexual relations once again repulsive to him, Duncan has only Chief, now a stallion, as an agent to manifest his masculinity. He breaks the horse to the saddle, then begins to gait him. Accepting her characterization of Nettie, Duncan often visits Aunt Virgy on his daily training of Chief. Once, during a full moon, he rides to the *unheimlich* landscape across the river:

> At the mouth of the hollow Duncan pulled him [Chief] up. Ahead, on uneven ground gutted with sinks and gushes like old wounds healed over but never filled, was a thicket. It was sparse, dwarfish, largely composed of the dead and bone-gray skeletons of trees. Here and there a bleached trunk stood as though strangled in the confusion of its own recoiled and twisted roots. Among the ribbed and crisscrossed shadows white chunks and ledges of rock stood out bare to the moon. Duncan sat for a time gazing at the sight. Chief was very still under him. Until, with a small start of his body, the horse's head, his ears, went up. Duncan listened. The sound, whatever it was, had been too fine for a man to hear. Chief began to paw, sprinkling bits of chirt behind them. Duncan turned him and went back the way they had come. (240)

The scene of the "thicket" at the "mouth of the hollow" "bare to the moon," invested as it is with overtones of menstruation, cicatrization, and parturition, must reflect the image of the *unheimlich* female genital that lurks in Duncan's unconscious. Again, Chief's restlessness indicates that he feels endangered.

On one of his night rides Duncan stops to see Aaron, who begins his campaign to involve Duncan in his criminal activity, delivering a load of his moonshine. Dismounted, Duncan holds the reins of the horse (242); apparently Aaron senses the horse's capacity to recognize peril, for he persuades Duncan to enter his shack, thus separating himself from Chief, where he offers Duncan money to work with him. At that moment, Chief causes a "commotion" that draws Duncan back outside. This time Duncan demurs, but offers Aaron the use of his truck for the delivery, promising to help him "sometime." – Right now, Duncan is preoccupied with entering Chief in the annual horse show at the country fair (244). He sees the horse as the manifestation of his own masculinity (and conversely the denial of his castration complex). That Freud's "special powers" are there to work against him is evident when he sees fellow contestant Dicky Jordan riding a "gelding" (245), therefore becoming a gelder. Desperate that Chief make a good showing, Duncan rashly employs the crop in an effort to calm him; instead, Chief throws Duncan, becomes ungovernable, seemingly setting his gait by "Over the Waves" now being played by the carnival calliope (248-52). Duncan remounts the horse, but the situation is still out of his control. Chief has broken another horse's leg, and Duncan has struck Logan's son Bantam on the face with his whip. When a deputy sheriff pulls him off Chief, Duncan punches him in the face. Chief then bolts, his significant destination the Jordan farm, where he wants to fight the Jordan stud and mount a Jordan mare. Before he is jailed, Duncan is able to prevent Chief's ambitions (256-59). In his cell Duncan hears Aaron whisper from outside that he will break him out, if Duncan wants him to. Still innocent of Aaron's intentions toward him, Duncan gratefully refuses Aaron's offer, saying that he will "get out the easy way tomorrow" (261).

Now Duncan does accompany Aaron on a whisky run to Nashville (266). Apparently Aaron thinks that he has so completely seduced Duncan that he can reveal his sole purpose, to harm humans. But Aaron's violent treatment of his Nashville customers causes Duncan to reflect: "It was not the act itself, its curt brutality, which mainly depressed him; it was what the act, and Aaron's whole behavior, revealed. In a way he felt he had been betrayed by Aaron. Or rather, not by Aaron, who had never dissimulated; but by his own deliberate blindness in creating an image which did not match, or only in part matched, facts which already had been apparent" (275-76). There is the indication that Duncan's "blindness," his castration complex, had first induced him to see Aaron as an admirable and friendly "double" who embodied the thought processes and behaviors of primary narcissism that were stripped from him when his relationship with the good mother was severed. A comment by Freud is apt: "When all is said and done, the quality of uncanniness can only come from the fact of the 'double' being a creation dating back to a very early mental stage, long since surmounted – a stage, incidentally, at which it wore a more friendly aspect. The 'double' has become a thing of terror, just as, after the collapse of their religion, the gods turned into demons" ("Uncanny" 236). – In the following weeks Duncan remains cool to Aaron, although he admits to himself that he misses their old companionship. For recompense, Duncan takes Chief on long rides, occasionally to the haunted landscape across the river which makes him shiver, even as it continues to make Chief skittish (278-79). Duncan also visits Aunt Virgy, whose tales of old times lull him into dreaming: "Each time the impression was nearly the same: the dreams began in a contentment that gradually was dispelled by the threat of an unnamed evil, an evil with which he had neither the knowledge nor the strength to cope." Once he wakes up thinking of the crow, and when he asks about it, Aunt Virgy alleges that it is not around, but Duncan sees it on its customary perch. The day comes when Chief apparently breaks down his stall door, goes to the Jordan farm to fight the stallion, and is shot dead by Dicky Jordan (285).

Now totally blind, Aunt Virgy freezes to death outside her cabin, her hand offering evidence that the crow had pecked her. The crow flies away after the body is discovered. Apparently the "special powers" deem that Aunt Virgy is no longer crucial to their design. Duncan has been sunk in apathy since Chief's death, but begins to have "on occasion moments when he felt a certain unrest, of the kind one feels under a fixed and unseen gaze" (293). One night, as he attempts to get warm by the hearth, he became conscious of a certain unfocused discomfort. In time he realizes that Aaron, unaware that he can be seen, is outside spying on him. Then, realizing that he has been seen, Aaron knocks at the door, giving Duncan the impression "that Aaron was something, a spirit, tossed there, suspended a moment in that tiny square of light by the north wind that whirled him in bitter and eternal darkness somewhere over the roof of the world" (298). Duncan's perception seems to be colored by the Milton he has been reading. But his whole world has been uncanny for so long that his impression of Aaron seems unexceptional to him. – Aaron offers a flimsy reason for his visit: he needs Duncan's help at his still. Ignoring his earlier intuitions about Aaron, Duncan eventually agrees to help. The still is barely reached when Aaron begins his attack, first expressing sympathy for Chief's death, then musing that it was Dicky Jordan who killed him. Then he tells Duncan that Dicky had bragged to him of his sexual prowess with Nettie: "Said he knew she wouldn't stay [with Duncan], though, after what he give her" (303). He adds that Nettie is once again Dicky's mistress. – Both lines of Aaron's attack insinuate that Duncan is dominated by a castration complex. As Aaron pressed his argument "his voice was still controlled, but quick, lancelike. He seemed to lean toward Duncan with the words: 'Set on it then, by God. Don't even stir. Spread your legs out and let him cut your cods clean off... if he ain't got them already. What in the hell are you –'" (305). After Duncan's interruption, Aaron finishes his question, "– a gelding?" neatly implying that he understands the deeper reason for Duncan's attachment to Chief. Thus goaded, Duncan decides that, if Aaron will help him, he will kill Dicky. Then he gets drunk drinking Aaron's moonshine. – The next day before nightfall, as Duncan waits to return to the still, he watches his life pass before his eyes, seeing himself as a child, Nettie, his first wife, his father, Garner, Margaret Mary, Dicky. So completely is his unconscious dominated by repression, though, that he does not picture the one whose actions precipitated the action that he is about to take. Although he recognizes that Aaron "may have schemed and goaded," perhaps even realizes that the shotgun Aaron leaves in his doorway is an obvious attempt to shame him for his castration complex, he feels that he has been fated to kill, by what "special power" he does not consider.

    After Duncan kills Dicky, he and Aaron bury the body. Then they return to the campfire at the still: "as the fire burned down they moved closer to it. At the last he could feel the very warmth of Aaron's body close to his side" (316). The scene ends with more suggestiveness. Duncan says, "I'd like to help you, whenever you want me to. Come get me any time," to which Aaron replies, "I'm obliged to you," with

Duncan catching "the ghost of tenderness in his face" (317). If Duncan's behavior hints of a homoerotic motivation in this scene, Aaron knows that that inclination had its origin in his early relation with his mother. Thus he adopts a maternal behavior toward Duncan, sitting over him as he sleeps, then soothing him when he wakes: "patiently, as though Duncan had been a child, Aaron laid his fears. All of them, until, in a pause, Duncan was left with a sense of release, of absolution almost. In this sudden bath of innocence he floated" (320).

During Duncan's bedridden crisis his sense of innocence soon vanishes, being replaced by dreams of "familiar faces, but distorted now, grown vile, hideous in the last festering stage of putrefaction. His lids would not shut out the sight; it met him whenever he turned. Aaron's hand was on his shoulder" (321). For all of his maternal posture, Aaron has become the uncanny "double," the shadow. When Duncan becomes aware that Aaron is with him, he first discovers his presence by seeing his shadow on the ceiling. As long as he remains in the room Aaron is first detected by Duncan by his shadow (321, 322 twice, 323). Aaron the shadow, representing the "evil and base side" of Duncan (Cirlot 277), becomes for Duncan "the uncanny harbinger of death" ("Uncanny" 235). When Aaron returns, he brings Duncan not a jar of maternal mash, but the distillation of such mash. The scene describes how Duncan's maternal need is distilled into his homoerotic inclination: "The neck of the jug was warm where Aaron's hand had held it. All at once the gift seemed a great thing. He looked up at Aaron with a gratitude that displaced even the urgency of the question in his mind," i.e. what was the public response to Dicky's disappearance (324). Duncan's desire for connection transcends his instinct for survival.

In a few days, learning from his brother-in-law that the sheriff suspects that Aaron is Dicky's murderer, Duncan rushes to his cabin, only to find it deserted. In his subsequent agitated movements he discovers that he is being followed by Aaron's dog. At home he dreams of escaping with Aaron to South America, "a place with many springs and forests, of great trees with spirits in them, of the beating ocean and a sky as unblemished and high as heaven," a plan that they had dwelled upon during Duncan's crisis after the murder. "He thought of Aaron. Upon this image his mind closed tenderly" (340). Thus his fantasy of returning to the womb is conjoined with his romantic fantasy of an escape with his loved one. – When Logan, his father's loyal farm hand, comes to the house to say that he must leave his employ, he and Duncan see Aaron's dog. Logan remarks that he had seen the dog at the barn the morning that Chief had gotten loose. Duncan immediately realizes that Aaron had engineered his killing of Dicky. But immediately Duncan excuses Aaron: "Aaron had only to recognize in Duncan an incipient likeness of himself. His own life was his model; his purpose was to create another in his moral image, a fellow in his loneliness" (344). Duncan "regretted that Logan had come; he thought of Aaron's gentleness. He saw the jug standing yet on the floor by his bed. How warm the neck of it had been when he took it from Aaron's hand. Through the whole night they had been that way; there was nothing feigned in that. Now he shivered with the cold" (345). – Duncan sees "himself as a man half stricken at the outset, only waiting in ignorance for what was bound to fall. The cause long preceded Aaron. He had himself to blame for this" (347-48). Duncan correctly locates the origin of his character, but, of course, because of repression, cannot identify the factor which formed it. Retrieving Aaron's money, Duncan sets about to rescue him: "the thought of Aaron's glad face brought a kind of serene joy" (348).

With Duncan's help Aaron escapes from jail, but in doing so unnecessarily kills a deputy, again reminding Duncan of the character that Aaron asserts, in contradistinction to the character that Duncan projects onto him. Aaron immediately becomes dominant, insisting that they flee with a boat on the river rather than by truck. But the sheriff quickly divines their route, and he and his deputies rake the river with spotlights. Then the authorities employ a motorboat, which will quickly overtake the fugitives. Aaron and Duncan guide their boat "through a gap in the overhanging branches" up a small tributary (357), which is vaginal topography. Sinking the boat, they enter "a ravine that mounted between two steep hillsides. They climb "slick stairsteps of rock over which small cascades of water tumbled," to discover "a horizontal slit in the foot of the bluff under a ledge of rock. It was high enough for a man to get into on his belly. Into this they would crawl if the men came close enough" (360-62). As they wait, Duncan realizes where he is: "he saw a grove of dead and half-living timber, each trunk arrested as it were, in mid-gasp, in a choke of roots that struggled like so many serpents for entrance into the stone-cropping earth.... He remembered his night rides here, the chill he had felt always when he rode down into these flats. He had another wave of shudders" (363). Still, his repression prevents him from wondering about such a significant physical reaction.

When the authorities approach, Duncan and Aaron slide "feet-first" into the slit. As the sheriff approaches, Aaron, seemingly controlled by some violent force, slithers out to the edge of the bluff. There, as Duncan joins him, Aaron trembles "as with a half-governed fit," until his body is "bunched and pulsating" (365), as if like a snake. Coming close, the sheriff sees Aaron: "if anything the spastic movements of Aaron's body, the tic at the corners of his lips, had grown more violent" (366). Freud speaks of the "uncanny effects of epilepsy and of madness": "the layman sees in them the working of forces hitherto unsuspected in his fellow-men, but at the same time he is dimly aware of them in remote corners of his own being. The Middle Ages quite consistently ascribed all such maladies to the influence of demons, and in this their psychology was almost correct" ("Uncanny" 243). It must be Duncan's realization that Aaron is possessed by "demons" that prompts him to confess to the sheriff that he, without blaming "demons," killed Dicky; it must be the same realization that prompts him protect the sheriff by struggling with Aaron, during which action Aaron shoots him in the chest (368).

Aaron carries Duncan back to the boat, drags it to the river. But the sheriff kills Aaron. As Duncan lies dying in the drifting boat in the maternal medium, perhaps he realizes that he has been drifting all his life because of the maternal current. Thus he had lived uncannily in an uncanny world until his eyes were opened to the profound uncanniness of Aaron McCool. *The Innocent* is brilliantly conceived and brilliantly executed, for each succeeding scene deepens the reader's understanding of the controlling role of the uncanny in Duncan Welsh's life and death.

NOTES

1 While Freud considered but rejected the possibility that it was woman whom man feared as the castrator, he was bound by other tenets of his psychoanalytic system to identify the father, not the mother, as the threat of castration perceived by the child ("History" 86). Many later critics, including Creed (158-66), have considered this identification a shortcoming in Freud's castration theory.

2 Thus Creed: "... Kristeva argues that the subject's first contact with 'authority' is with the maternal authority when the child learns, through interaction with the mother, about its body: the shape of the body, the clean and the unclean, the proper and improper areas of the body. It is the concept of the 'maternal authority' that, in my analysis of the monstrous-feminine in horror, I will expand and extend into the symbolic in relation to castration" (12).

3 The presence of humans associated with animals who seem to think like humans – Aunt Virgy with her crow, Duncan with his horse, Aaron with his dog – contributes greatly to the uncanniness of the world of *The Innocent*.

4 To support his contention that "the wilderness has always been a source of the uncanny for American writers," Lloyd-Smith cites, among other texts, "The Bear" (151).

5 Creed writes: "According to Freud, every child either watches its parents in the act of sexual intercourse or has phantasies about that act. These phantasies are about origins: the primal scene represents to the child its own origins in its parents' lovemaking; the seduction phantasy is about the origin of sexual desire; and the phantasy of castration pictures the origins of sexual difference." In "From the History of an Infantile Neurosis" Freud left open the question of the cause of the phantasy but suggested that it may initially be aroused by "an observation of the sexual intercourse of animals" (59). The point is that Duncan, even at the moment that he is controlled by an instinctive drive, is still haunted by repressed thoughts. On the spot where he is causing life, Aunt Virgy had, during the war, caused death.

WORKS CITED

Cirlot, J. E. *A Dictionary of Symbols.* Tr. Jack Sage. New York: Philosophical Library, 1962.

Creed, Barbara. *The Monstrous-Feminine: Film, Feminism, Psychoanalysis.* London: Routledge, 1993.

Dijkstra, Bram. *Idols of Perversity: Fantasies of Feminine Evil in Fin-de Siècle Culture.* New York: Oxford UP, 1986.

Freud, Sigmund. "From the History of an Infantile Neurosis." *The Standard Edition of the Complete Psychological Works of Sigmund Freud.* Ed. James Strachey. London: Hogarth, 1957. Vol. 17. 1-122.

—. *The Interpretation of Dreams. SE.* Vol. 4. 1-338; Vol. 5. 339-565.

—. "Leonardo da Vinci and a Memory of his Childhood." *SE.* Vol. 11. 59-137.

—. "On the Universal Tendency to Debasement in the Sphere of Love." *SE.* Vol. 11. 171-90.

—. *Three Essays on the Theory of Sexuality. SE.* Vol. 7. 123-243.

—. "The Uncanny." *SE.* Vol. 17. 217-52.

Grant, Frederick C., and H. H. Rowley, eds. of revised ed. *Dictionary of the Bible,* ed. James Hastings. New York: Scribner's, 1963.

Gutheil, Emil A. *The Handbook of Dream Analysis.* New York: Grove, 1951.

Jones, A. "St Matthew." *A Catholic Commentary on Holy Scripture.* Ed. Bernard Orchard. New York: Nelson, 1953. 851-904.

Kirschner, Lewis A. Rev. of *The Skin Ego,* by Didier Anzieu. *International Journal of Psycho-Analysis* 71 (1990): 543-46.

Lloyd-Smith, Allan Gardner. *Uncanny American Fiction: Medusa's Face.* New York: St. Martin's, 1989.

Phillips, Adam. *On Kissing, Tickling, and Being Bored: Psychoanalytic Essays on the Unexamined Life.* Cambridge: Harvard UP, 1993.

Power, E. "Exodus." *A Catholic Commentary on Holy Scripture.* Ed. Bernard Orchard. New York: Nelson, 1953. 206-28.

Rose, H. J. *A Handbook of Greek Mythology.* New York: Dutton, 1959.

Rycroft, Charles. *Anxiety and Neurosis.* London: Pelican, 1970.

Thomas, Clayton L., ed. *Taber's Cyclopedic Medical Dictionary.* Philadelphia: Davis, 1981.

Vauthier, Simone. "Gratuitous Hypothesis: A Reading of Madison Jones' *The Innocent.*" *Recherches Anglaises et Americaines* 7 (1974): 191-219.

A DECLARATION OF INDEPENDENCE:

FOREST OF THE NIGHT

George Garrett

In a remarkably open and altogether interesting essay about his life and his work, written for *Contemporary Authors: Autobiography Series* (Vol. 11, 1990, 171-87), Madison Jones said of this book, his second published novel: "*Forest of the Night* would turn out to be, I believe, the least successful of my novels. Yet I sometimes feel that it could have been my best." He goes on to say that the last third of the novel suffers from his own impatience, that its last part is, as a result, hurried and not fully realized. He is entitled to that judgment. He wrote the story and he alone knew and knows now what he hoped to achieve with *Forest of the Night*. But, by the same token, the sympathetic reader is entitled to deal with the experience at hand, what the book in fact is, not what it might have been. If that reader happens to be, as I am, a teacher of literature and a novelist himself, he may feel, as I do, that the author's judgment of the work is too severe and finally not strictly relevant to the reader's experience.

It is entirely in character and appropriate that Madison Jones should demand more from the story than he feels he created and presented. On the other hand, the engaged reader might well argue that the novel, public property as it has been since 1960, requires a quickly moving narrative line for its final act, some change and even relief from the tightly focused intensity of the first two-thirds. And a reader, this one, would have to report that there is no novel, even among the acknowledged masterpieces of the canon, that does not at some point reward the reader and his involved impatience with a more rapid working out of the established premises and promises. Otherwise there would never be an end to any of them. And – and I suspect Madison Jones knows this well – if a serious and gifted writer were ever able to achieve in any one work the perfect model of what he has imagined, there would be no good reason to create another.

What we learn from the experience of writing a novel is how we should have done it in the first place. If the novel is, in Jones's terms, "successful" (by which he clearly means not the success of sales or critical appreciation, but purely and simply, aesthetic satisfaction), it is because the writer has managed, by craft and art, to camouflage overt and inherent flaws and to disguise the undeniable truth that this is only one way among many possible ways that a given story can be viewed and told. We aim always for the sense of inevitability with the neatness of a balanced equation, yet we always know that there is a kind of trickery or magic, smoke and mirrors, involved – the successful novel only *seems* inevitable. That is the most that we can ever hope for, though, of course, we begin and begin again and again, always hoping for something more. All of which adds up to the desperate wisdom of the Wizard of Oz when Judy Garland and the others discover his duplicity: "Pay no attention to that man behind the curtain."

As for the other more mundane ways of measuring success, *Forest of the Night* seems not to have sold a great many copies, at least not enough to give Madison Jones the one thing most writers hope for, the gift of more time and freedom to get on with their work. It was not reviewed as widely or as well as his first novel, *The Innocent*, which had earned respectful attention, including a highly favorable notice in *Time* ("South in Ferment," Feb. 25, 1957). *Forest of the Night* was by no means ignored, but did not earn as much national space or as unmixed praise as his first novel had. *Kirkus* praised the immediacy and authenticity of the story while complaining about the "brutality" of it. *Library Journal*, perhaps more influential then than now, was not very helpful, inaccurately describing the book as "a portrayal of small town drudgery," and faulting the writing for "a style full of introspective platitudes," concluding in final judgment that it was "a waste of reading time." *Forest of the Night* earned a positive, if mixed, notice in the *Herald Tribune Book Review*, complaining that the book was "too dark."

This kind of thing, though it may hurt the writer's feelings, is chiefly important in another way. Publishers tend to take the initial reviews more seriously than larger and longer views. The chief concern of the publisher is the "shelf life" of the book at hand. In 1960 the shelf life of a novel, other than a bestseller, was about four months. Now it is more like four weeks. Madison Jones's relationships with publishers are typical enough to be emblematic of most of the serious – or, to use the more recent term, 'literary' writers of our generation. With the notable exception of a mere handful of American writers – John Updike is an example – most of our novelists have moved restlessly from publisher to publisher according to the critical and commercial success of their books. I count seven different publishers for the works of Madison Jones, four of them from among the major commercial publishing houses of the times – Harcourt, Viking, Crown, and Doubleday. The truth is that it is a fairly stable record for our era. My own record is probably more typical: sixteen different publishers, five of them large commercial houses. In his autobiographical essay for *Contemporary Authors*, Jones shows himself to have been cheerfully innocent at the outset of some of the problems and details of modern publishing. He earned only three rejections of *The Innocent* before Harcourt Brace accepted it and those rejections troubled him more than they might have if he had known the publishing histories of many of his contemporaries.

More important to the writer, at least before mergers and conglomerates took over American commercial publishing, was serious critical attention conferred by literary critics of reputation and integrity. Their criticism could make, or break, careers. Their essay-reviews and critical pieces, if any, come on the scene too late, usually, to have any direct effect on sales and journalistic reviews. The major literary reviews and quarterlies appear months, sometimes years after a given book had come and gone. With the support of his mentors and admirers, people like Donald Davidson, Allen Tate, Andrew Lytle (to whom *Forest of the Night* is dedicated), Walter Sullivan, and Monroe Spears, and friends like Flannery O'Connor, Madison Jones received a good deal of respectful critical praise. Two books in particular led to considerable encouraging attention. *An Exile* (1967), which became a film, *I Walk the Line*, with Gregory Peck, and *A Cry of Absence* (1971) which earned a prominent place on the *New York Times Book Review*'s bestseller list. Perhaps most important and helpful was "A New Classic," by Monroe Spears (*Sewanee Review*, Vol. 80/1, 1972, 168-72) in which Spears celebrated *A Cry of Absence* as "an authentic, pure, and deeply moving tragedy," and praised the novel as "a major work of art."

Partly because of the well-earned attention given to *A Cry of Absence*, the earlier and less conventionally successful *Forest of the Night* has subsequently received less critical attention than it might have. Ashley Brown's piece in the special edition of *The Chattahoochee Review* (Vol. 17/1, 1996, 67-73), "Experience in the West: Madison Jones's Immersion in History," is an outstanding and valuable exception, as is M. E. Bradford's earlier "Madison Jones" in *The History of Southern Literature*, edited by Louis D. Rubin, Jr., 1985. Bradford wrote of *Forest of the Night*: "There is no more powerful exposé of the myth of the New Eden in our literature." Not long after the original publication, critic Arthur Mizener, in a chronicle review, "Some Kinds of Modern Novel," of eight recent historical novels for *The Sewanee Review* (Vol. 69/1, 1961, 154-64), praised *Forest of the Night* as the best of the lot, though he somewhat undercut the praise with extended comments on the limits and faults of the historical novel as a form. Ashley Brown's important piece places *Forest of the Night* in a Southern literary context: "Lytle and his contemporaries almost inevitably wrote novels about the history that was accessible to them.... But the next generation, that included Eudora Welty and Peter Taylor, then Elizabeth Spencer, were seldom interested in the historical subject, and Flannery O'Connor and Walker Percy (a late-comer to fiction) shunned it on principle. This is largely true of Madison Jones; the exception among his books is *Forest of the Night*...." (Bear in mind that Brown's essay appeared before *Nashville 1864: The Dying of the Light* was published.)

The conventionally correct, and probably the most fruitful way to talk about *Forest of the Night* is to deal with it, both in general and in detail, within the context of all Jones's work so far. Certainly, as critics and reviewers early and late have noted, there are close connections among all his work, more intensely so than is the case with many of his contemporaries. In an essay published in *Southern Fiction Today: Renascence and Beyond* (1969) edited by George Core ("The New Faustus: The Southern Renascence and the Joycean Aesthetic," 1-15), Walter

Sullivan, dealing specifically with *An Exile*, writes: "The novel is clear, and the book like all of Jones's work is full of bucolic imagery, of sequences flagrantly calculated to show the evil of urbanization and the questionable nature of material progress." Thus Sullivan assumes, and it proves to be a safe and useful assumption, that there are both thematic and technical kinships in all of Jones's books. It is an observation made by an anonymous critic for *The Virginia Quarterly Review* (Vol. 44/1, 1968, viii) likewise commenting on *An Exile* and its relation to the other stories: "Not many present-day writers are able to evoke an atmosphere of terror so overwhelming nor to conjure so artfully a sense of anxiety and dread."

Others have noted the similarity, with variations, of his protagonists to each other. And there is some value in comparing and contrasting Jonathan Cannon of *Forest of the Night* with Duncan Welsh of *The Innocent*, Percy Youngblood of *A Buried Land*, Hank Tawes of *An Exile*, Hester Glenn of *A Cry of Absence*, Jud Rivers of *Passage through Gehenna*, etc. Though they are each distinctly different, and aptly representative of their particular times, they have in common, whether they realize it or not, the wound of Original Sin. Madison Jones has been unflinchingly explicit about this. "Adam ate of the tree of the knowledge of good and evil and was cast out forever, and we all share his condition. Evil is a prime fact of our existence: we may be forgiven for it but we cannot escape it" (*Contemporary Authors* 180). Speaking of Percy Youngblood in *A Buried Land*, he points out the pattern that links him to other protagonists: "Here my hero, in flight from a world he finds intolerable, like Duncan and Jonathan before him, commits himself to a different world where imagined redemption lies. But what awaits him is not redemption. No worldly rejection can separate us from the evils that are ours." The allusion is to the passage (on the reverse side of the theological coin) of St. Paul in the eighth chapter of Romans: "For I am persuaded, that neither death, nor life, nor angels, nor principalities, nor powers, nor things present, nor things to come, nor height, nor depth, nor any other creature, shall be able to separate us from the love of God, which is in Christ Jesus our Lord."

Jones tells us in *Forest of the Night* that he set out to write "a terrible ballad or legend," "a controlled nightmare," "a story about the making of a Harpe." It was originally to be a story of the Harpe brothers, savage and brutal outlaws of Tennessee and the Natchez Trace in frontier days. But the story of the Harpes, told directly, was limited by being too well known. So instead, though the Harpes do, indeed, appear in person and in character, he wrote of a young man of high hopes and Jeffersonian ideals and of admirable character who, bit by bit, slowly and surely, and in spite of all his better angels, becomes a kind of Harpe, himself and is, in fact, taken by others to be one of the Harpes. And in the feverish nightmare of the final part of the story, he comes to suspect that this is somehow true. Here is what Madison Jones had to say about the essential weakness of his central character in *Forest of the Night*: "My hero, Jonathan Cannon, is a young idealist smitten with Rousseauesque ideas (ideas that entered importantly into the thinking of makers of our constitution) about the goodness of man in the state of nature, and evil as mere negation created by the dead hand of the past" (181-82). Jonathan's initiation comes in the opening scene when he tries to comfort and help a terribly wounded and dying Indian who uses the last of his vital energy and strength to try to kill Jonathan.

Jonathan has come west into the wilderness, coming from Virginia in the year 1802 in the hope of being a schoolmaster in Nashville or one of the settlements. As he tells Judith Gray, who will become the woman in his life: "Someday there'll be schools for everybody – free. That's what President Jefferson wants.... Did you ever think what a difference it would make if there were schools for everybody, rich and poor? I don't believe most people dream how much good it would do" (35). Badly wounded by the dying Indian at the outset of his story, Jonathan imagines his father's voice explaining what has just happened: "He was blind with pain and in his blindness blamed you because you are a white man. You see how blindness inspired the act. Or, rather, delusion, nothing. It was an act without any real cause… Without his blindness, what object could he have avenged his suffering upon? Because the blame lies with everybody and nobody. Whom would he have attacked? He could have done it only in blindness. And who can blame a blind man for not seeing? To understand is to excuse. Not to excuse him would be to keep the evil alive" (15-16).

Evil turns out to be alive and well in Tennessee in 1802 and awakes in the heart and soul of Jonathan Cannon whose enlightened views are tossed aside as he is inexorably reduced to a kind of brutal and loveless savagery. It is a dark story set in a dark world. It is, in Ashley Brown's words, "suffused with death." But, even so, through it all there is an older man, Eli, friend to Jonathan, an exemplary man of courage, honor, and simple purity of character who sees what is worthwhile about Jonathan and who manages, several crucial times, to save him from others and himself. Finally asked why and what for by Jonathan, Eli allows: "Like I owed it to learn you something." Jonathan answers: "You couldn't have taught me anything.... And it's too late now." To which Eli says, "Maybe it ain't... for you. It'll get to where you can live with it if you keep on living. But just don't never forget it" (302). Not exactly a conventional happy ending, then, but also not without some solace. Life is at least possible "if you keep on living."

Synopsis – and the best I have seen is in Ashley Brown's essay – does not begin to do justice to the power and subtlety of the story line, a well-made, virtuoso narrative rich and full with incident, urgent suspense, and complex, fully dimensional characters. Similarly a more abstract approach, focusing tightly on the basic themes and ideas which are dramatized in and by the narrative, tends to be schematic at the expense of the experience. Like all art, the novel has to be taken, first of all, as a sensory affective experience. It has to be felt before it can be considered analytically. The problem for the writer, and the reader, is compounded when the work is historical and set back in time far enough to be at least somewhat alien to the reader's experience. The writer cannot allude to or easily summon up an alien and vanished world. It must be created by credible and authentic concrete details, by vivid sensory engagement. Here Madison Jones's acute sensitivity to nature, not the sentimental pastoral of the urban dilettante, but hard scrabble knowledge of a working farmer joined with an awareness of the mystery and implacable indifference of nature to our comings and goings, all our doings, pays off handsomely. From beginning to end of this story, the vast wilderness, touched hardly at all by the lonely farms and the few rude settlements that pass for civilization, broods over the action of the story. It filters through the leaves of tall trees and pays out shapes and shares of light and shadow. Most of the story comes to us through the perceptions and consciousness of Jonathan. But it is not entirely a third-person, limited point of view. Rather it is omniscient and the first consciousness that we encounter is that of a bear "standing in shaggy, brutish immobility," not so much a symbol of the wilderness as the creature of it:

> Then he stood upright. To a human eye the action might have suggested mockery; or else some secret power of metamorphosis in brute nature. The bear's posture revealed his age, the scars and slick, black patches of hide, the breast of an old warrior. Standing so, he seemed the type of the great passionate sire, begetting and murdering his kind throughout all the wilderness. Now his head, tilted a little upward, swung to left and right in deliberate inquiry. It stopped. He was all attention to something beyond the reach of human ears. With dignity he dropped onto four feet again. He angled across the road at a casual, lumbering walk. Before an opening between two trunks he paused and looked back down the road. (4)

Who sees the bear? Only the invisible narrator and the reader, not even Jonathan, who is coming down the road breaking the silence. Much later in the story he is clawed by a bear that might as well be the same one.

There are other abrupt switches of point of view, here and there, as needed; and at the tag end of the book, as Eli and Jonathan wait for some Indians to ferry them and their horses across a river, it is the Indians, like the bear of the beginning, who are the observers: "They waited close to the water's edge. As the boat slipped in toward the bank, the Indians stopped their poling. They stood upright, without motion now, and fixed upon the two white men the brooding gaze of the wilderness" (305).

During a considerable part of the story Jonathan suffers from a nameless fever and thus his perceptions are (long before "magic realism" came to North American attention) distorted and hallucinatory. At times he hears voices. So did the author, who writes in his autobiographical essay – "There are times in the woods when unexplained voices call to you." The triumph of *Forest of the Night* is that the author has managed to translate those voices for us into a living language and to create a compelling, vividly realized story that questions some of our most cherished and comfortable assumptions.

Madison Jones has continued writing fiction, a series of important and influential books, all of them aesthetically successful, several successful in more mundane terms. The question that inevitably arises among readers, if not often from veteran professional writers, is how has he done so much so well and yet not (yet) been appropriately recognized and rewarded. It is a question too complex to be easily answered. But a few things can be said. Like others among our finest literary writers, he has become the victim of new trends and the economics of commercial publishing. There has also been a critical change, a movement away from interest in and appreciation of the South and its writers. Once again, as in the years from 1865 at least until the turn of that century, Southern writing is respectable in literary circles only insofar as it confirms presuppositions devoutly maintained by others. Since there is no way to deny the achievement of the earlier generation, the generation of Faulkner and the Fugitives and others, it is easier to write off the generations that have followed after. After *Forest of the Night* came the decade of the 1960s which witnessed the transformation of everything, from high art to soda pop, into political statement. Which witnessed new threats to literature from all sides, from death by theory to the rapid contagion of functional illiteracy. Which witnessed a radical change in American values and the rapidly spreading fungus, on a global level, of a vulgar popular culture that celebrates and hugely rewards rock stars, rap singers, slam dunkers and honors celebrity for its own sake. Reviewing (Southerner) Tom Wolfe's *Hooking Up* in *The New York Times Book Review* (5 November, 2000, 6) Maureen Dowd points out the obvious – that his satire cannot keep up with American reality: "By the time we got to the Molière bedroom farce of Clinton and Lewinsky, America had grown so wacky and gossipy and shameless and solipsistic and materialistic, [that] satire was simply redundant." It is as if the very wilderness that Jones created in *Forest of the Night*, having vanished, has reappeared as inward and spiritual in an urban setting.

If so, then where is the place in all our culture for the serious and gifted writer who dedicates his life and art to the exploration of serious issues? There is, of course, no answer. Except for the undeniable fact that good work has been done and continues to be done and is waiting to be found. Except for the fact that there can still be a collection of essays like this one on Madison Jones's work, where we speak to each other about what matters to us.

CLEANSING THE HOUSE:

RACE AND CULTURE IN *A CRY OF ABSENCE*

Jewel Spears Brooker

Madison Jones is a novelist obsessed with a particular place, a particular time, and a particular theme. For more than half a century, from *The Innocent* (1957) to *Nashville 1864* (1997), he has focused on the American South in the nineteenth and twentieth centuries, and whatever his particular subject, his more general theme has always been the continuing effect of the Civil War upon the culture and the psyche of his region and its people. The background for all of his novels includes the nineteenth-century collapse of social and political order in the United States and the ensuing four-year catastrophe pitting brothers against brothers. His narratives assume, further, that the war did not end racial and class divisions within the region, but, rather, that it nurtured old resentments and bred new ones, wounding the psyches of children not yet born, for generations to come. Jones repeatedly uses this legacy of resentment and violence as the dark canvas for his portraits – aristocrats, white trash, blacks, deputy sheriffs – all those forlorn figures haunted by the unresolved quarrels of their fathers. In *A Cry of Absence* (1971), Jones offers a penetrating exploration of Southern culture in the middle of the twentieth century. By disclosing the history of the Cameron and Glenn families, and by dramatizing their present struggles and those of their children, he reveals that the scars of the old conflict still shape regional politics and skew personal destiny.

Jones's assumptions about violence and culture can be illuminated by looking at them in terms of René Girard's work in *Violence and the Sacred* (1972) and *The Scapegoat* (1982). Girard argues that there is a close relationship between violence, particularly fratricidal violence, and the development of culture. He maintains that cultures go through cycles, each of which can be analyzed into several distinct stages. The first stage, characterized by political and social stability, is a period in which the hierarchies that hold communities together and keep violence at bay are intact. The second stage, characterized by turmoil, is a time in which hierarchies once taken for granted are disturbed or destroyed. The third, characterized by accelerating violence, sees the emergence of rivalries triggered by the collapse of authority. And the fourth, characterized by crisis or catastrophe, clears the stage and allows for the reconstitution of relationships and the rebuilding of institutions.

Girard makes much of the social and political leveling associated with crisis. He insists that "peace and fecundity depend on cultural distinctions; it is not these distinctions but the loss of them that gives birth to rivalries and sets members of the same family or social group at one another's throats"(*Violence and the Sacred* 49). When social and political differences are weakened or dissolved, the phenomenon of "enemy brothers" emerges, leading first to rivalry and then to violence. Girard's paradigm includes a number of important assumptions about the nature of violence. First, he argues that violence originates in "mimetic desire," i.e., it comes from noticing and copying the desires of others. Second, it tends to be reciprocal, i.e., it feeds on itself through the back-and-forth of rivalry. Third, violence between individuals is contagious and usually leads to a more general crisis involving the community. And fourth, under certain circumstances, violence can be the cure for violence. For violence to be curative, for violence to stop violence, it must assuage rather than feed the desire for individuals to avenge themselves. In ancient times, curative violence involved convergence by a community on a scapegoat or surrogate victim, who became the focal point for community agitation. In modern times, curative violence is administered by the courts or a higher authority on behalf of the victim. If individuals trust their institutions, especially, their judicial system, they are far less likely to take the law into their own hands. Girard supports his theories about violence and culture with numerous examples of antagonistic brothers – Cain and Abel, for example, or Romulus and Remus. In these and other cases, fraternal enmity leads to a crisis in which one of the brothers is killed or expelled, or in which a scapegoat is killed in the name of the community. After the catastrophe, differences are reasserted, hierarchies re-established, and culture rejuvenated.

The background crisis in *A Cry of Absence*, the Civil War and Reconstruction, fits remarkably well into the cultural patterns outlined by Girard. The crisis in the foreground, the struggle for racial integration in American schools, can also be understood in Girardian terms, and as will be evident in the ensuing discussion, the racial and fraternal conflict dramatized in the plot is intelligible in terms of Girard's model of conflict and crisis. The controlling image in Jones's novel is one of literature's oldest – a ruined house. This image enables him to deal simultaneously with several temporal layers as he explores the connection between moral corruption and cultural crisis. He uses the image much as it was used in the Old Testament and Greek drama. The house of David or the house of Atreus stands not only for a palace, but also for a family, a dynasty, and a culture. Because such houses have a Chinese-boxlike structure – i.e., a person exists within a family which exists within a community which exists within a culture –, it is almost inevitable that references to the "house" contain implications both about its occupants and about the culture in which it exists. Other southern writers, notably William Faulkner, have also used the house image to deal with family identity and cultural decay. One thinks of the Compson family, for example, in *The Sound and the Fury*, or of Miss Emily Grierson standing in the shadow of her father in the doorway of his house in "A Rose for Emily."

In *A Cry of Absence*, Jones spotlights three literal houses – all in the same general region of the old south, all built about the same time, all formerly splendid. Two of the houses are in ruins; one is still intact but besieged by destructive forces. The first is the ancestral plantation of the Cameron family; the second is the Cameron Springs home of his heroine, Hester Cameron Glenn; and the third is the birthplace of a Civil War hero, General Luther Brownfield. Metaphorically, these houses are all used to comment on the moral and political condition of the town and region in which they are located. Thus, the ruined plantation is an image of the ruined Confederacy, and the town house of the Cameron family is an image of the town of Cameron Springs. Jones's metaphor not only points toward more inclusive houses such as the town and the region, but toward the families and individuals who occupy the houses. Thus, the ruined Cameron estates can be seen as registers of the ruined family and, within the family, of the matriarch Hester.

The situation in the houses in *A Cry of Absence* reveals another important parallel with ancient thought. In Greek drama, the house image carries with it the idea of an inter-generational curse, a combination of pollutant and punishment associated with the sins of one's ancestors and passed from generation to generation. The Greeks believed that a family could inherit moral liabilities, much as moderns might believe that a family inherits financial obligations. In the house of Atreus, for example, the family of Agamemnon inherits a curse related to inter-generational violence. Parents kill children and children kill parents, and this happens again and again, generation after generation. This curse began with the crimes of Agamemnon's great grandfather Tantalus, and in the *Oresteia*, the chorus reminds us that it has persisted into the present generation, with Agamemnon killing his daughter Iphigenia to gain good winds for his trip to Troy. When he returns from the war, he is murdered by his wife, who is in turn murdered by their son Orestes in his role as avenger. This curse is inherited, but it is also in subtle ways chosen and thus it incurs further consequences. The cycle is finally checked when Apollo and Athena arrange for Orestes to be tried in a legal proceeding in the Aeropagus, a trial that ends in his acquittal.

The modern equivalent of a curse on the house is clearly present in *A Cry of Absence*. In this case, the guilt passed from generation to generation is related to race and it manifests itself by conflicts between brothers. The racial curse begins with the institution of slavery as the basis of the economy of the south and culminates in an archetypal (and Girardian) conflict of brothers in the Civil War. The idea of a curse includes the notion that it is repeated generation after generation; in the language of the Old Testament, "the fathers have eaten sour grapes, and the children's teeth are set on edge" (*Ezekiel* 18.2). Jones has long shown an interest in family conflicts that persist over generations. Drawing on decades of immersion in southern studies and decades of lived experience in Alabama and Tennessee, he focuses on race relations in the states that were part of the Confederacy before the Civil War. He prods the reader to reflect on poignant and painful chapters of southern history – slavery, the War Between the States, Reconstruction, and court-ordered integration. And he uses language and images that remind the reader that violence within families (civil wars) and between races has happened here before and will happen again. The self-repeating nature of the fraternal and racial violence suggests that it is a regional legacy, a curse with a life of its own. The events figured in *A Cry of Absence* are a confirmation of the curse – brothers destroying brothers, whites and blacks at each others' throats. The novel is set in the deep south in the hot summer of 1957, three years after the watershed *Brown vs. Board of Education* decision by the United States Supreme Court, a ruling that precipitated a crisis in the south by mandating racial integration in American schools.

My thesis in this essay has two interrelated parts. The first is that the underlying conflict in *A Cry of Absence* is a conflict of brothers, a conflict only one can survive. This conflict, profoundly Girardian, is evident in the Civil War background, in the Cameron Springs conflict over integrating schools, and most vividly, in the defining conflict between the two sons of the Cameron/Glenn family. The second part of my thesis is that Jones uses the "house" as a symbol of the deteriorating condition of the South over several generations. This house, like its ancient prototypes, carries a curse, racial violence, the most graphic symbol of which is the horrific racial murder around which the plot turns. The curse is both inherited and chosen by this house, both a punishment for old sins and a choice that will bring unimagined agony. Jones shows that larger cultural conflicts, all roughly Girardian, are replicated within Southern houses, Southern families, and most movingly, within the heart of his Southern heroine. In the antebellum houses represented by Fountain Inn, reciprocal violence had led to Civil War, a bloody conflict between brothers, at least in part over the issue of race. The war resulted in the defeat and humiliation of the south, and that humiliation has made the antagonism an indelible part of regional memory. Collective memory of the war is inseparable from the curse, and in each subsequent generation, the conflict repeats itself on a microcosmic level, within communities and families. In the present time of the novel, that is, the summer of 1957, mob violence has resulted in the erosion of distinctions and the proliferation of violence within the community.

"In such a world, what could a person do except cleanse his house and shut his door against the stink of dissolution" (*CA* 15). The racial conflict in the community culminates in the murder of a black youth, and the fraternal conflict in Hester's house culminates in the death of the son she loved most intensely. The conflict within Hester herself is also destructive, leading to her suicide.

As a born and bred southerner, Jones clearly understands the difficult issues for people on both sides of the fraternal and racial divide. One of his major achievements in *A Cry of Absence* is the combination of genuine sympathy for his characters with unflinching criticism of their racism, whether blatant or subtle. Jones appreciates the burden that history and circumstances have placed on his heroine, but nevertheless, he implicates her in the horror at the heart of his story. By unmasking the killing of the black youth as racial scapegoating, by revealing Hester's shaping hand on the child who cast the stones, he reveals the insidious racism hidden in her convictions about the preservation of tradition. In the course of the novel she comes to realize all of this herself and also to accept her responsibility in the death of her son. Hester is not, however, the villain in this novel. Far worse are those who try to evade responsibility for their sins and those of their fathers by turning their black brothers into scapegoats and those in the judicial system who are too weak to secure the public confidence that is essential in curbing reciprocal violence. So violence continues unchecked, first with Cam's death and then with Hester's. Racial turbulence persists, and as the novel ends, a white man shoots a black man who is in a car with a white woman, and blacks take revenge by savagely beating a white deliveryman.

Of the many houses in *A Cry of Absence*, three are particularly important in interpreting the novel. The first is the Cameron Springs home of Jones's heroine. The second is Fountain Inn, a nearby plantation which was her ancestral home and is now in ruins. And the third is an antebellum mansion, once the home of Civil War General Luther Brownfield, but now occupied by white trash. Jones provides descriptions not only of the interiors of these houses, but also of their exteriors, their grounds and neighborhoods. And within each house, he places families and individuals. Jones includes in his representation the blacks who live in the house or the environs, thus enabling his reader to observe how racial problems exist within houses and across generations. The systematic interrelatedness of the houses is supported by Jones's double focus on interiors and exteriors. There are parallel houses, co-existing in time and space, and there are others that are nestled within each other in a context that is in turn part of a larger context. The Cameron house, for example, is contained in the American south, which is contained in a larger house, the United States. The south, in turn, contains smaller houses – states and towns and plantations and families. Within these houses, there is temporal succession, with houses rising and falling across the years. The Confederacy, a great house now fallen, is a backdrop in most of Jones's work, as it is in the works of Faulkner and other Southern masters. It is full of ghosts who even today linger in the chambers and corridors of the region. Hester Cameron's tragedy is inseparable from the dismantled Confederacy, for the moral and regional alliances sealed by the Civil War are replicated in the struggles of which she is a part.

The house in which the action begins and ends is an imposing edifice on tree-lined Hampton Street in the town of Cameron Springs. It is the home of Hester Cameron Glenn, and her two sons, and its history is closely identified with that of the town itself. Hester's great grandfather, the Civil War General for whom the town is named, built it in 1850 as his town house, and in due course, he gave it to his son, Hester's grandfather, who in turn bequeathed it to Hester's father, from whom she received it. Portraits of illustrious ancestors keep watch from its walls, portraits before which Hester often pauses to gain strength in dealing with her wayward sons. The interior of the house includes, downstairs, a kitchen, used not only for eating but for conversations, and upstairs, the bedrooms of Hester and her sons Ames and Cameron. She is often seen or imagined by her sons as framed by the window of her bedroom, a lonely figure looking out on a confusing world. Her youngest son's room, remarkable for its neatness, is mute testimony to his penchant for order, his inclination to believe that everything has its place. Her eldest son's room is usually unoccupied, for he is a college student, infrequently at home. Ames exists in a liminal space between his family's home and the outside world, looking out and looking in by turns, depending on whether he is at home or at the university. If Ames is caught between inside and outside, Hester is caught between then and now, past and future, a dilemma figured in the history of her house, which extends back to antebellum days and forward into an unknown but very different future. With the help of her black hired hands – Lucius (her gardener) and Willodean (her housekeeper) –, Hester meticulously maintains the house, inside and out, and at the end of the novel, she leaves it to her surviving son.

The immediate context of Hester's house, its yard, is a beautiful and intimate garden, a bower of camellias and sasanquas in which she can relax with the newspapers or wait for her sons to return home. This garden, a sanctuary, is surrounded by hedges that clearly mark the line between her world and that of the town. The sense of harmony and order that characterizes Hester's house extends to racial relations within her house. She remembers approvingly that her father, a former mayor of Cameron Springs, had sheltered a black man who was fleeing from a mob, and she herself is a model of kindness in dealing with her black helpers. She respects Lucius, who has been with the family for a long time, and quietly pays for his wife's operations. He, in turn, is devoted to her and her sons; he is totally dependable. He knows that he is free to leave, free to head north, but he chooses to stay as the maintenance man for Hester's house and garden. Both Hester and Lucius believe that fate has put them in place and that it is best not to try to rearrange social and racial boundaries.

Hester Cameron Glenn has passed most of her life in the house on Hampton Street, but the house she lives in is less important than the house that lives in her. She spent her childhood summers with her Cameron grandparents at Fountain Inn, their plantation home, and like the speaker in Dylan Thomas's "Fern Hill," she recurs to these "lamb white days" of early childhood with a profound sense of loss. Fountain Inn was built by her great-grandfather, and though she spent only a few summers there, she remembers it as her true home, "as if she had lived there a dimly remembered primal life before this present one had dawned" (CA 91). Fountain Inn is now a ruin, but in her imagination, it retains its power, recalling not only lost splendor, but also lost innocence.

Hester's ideal reconstruction of Fountain Inn is described in detail at the beginning of part II of *A Cry of Absence*. It is crucial to notice that while Hester would have had memories of Fountain Inn, she would not have had memories of the antebellum south. She is forty-eight years old in 1957, and thus was born about 1909, nearly half a century after the end of the war. The memories she cherishes and protects have at least three layers – the first composed of her recollections of early childhood summers at Fountain Inn during the First World War, the second composed of her family's memories of an antebellum world, and the third composed of what she as a child imagined when hearing family stories. Her personal vision of the earlier world takes shape largely from stories told by her grandparents and their black servants, mostly former slaves. The grandmother tells about the childhood of Hester's father. The grandfather, whose shining cavalry sword hangs above the mantel, tells stories of heroes such as Lee and Forrest and Jackson. He also tells Hester and the other grandchildren stories from the Old Testament, reading aloud about God's chosen people – Abraham and Moses and the children of Israel. And Old Burtie, the black housekeeper who is a contemporary of the grandparents, loves to entertain the children with inexhaustible stories of her "wonderful life" in the old days.

Importantly, then, Hester's Fountain Inn is an ideal constructed of her own memories and her memories of the memories of defeated soldiers and former slaves. And even more vivid than her memory of what she experienced in those summers of yesteryear is her memory of what she imagined.

> When Hester was a very young child she had imagined that the Lord had laid [Fountain Inn] out with His own hand – the patterned garden beside the house, the orchard behind, a fence here, and there a swooping meadow half shady with water oaks. Down the incline toward the gate, as it had done from the beginning, the drive divided itself to pass around the first and greatest of pecan trees. Boxwood balanced boxwood along the front walk and twin urns stood like counterweights at ends of the broad porch step. Who but the Lord could have raised those columns up – and so long ago that the big crossbeam now faintly sagged in the intervals between them? (*CA* 89)

Her childhood Eden is beautiful, orderly, timeless. In this time out of time, beauty was inseparable from balance, from pattern, from clear boundaries. For this paradise lost, Hester devised an alternative creation story, with God himself as the maker of Fountain Inn – the divine architect of its main house, its outbuildings, its wonderful gardens, its noisy animals: "When God made the house and set down in their places behind it the barn and the smokehouse and the four log cabins across the field in a stand of chinaberry trees, there was not a sound in all the world. Then he made birds and chickens and cows, so that when he made people the sounds were already here, whistling and crowing and bawling in the fields." Having made the animals of Fountain Inn, God then created the people – male and female, black and white, rich and poor. "Then he made people: the white ones first, to live in the house, and then the black ones, to feed the stock and farm the cotton that the white people showed them how to plant. It was all exactly as His hand, in that original silence back at the beginning, had made it to be" (*CA* 89).

Hester's paradise includes a divinely ordained social/racial order. She remembers the "cries of colored children" at play and the wonderful time she had with them. She remembers seeing the black workers going about their duties, and hearing their wordless voices "mellow like echoes in a drum." She remembers Old Burtie working in the kitchen or ironing on the veranda. The key to harmony in this primal world is that all of the people at Fountain Inn, even the children, know their place and accept it as inherent in creation; it is a system based on hierarchy and difference, and as long as the differences are respected by all, everything works beautifully.

For Hester, Fountain Inn is not simply some place that used to exist but no longer does. It is a present reality. The sounds still reverberate in her mind – the crowing of the rooster, the swish of the water in the bucket, the ping of the milk in the tin pail, the crunching of the mule eating corn, and much more. The centerpiece of Fountain Inn, the showpiece for which the plantation is named, is a fountain, designed so that "the mouths of four little angels sprayed water into the circular basin around them – cold water, spewed up from deep in the earth" (*CA* 90-91). Through the years, Hester has continued to hear its gentle splashing, its rhythmic soothing music. At moments of stress, she slips back into her first world, replenishing her nostalgic imagination by visits to the ruins. That world is never more than a glance away, for she lives in the home and town built by her family, and most of all, she sees in her youngest son Cam a reincarnation of the virtues of her first world.

The third house which is important for the structure and symbolism of *A Cry of Absence* is the birthplace of a Civil War hero, General Luther Brownfield. Assuming that the General had been middle-aged at the time of the war, he would have been born around 1820, and so by American standards, the house, located just outside Cameron Springs, is rather old. The Cameron Springs Heritage Society is interested in restoring this historic house, and they send Hester, who is the Society secretary, to visit it. As she approaches, the reader sees the property through her eyes. The dismal scene mocks the agrarian ideal that improvement of the estate is incumbent on landowners. The yard is covered with weeds and the big oak trees near the house are dying. And the exterior of the house has been neglected. "Here and there a board was missing, like wounds in the side of the house. What window screens survived were rotten tatters, and many of the panes had been replaced by pieces of cardboard and rag. Around back she saw the remains of the kitchen steps lying detached from the rest of the house, in their place a chunk of yellow stone. On the ground lay refuse – tin cans, bottles, cobs, and blackened cabbage leaves – over which flies crawled and a few bantam chickens pecked" (*CA* 45-46). In one of several details that suggest a parallel between this estate and Fountain Inn, Hester notices the remnants of a fountain protruding out of the weeds. This symbol of lost elegance and fruitfulness impresses her as the "saddest sight of all," and reminds her that, in her afternoon nap, she had dreamed of the fountains of Fountain Inn.

The interior of the Brownfield house is as depressing as the exterior. The plaster is falling and the floor has holes. The rooms have almost no furniture, but are cluttered with trash. The mahogany has been stripped from the mantels, presumably for its cash value in the market. The upstairs rooms have torn ceilings and littered floors. The roof is rotten, allowing pinpricks of light to filter in from above. The floorboards protrude, causing Hester to trip. She pauses before an open window, from which she has an overview of the dismal estate and crumbling fountain. Closing her eyes, she superimposes on this ruin the beautiful fountains of Fountain Inn in its glory.

General Brownfield's family no longer owns the house. It is now occupied by white trash – Hollis Handley, his son Pike, his fifteen-year old daughter, and his incestuously produced infant child/grandchild. The property, which is heavily mortgaged, now belongs to Handley, who fails to do even minimal maintenance. Handley, who exemplifies sloth, is an evil figure whose life has been shaped by envy of those above him, such as Hester, and resentment of those whose skin is black. His gaze is one of the horrors of this novel, as he leers at Hester and gloats about his newfound equality with her, based on the friendship of their sons. A vicious racist, he assumes that he and Hester are also bound by the fact that they are both white and thus have a common enemy. He fears that the government and civil rights advocates are re-drawing the social and political map. "Naw, it ain't the same anymore. The rich and the poor is teaming up. Got to. Else the black niggers be taking everything over – yours and mine, too. Getting more smart every day and the gover'ment right in behind them shoving. No ma'am, we got to see to it – all of us has. 'Cause it's going to have to be some niggers showed a thing or two" (*CA* 50).

Referring to the murder of the black youth, Handley adds "We already done showed the first one" and then using words that will be echoed by Hester's own son, says of the murderers, "whoever it was, they was shore-God doing all us white people a favor."

The problems in this house are myriad, but all can be associated with a lack of understanding of the importance of respecting difference. Handley does not recognize the difference between nature and culture. He allows the wilderness to transgress its boundaries and reclaim the estate. He does not respect the differences which should exist within the family, differences between father and daughter, thus appropriating his daughter as a sexual partner and breeding children from the womb of his own child. He does not acknowledge any difference in class or economic standing, and thus he considers himself to be Hester's equal, and his son Pike to be the equal of Cam. In regard to race, he moves in the opposite direction. He finds the idea of equality with blacks intolerable, and so he magnifies the difference of skin color into a powerful barrier.

People, of course, are also houses. Destroy this house, says Christ of his body, and in three days I will raise it up (*Mark* 14:58). "One need not be a Chamber – to be Haunted," says Emily Dickinson, "One need not be a House – /The Brain has Corridors – surpassing/Material Place" (*Complete Poems* 670). Jones escorts his readers to the innermost sanctum of his houses by taking them into the mind of his heroine. Hester's mind is from one point of view the smallest and most intimate of Jones's chambers, but from another, the most comprehensive, for it contains not only her own private thoughts, but also the history of her family and her region. Her mind encapsulates the central conflict of *A Cry of Absence*. The major conflict, implicit in the struggle between Hester's sons, is between those who see integration as a moral imperative and those who see it as part of the dismantling of tradition. Hester is not only on the wrong side of a historic battle about civil rights; she is also on the losing side. And although she is a principled segregationist, her position puts her in company with some of the most morally degenerate members of her society. On the other side stand strangers in the house; self-righteous zealots bent on social and moral engineering. The social/moral conflict in the town mirrors the division in Hester's house, shown in the archetypal Jacob-and-Esau relation of her sons – Cam, seventeen and the star baseball pitcher for the local high school, shares his mother's sense of tradition and empathizes in her distress; whereas Ames, twenty-one and a student at the state university, sees his mother as an anachronism blocking progress in human rights. This antagonism between her sons, profoundly Girardian, is fought not only in the Hampton Street house, not only in the Cameron family, but most poignantly, within Hester herself. Her body is the house which sheltered them before they were born, her womb the chamber in which they were first loved, her heart the tiny room in which they struggle to the death.

Jones constructs his novel in such a way that he offers three perspectives on his heroine. The first is Hester as she sees herself, shown by giving the story over to her point of view, by allowing her to reveal in her own words her anxieties about race and her warring sons. The second and third perspectives, which supplement and complicate the first, are achieved by merging Hester with and differentiating her from her boys. The second is Hester as she exists in her unconscious, in her vague but powerful instincts, shown by transferring her more primitive self to the characterization of her youngest son; and the third is Hester as she is seen by outsiders, shown by arranging her point of view in counterpoint with that of her eldest, less sympathetic, son.

The first perspective, Hester's self-portrait, is the one that most poignantly conveys the cry of absence. It is created by giving the reader access to her mind and heart, to her nightmares and her aspirations. For thirteen chapters, roughly one-half of the novel, everything is filtered through Hester's consciousness. The woman that emerges from these passages is loving to her sons, charitable to her servants, reverent towards her ancestors, responsible towards her community. This is the Hester who thinks and plans, the consciously constructed self she encounters on waking and sees when she looks into her mirror. In the opening scenes of the book, Hester herself does not come across as particularly attractive – her defensive posture, her aristocratic bearing and manners, her understanding of history, her brooding pride, and even her virtues conspire to make her seem less than she is. As the novel moves forward and her integrity is tested, however, she proves her nobility, in part by the quiet dignity with which she endures pain and sorrow, in part by the total acceptance of responsibility for even her unintended wrongs. In a striking scene at the end of the novel, Hester, numb with grief after burying her son, goes to her critics, the Delmores, on an altruistic mission, to warn them of possible danger to themselves. In language so simple and straightforward that it makes the reader wince, she acknowledges not only her son's guilt but her own. In this complex moment of generosity, grief, and self-castigation, she is met not with sympathy but with judgement. In allowing the Delmores to judge her so harshly, in allowing them to be insensitive to her pain and her courage, Jones disarms his readers, making it impossible for them to toss a single stone.

But there is more to Hester than meets the eye. Jones greatly complicates his portrait by supplementing it with glimpses of her hidden self. In one of the finest technical achievements of this work, Jones concentrates the mother's unconscious desires in her youngest son and shows the effects of those buried longings in her son's primitive crime. Cam is, to borrow a term from Conrad, her secret sharer. He carries the maternal family name and is consistently associated with Hester and her values, while his older brother is associated with the wayward father and the values of the hostile outside world. In the words of the oldest survivor of the Cameron house, Aunt Minnie: "He [Cam] is a Cameron, all right. Like all the Cameron men. It's Ames who is like his father" (*CA* 79). Hester's special bond with Cam is evident in the first chapter of the novel when, distressed by the rudeness of the ladies at a luncheon, she retreats to her bedroom and is comforted by her youngest son who at once senses her unhappiness and longs to alleviate it, promising her that "they won't break us" (*CA* 11). Later as she recalls the bitterness of her failing marriage, she remembers her young sons and her vow that she would be their shield. Fearing that she might have slighted Ames, "in so many ways, indeed,… his father's child," she knows that she has not slighted Cam. In language echoing St. Paul's discussion of God's preferential love for Jacob, she reflects that "before he was born,… she already had loved him… with a kind of all-enfolding love" (*CA* 97). She does not hide from herself the preferential nature of her love, and when she remembers her past, she recalls that in the miserable last year of her marriage, she moved from her husband's room to her baby's; indeed, it became her own, "for always she slept there, taking the little boy into her bed, against her breast, to keep him, and her own heart, warm" (*CA* 98). As he grew, she took enormous pride in his clean-cut good looks and, ironically enough, in his pitching ability; and she took comfort in his empathy with her and in seeing replicated in him her love of the old ones, her sense of tradition.

   This powerful primeval bond between mother and son carries the potential for horror, a fact substantiated by the racial murder and its aftermath. The child has absorbed not only the mother's virtues, but also her prejudices, and he commits a most heinous crime in defense of what he imagines that his mother loves. After the murder, Cam insists that he was acting for her and their ancestors, that he was protecting the honor of the house. As Henry II conveyed to his knights his longing to be rid of Thomas à Becket, so Hester has conveyed by her joys and sorrows the need of relief from those who seem to be tearing her world apart. Using the skill that has made him a baseball star, Cam moves in perfect obedience to what he feels is a wordless command. When Ames tells Hester that Cam is the killer, she confronts her youngest son with the allegation. He denies it, but insists that "whoever did that, did this whole town a favor." Hester protests in horror, and he responds, "Mama, you can't tell me you're really sorry it happened" (*CA* 85). Later, they visit Fountain Inn together, and he tells her that all white people should be glad the murder happened. For a moment, a crack appears in the mother's faith, and she responds, "You sound so cynical, sometimes. And cold" (CA 115). In the climactic chapter of the novel, Hester knows what Cam has done, and he knows that she knows. He explains, "You won't believe me, but I always did like I thought you wanted... I've always tried to be the best, like you wanted me to" (*CA* 190-91). Thinking, "What are you, where did you come from? How did you come from my blood?" Hester insists that what she really wanted was what she had taught him – "Goodness and honor and respect." Both are right, of course, for she is speaking of her willing self and he of her longing self. Cam then broadens the unintended indictment to include the revered grandparents, "If those old people were still alive, you know they'd be glad it happened." She begins to see him as already lost, as a shade among the living, as "a shape barely visible against the gray daylight," and she asks him to turn himself in to the sheriff. When he demurs, she commands him to remove himself from her presence. Realizing that she would prefer to see him dead, he again acts as her surrogate and takes his own life. This child has absorbed her deepest desires like a sponge and, even in death, takes his orders from her darker self. Understanding that she is responsible not only for his life, but also for his death, Hester acts as her own executioner. Mother and son are so closely identified that it could not have been otherwise. It is inconceivable that she could have survived him. By identifying Hester and Cam so intimately, Jones is able to explore the Cameron family, particularly Hester, in a psychological depth worthy of Dostoevsky.

 The third perspective on Hester, the outside view, Jones provides by splitting the point of view between her and her eldest, generally unsympathetic, son, Ames. Some outside view, that of the Delmores, for instance, would have been too harsh. Others, such as those of her friends in the Cameron County Heritage Society, would have been too partisan. Ames, who has one foot in the home circle and one in the larger world, is perfect, for he can temper judgment with sympathy, sympathy with criticism. Eleven chapters of the novel are filtered through his consciousness. Hester speaks first and most, but he speaks in counterpoint to her and, as the only survivor in her doomed house, he has the last word. Hester's thinking and values incline toward an ideal timeless world, but they are immediately criticized by someone who lives most of his life in the time-tarnished real world of the local bar, political action committees, and the university. The point of view alternates between the two, establishing a dialectic not only between mother and son, but between the mother and the absent father, between the aristocratic Camerons and the middle class Glenns. The dialectic created by this split point of view is generational, with Hester speaking for the illustrious dead and Ames speaking for the contemporary and future man on the street.

By means of this bifurcation in point of view, Jones is able to establish a dialectic on history, which Hester feels in her bones and gets from her Heritage Society and which Ames sees in town, hears about in citizens' meetings, and reads about in his university textbooks. There is a dialectic on race, with memories by Hester of her own and her father's amiable and charitable relations with blacks juxtaposed against experience by Ames of riots and racial discord. Hester remembers Cam at twelve pitching balls on a playing field, but Ames remembers him tossing balls in the throwing gallery of a country fair where the target in the hole was a human head, a grinning black face. Hester does not believe that Cam is a killer, but Ames, having grown side by side with him, having struggled with him in the family agon, knows that he is capable of murder; and having seen him at the fair and on the ball field, Ames instantly connects his brother's powerful arm with the arm that stoned the black youth. Ames makes it his mission to force his mother to accept the "truth" about his younger brother. Once she has done so, he tempers his criticism with pity. When at the end of the book the Delmores exult in Hester's humiliation, he becomes protective and tells them to leave her alone. After Cam's death, he supports his mother's fragile arm and feels her pulse beating as if it were "the blood of his own hand" (*CA* 271).

It is the argument of this paper that Jones uses the ancient image of the house to convey the decadent state of the south, especially the "new" south of the 1950s and 1960s. The image serves as structural frame and thematic center for the violence that constitutes the action of the novel. Aesthetically, the image tends to be spatial and static, making it the perfect complement of the temporal and dynamic action it enfolds. Within a context in which there is a dissolution of differences, Jones plots rapidly moving violence which includes midtown bombings, racial assault, racial murder, and suicide; he also shows the interlinking of violent acts, with violence breeding violence. Because the violence is a recurrent version of an old crisis, it can be seen in terms of the working out of a curse, a version of which seems to revisit the region generation after generation. The curse can be identified as the fraternal and racial strife which replicates in miniature the conflict that erupted into America's bloodiest war almost exactly one century earlier. The characters are variations of what René Girard calls "enemy brothers," antagonists both akin and different whose desires lead to accelerating violence. Hester's sons are locked in a struggle which one will not survive. Blacks and whites are engaged in a parallel battle, as are northerners and southerners, and in each clash, one party will be humiliated or annihilated. All of these destructive quarrels are, at bottom, family feuds, all related to the never forgotten war of the 1860s.

In Girard's theory of crisis, a blurring of boundaries (a sudden diminution of structure) is one of the markers of approaching violence. The situations in the various houses in *A Cry of Absence* could be characterized in just such terms. At Fountain Inn, differences were accepted and for the most part respected. It was a hierarchal world in which everyone had a place and seemed to accept that place as divinely ordained. The attempt to subvert those structures led to the cataclysmic violence of the war. In the Brownfield house, differences of all sorts are disregarded. Handley transgresses the boundary between father and daughter, and also between himself and Hester; at the same time, he is spurred to violence by his fear that the line separating whites from blacks is dissolving. He responds with malice to all who disagree with him. His mirror opposite can be seen in the Delmore family, the newcomers who wish to force integration on the town. They refuse to acknowledge any difference related to race or class or tradition, and they too are willing to use violence to force others to accept their point of view. In the Hampton Street house, an awareness of difference is intact, but it is challenged from without, by the Delmores, and from within, by warring sons. Hester is caught between her sons, as she is caught between the Handleys and the Delmores.

A Cry of Absence begins *in medias res*, with a community trying to cope with dissolving boundaries and sporadic violence. When there is general confidence in the justice system, such situations can be controlled by effective law enforcement. Injured parties can turn their grievances over to an impartial higher authority, and thus they are not tempted to take the law into their own hands. In this novel, there is no faith in local law enforcement, which is represented by Monk and Larch, two racist deputy sheriffs. Furthermore, there is little confidence in the courts; it is the attempt of the United States Supreme Court to force school desegregation that precipitates the violence. This breakdown in confidence that justice can be achieved through the law leads to the adoption of more primitive ways of coping with injustice, that is, to scapegoating. Scapegoating involves the murder or expulsion of a single person, with whom the disorder in a community can be associated. If the scapegoating is successful, if the sins of the community are transferred to the victim, the violence is curative, that is, it will be followed by an interval of peace, allowing for the restoration of order. If it is not successful, it becomes one more episode in a chain of reciprocal violence.

In *A Cry of Absence*, the murdered black youth, Otis Stevens, is a classic example of a scapegoat. He is murdered by white youths, not because he is a wrongdoer, but because he is a symbol of the transgression of boundaries thought to be necessary to the social order. After two years in a northern college, he returns home, bent on "liberating his people." His efforts involve "exhortations at meetings in Negro churches and... instances of rudeness toward white people on the streets" (*CA* 18). Even Ames, who deeply sympathizes with the civil rights agenda, finds him obnoxious. As a troublemaker and a member of a demoralized and disliked minority, Stevens fits the age-old profile of a scapegoat. Like most scapegoats, he is considered unclean, and is murdered from a distance, so that the murderers can avoid physical contact. He is stoned, chained to a tree and "rocked" to death by Hester's son Cam and Handley's son Pike. In another echo of ancient scapegoat incidents, including the murder of Jesus, the torturers taunt the victim, turning the murder into sport, "like one of them throwing galleries at the fair" (*CA* 18).

One of Jones's triumphs in *A Cry of Absence* is the combination of an indictment of the south for recurrent racism and a projection of genuine love for the region. The love is shown in several ways, from his descriptions of gardens to his characterization of Hester. The indictment is shown, principally, in the unmasking of scapegoating. The narrative (not the narrator, but the unfolding plot) takes the side of the victim simply by showing that his death was a heinous crime. The story reveals that Otis Stevens was innocent, and in showing this, it not only exonerates him but condemns his far more attractive killer, Cameron Glenn, the handsome southern all-star. Jones underscores Stevens's innocence by paralleling him with Stephen, the first Christian martyr. This identification is suggested by numerous parallels – his name, his speeches in churches, and his condemnation of his contemporaries, their angry response, and the manner of his death. The Biblical Stephen was an irritant, one who dared call the Jews to task for their sins. Enraged by his address to the Sanhedrin, they cast him out of Jerusalem and stoned him (*Acts* 7). Otis Stevens, though by no means faultless, is also calling the community to account, and he is also cast out and stoned. The connection with the Biblical Stephen is explicit within the text of the novel. In a discussion of the murder, Ames reminds his mother that the last time she went to church with her two sons, the sermon was about the stoning of Stephen. Ames wonders whether or not the trigger for this horrific crime might have come from the sermon (*CA* 38).

The death of Otis Stevens fails as a scapegoat event, for it does nothing to assuage the violence in Cameron Springs. It fails for complex reasons, one of which is lack of unanimity regarding the violence and another of which is collective self-deception about the history of the south before and after the Civil War. Unanimity, according to René

Girard, is a crucial element in scapegoating. In order for the turbulence in the community to be transferred to an individual, the community must converge as one on the victim. Cam claims that he is "doing a favor" for the entire community, at least for all whites, but in fact, he is acting only for himself and the darker elements of the community, such as Handley. Hester, for whom he thinks he is acting, is horrified by his ability to murder in cold blood, and in the most poignant scene of the novel, she realizes that the son to whom she has given birth, whom she has fed and nourished and protected, whom she cannot stop loving, is a moral monster. And the "old ones," those revered ancestors in whose name he acts, would also be appalled. Cam's argument that he is acting on behalf of all white people, including his mother and his ancestors, is an example of what Jean-Paul Sartre in *Being and Nothingness* (1943) refers to as bad faith (*mauvaise foi*). Bad faith is basically a lie to oneself, a self-delusion that is mysteriously willed into existence and for which one is accountable. In *A Cry of Absence*, it operates in both individuals and the community at large. In killing Otis Stevens, Cam not only deludes himself into thinking that he is acting for the good of the community, but also into thinking that the victim is the villain in the story. The murderers do not understand that they are repeating the sins of their fathers, and that their black victim is a scapegoat representing not himself but his race.

Both the fact of scapegoating and its failure are important in any understanding of Jones's fine novel. By refusing to allow the narrative to affirm the side of the community (Hester, tradition), Jones leaves no doubt that racism was a major factor in the battles of the 1950s and 1960s. He does not flinch before the truth that bad faith is rampant in southern houses and that innocent people, especially blacks, are being sacrificed to assuage old wounds. At the same time, he refuses to strip his heroine of her dignity and to join the crowd tossing stones at her. It is this combination of sympathy and criticism that gives his narrative its moral and ethical fiber. As *A Cry of Absence* ends, Ames, the only surviving Cameron, stands surveying his ruined house, while outside, the violence continues, with whites and blacks alike still entangled in the dark and bloody web of the curse. This conclusion could be seen as a prophecy that the violence will continue until his fellow southerners cleanse their houses and his government restores faith in American justice.

WORKS CITED

Dickinson, Emily. *Complete Poems*, ed. Thomas H. Johnson. Boston: Little, Brown, 1960.

Girard, René. *The Scapegoat* (1982), trans. Yvonne Freccero. Baltimore: Johns Hopkins UP, 1986.

—. *Violence and the Sacred* (1972) trans. Patrick Gregory. Baltimore: Johns Hopkins UP, 1977.

Jones, Madison. *A Cry of Absence*. New York: Crown Publishers, 1971.

Sartre, Jean-Paul. *Basic Writings*, ed. Stephen Priest. London: Routledge, 2001.

NOBODY IS INNOCENT:

SEASON OF THE STRANGLER AND THE SHORT STORY SEQUENCE

Hans H. Skei

Madison Jones published *Season of the Strangler* in 1982, well into a long writing career that had produced such remarkable achievements as *A Cry of Absence* and *A Buried Land*, to mention two of his very best novels. *Season of the Strangler* is a very fine book, and our appreciation of it has little to do with how well it works as a novel or as a short story sequence. The book is well-structured and written with complete control of narrative techniques as well as of style. It may fail as a novel, if we have rigid demands as to plot development, chronology, and a final revelation or resolution of conflicts. It may fail as a short story cycle because the unifying strategies are too few and the intratextual links rather sparse. Yet the stories in *Season of the Strangler* are contained within a narrative frame, and they share the time-space of the fictive town of Okaloosa in 1969. Scholars of the short story sequence seem to have felt a compulsion to make story cycles unified. We should rather approach a sequence of short stories such as *Season of the Strangler* with an open mind and see how it manages to get the best of two genres: short story and novel, or to see how creative and productive the tension is between individual stories and the whole.

We have twelve stories that all reach a form of closure and may be seen as relatively autonomous. Yet they share a narrative frame, they all relate to the same place and time and – not the least – the strangler and his evil acts are central to all stories. This relative autonomy within the larger framework is a decisive element, and I do think that some of the stories in *Season of the Strangler* could stand alone, e.g. in an anthology, whereas others are more in need of the support of their neighbors to explain the atmosphere of tension and terror, long before the strangler is mentioned in those particular stories. We could say that the fourteen units in the book, Prologue, twelve chapters or stories, Epilogue, simply create a fairly long prose narrative, arranged so that chronology and plot development for the text as a whole are reduced to a minimum. The book gives numerous textual signals that it is both a novel and a short story sequence at the same time, and accordingly I shall try to give a reading that will profit by my seeing the book as a novel *and* as a somewhat unified sequence of stories. If we look at individual stories and the way they cross the borders of each other we may be in a better position to explain the richness of this text. One should nevertheless be free to give more extensive treatment to stories that are important in themselves and as structural units of the book as a whole. The text organizes itself so that a very dramatic series of events, five stranglings of women in a small town, is a structuring device in relation to which a number of characters and events are presented. Within the chosen place and the chosen time span the narrator points a searchlight at human beings, who under the terror of a strangler see their lives threatened, shattered, destroyed. Rumors contribute to this, and most of the characters we meet in this book do not face the new situation with courage or grace.

In my understanding the novel is one of the most inclusive and flexible of all literary forms, always changing, renewing itself, always creating itself anew. Therefore I would have no problems using novelistic terms in a reading of *Season of the Strangler*. But the book gives so many signals that it is something more than a novel, if not radically different from what a novel obviously could be. And I think the textual signals indicating that this is both a novel and a sequence of short stories must be taken seriously. The very word "season" in the title indicates some of the cyclical movement in the text itself. The Prologue and Epilogue provide a frame, which opens and rounds off the text, almost bringing closure to it, but certainly creating a circular movement. The book has twelve chapters, numbered from 1 to 12, but each chapter also has a separate title, almost as if it were a short story. Chapter one functions well both as an opening chapter of a novel and as a completed short story text. From chapter two onwards, we expect as readers to find development, continuity, progress. Instead we find that the text circles back to the same beginning in time, introduces new characters, and tells a story independent of the previous chapter, but interdependent in the sense that people as well as stories relate to the strangler and live in the same city or on the same street. Repetition, and repetition with variation, new stories with new characters, but a few times characters in one story show up in a later story, and a few stories are directly linked through shared characters or because an event in one story becomes the starting point in the next. *Season of the Strangler* is a hybrid form, not somewhere between the novel and the short story collection, but a form that benefits from both genres. Hence, we might profit from a discussion of the so-called short story cycle, which I prefer to call short story sequence, which theorists situate somewhere between novel and story collection, and which I think might offer us better tools for our interpretive work with the text. As I have tried to indicate, a text that deliberately and persuasively wants the best from two genres must be approached with an open mind, also, because the short story sequence, by its very nature, is an open form.

Forrest L. Ingram claimed that he discovered a new literary genre, the short story cycle in his 1972-book *Representative Short Story Cycles of the Twentieth Century*. Ingram discusses the balance that must be sought between the individuality of each story and the demands of the larger unit and points to patterns of recurrence and of development that operate concurrently. His essentialist definitions become rather rigid and normative, and the concept of unity with numerous unifying factors seem to have been basic also to Susan Garland Mann in her *The Short Story Cycle: A Genre Companion and Reference Guide* from 1989, whereas later theories have tried to be more relational, more open, for the great possibilities of variety and renewal the form offers. Robert Luscher states that a short story sequence – he prefers this term because the reader's experience of these books is sequential – "should be viewed, not as failed novels, but as unique hybrids that combine two distinct reading pleasures: the patterned closure of individual stories and the discovery of larger unifying strategies that transcend the apparent gaps between stories" (Luscher 150). He also lists a number of simple textual strategies – a title, preface, an epigraph, or framing stories – and "more organic unities such as common narrators, characters, images, locale, and themes." Rolf Lundén in his 1999 study, *The United Stories of*

America, insists on the open nature of the short story composite, so that the inherent tension between discontinuity and fragmentation on the one hand and the totalizing demands on the other, informs his reading. *Season of the Strangler* obviously qualifies as a short story sequence, or, rather, benefits from a reading in which we emphasize the autonomy of individual stories *and* the unifying strategies that provide coherence and unity. We should, so to speak, read each story as a short story and as a book chapter, which the textual signals ask us to do.

The brief prologue introduces us to Okaloosa, Alabama, population 38,400, and to the summer of 1969 that the people there are not likely to forget. The narrator then lists three reasons for this, apparently in order of growing significance: that summer produced the climax of racial unrest, and perhaps also the climax of a general unrest because old ways were displaced by new ones. Most importantly, the summer of 1969 was the season of the strangler, who left altogether five female victims dead, all but one were old women. No evidence of the strangler anywhere except a strand of black hair under one victim's fingernail. And rumors, alarms, and reports everywhere; anyone could be the strangler, windows and doors locked and barred, and hysteria and suspicion forced the police to question suspects that in their turn became victims, because of gossip, rumors, and fear.

The scene is set, the time-space of the novel is defined, and we expect stories of fear and accusation, innocent people charged with murder, set free, but somehow marked for life. We expect stories in which racial unrest and "the new ways" somehow contribute to the tension and drama. The twelve stories produce all of this, and more, and somehow it ought to be possible to see the strangler as a kind of catalyst, starting a process and letting us watch the disappearance of an old order, a traditional way of life with its basis in country life and not factories and shops and businesses in town and city. The tension between young and old, white and black, husband and wife, parents and children, is ubiquitous, and even if we experience this through individual characters, we should not be misled to think that the conflicts are limited only to characters who may appear as weak, uncertain of their role or place, and at a loss in a community with whose rules and regulations they cannot fully cope.

Fear, tension, anger, remorse are all intensified because of the strangler who murders his five victims between May 7 and early September – during the long, hot summer of '69 in Okaloosa. The season is especially hard to endure for old people who have moved from country to town, and whose memories suggest a better past with clear-cut rules and shared values. The book does not dwell on the memories of the past, but they turn up in the margins of many a story, in images of a stable and independent farm life, or as memories of good comradeship and respect between whites and blacks. Even in Okaloosa life had been much better, according to some characters, before the textile mills and the black workers. Seen from the black point of view – and blacks are protagonists in some of the stories – freedom and equality mean little, since the white man still does exactly as he wants. A couple of references to a brawl at the high school is the only concrete racial unrest described in any of the stories, although chapter eight or the story "Rage" is a close-up of a black character who is a small riot all by himself.

All these elements that we find at the center or in the margins of most of the stories contribute to the unity of the book, but the single most important unifying device is, of course, the strangler and the stranglings. From the first mention of the strangler in the Prologue, the fear of him accompanies us through all stories, whether he is hinted at, described, or simply there as part of the atmosphere in which people breathe and behave. As a rule, each story includes at least one reference to the strangler, or to the period when he was active, so that the stranglings become a point of orientation in time and place.

Let us take a closer look at the twelve stories, with emphasis on their function as chapters of a novel *and* as short stories in a sequence that ultimately signifies more than the sum of the individual stories put together. Our reading will concentrate on the narrative drive forward, the novel's deliberate movement towards a conclusion or resolution, but also on the cumulative effect of repetitions, parallels, unifying devices which all characterize a short story sequence.

The first story, "A Strange Land," inevitably opens on a brief note of the strangler and the effect he has on people: "Suspicion was everywhere that summer, eating away. *Somebody* in Okaloosa had to be the strangler and after those first two murders in May and June every week or so produced a new suspect who was taken more or less seriously for a while" (*Season of the Strangler* 3). This is a general introduction, not only to this first story, but to each and every story; an introduction to the sequence as a whole, and the narrator can pick and choose suspects, relate them to one or all of the five victims, open his stories well before the first murder and bring it up to and through the summer of the strangler. In most of the stories, however, there are references to one or more of the actual murders, and in the first story three of them are named, and the age (47) is given for the only one who is not an old lady. This woman, Ernestine Bell, is referred to in a number of stories, and the strangling of her is the more terrifying among characters we get to know, many of whom are middle-aged women, because she belongs to their age group. Also, the two murder victims in June, Emma Quick and Marilyn Barfield, are named in this story. This indicates the kind of interdependency between the stories. New stories may refer indirectly or implicitly to the murders in June, to the poor old victims of sexual assault and strangulation, but we know the names of them all after three stories or three chapters. This practice is an indication of the novelistic tendency of the book, in the sense that new chapters build on former ones. On the other hand, this is also a key element of the exemplary short story sequences, notably *Winesburg, Ohio*.

"A Strange Land" as a title seems to refer to Wiley Brownlea, the old farmer who now lives in Okaloosa with his son and daughter-in-law, who, in Wiley's view, lead an empty and shallow life selling land to build houses on, being members of a country club, and carrying on meaningless conversations about nothing. Wiley had been a farmer all his life, but old age and a broken hip forced him to sell his mortgaged farm and move in with his son on Bass Street. He had lost his best boy in the war, and it has indeed become a strange land where you cannot live off the land, producing goods, but live well by selling land you do not own. The story's center is really the family conflict, the nagging and impossible daughter-in-law, Agnes, and Wiley's many attempts to stay out of her sight and hearing. This is also what gets him interested in Ragar Wells, who for some time is suspected to be the strangler. Wiley watches Ragar for weeks, and after the first two murders in May and June, "Wiley had known for many weeks that Ragar was the Strangler" (4). Later, however, we see Wiley trying to help Ragar because his spying has told him that Ragar was home on the night of the murder of Ernestine Bell (a murder that took place in August).

In the opening story, as in most stories to follow, the stranglings seem to function more as a catalyst to strengthen conflicts, suspicions, uneasiness, fear and guilt among married people, whole families, outcasts and losers, youngsters struggling to find their place among friends and in society. The Summer of 1969 is also a summer of racial riot, a little delayed in Okaloosa as compared to Birmingham, and even if the text basically limits racial conflicts to the story "Rage," we get numerous hints of an unequal society and a town in which the textile mills have brought in new people who threaten old ways and upset the racial balance.

The strength of "A Strange Land" lies in the portrait of old Wiley Brownlea whom we follow to a home for the aged. He belongs to the past. He reads about the Civil War. He still mourns his best son. He misses his farm, his hunting dogs, life in the country. His confrontation with Ragar Wells, who so easily becomes a suspect because he once spent some time in an insane asylum, is perhaps as much a result of boredom as an effect of the stranglings, which only interest him in so far as he can scare his daughter-in-law by telling her about them. By implication the story praises the old ways of life and is critical of the new, although the story is rather limited in its perspective. We shall have to read more stories and see if they add to the first story's impression or contradict it.

In chapter two, "Loss," a housewife, Myra Nettles, married to the real estate agent Baxter, is the protagonist. She has just begun an intense affair with a man named Henry Gude, and the story centers on this adulterous affair and its ramifications. The stranglings are only there in the background, something Myra is aware of and afraid of, and which, finally and for subtle psychological reasons that bring out hysteria in her, leads to her accusing Henry Gude of being the strangler. The whole illicit affair is then disclosed, Myra runs away, and rumors have it that she and Henry Gude have found each other in places distant from Okaloosa.

We have seen two "situations" which are difficult in themselves, and which would probably have had their own dynamics and would somehow have had disastrous consequences, strangler or no strangler. The fear of the strangler and the ease with which anyone male and capable becomes a suspect are typical of all stories, perhaps with the exception of "Ashes." In chapter three, "Faith," we watch how the Reverend Harold Gates with his strong faith, which is ridiculed through the story's strong irony, and his fanatical beliefs, never doubts who the strangler is. He is directly responsible for the death of a black deafmute, Earl Banks, who is shot by the police. The story offers a strong and convincing psychological portrait of the Reverend, and it shows how Harold Gates is almost forced to act because the fifth victim, old Mrs. Gladys Stallworth, is a member of his congregation – and he has suspected the new janitor, poor Earl Banks, for a long time. Reverend Gates' position seems to have been threatened a number of times over the years. He has been accused of being a liberal in relation to the blacks, and he has serious problems with his children, who do not seek the company he would have preferred. It is almost a relief, for Okaloosa, and for us as readers, when he sets out for the West!

The fourth story is one of two with basis in the black community of Okaloosa. "Sim Denny" is the story of a black master cement-finisher who has worked all his life for white people. He owns his own house, in which his daughter Maybelle and her angry and frustrated husband, Herman, now live, so that Sim has moved to the toolhouse more or less permanently. Sim is victim of his age, a heart that troubles him, and of a son-in-law who thinks he is an Uncle Tom. Sim even has close and real friends among white people, and he is ridiculed for this even when his old friend William is dying and he is unable to be with him. At the core of the story is Sim's misunderstood and useless attempt to show that he believes in the "Movement" and is a black man of value. He withdraws his savings, more than $ 1,400, and donates the money to the leader of the movement. His daughter and son-in-law are shocked, but this is about the last thing Sim does, because he dies shortly after. The story covers the whole period of the five stranglings, from May when Rosa Callahan becomes the first victim of the strangler and a black person's hair makes Herman furious, till the fifth murder in

September. Herman's rage is the theme and makes up the bulk of chapter eight in *Season of the Strangler*.

"Sim Denny" begins by referring directly back to the death of Earl Banks in "Faith," whereas story five, "A Worldly Man," takes us to one of the aristocratic families in Okaloosa, the Carneys, of which only Dr. Charles Carney and his 19-year old son live in Okaloosa. Charles' wife is in the insane asylum, and the son Bruce is mostly away. In the background of the story looms the insane wife, but at the center is Charles' life as a well-to-do doctor and womanizer. He has a lasting affair with a married woman, Lorraine Williams, whom he is unable to get rid of when he is tired of her. More efficiently than in most stories in the book we here witness "one evil brew set going by his own hand" (82). A combination of the affair with Lorraine, the racial riots, the difficult family situation, a heart condition, and the threat of the strangler, has disastrous results. A strangling is seen as parallel to an embrace, Charles' ex-wife accuses him of being the strangler, and Lorraine is beaten up by her husband. Charles ends in hospital, but recovers, and, thinking only of himself, seems to return to a quiet life, and has, as always, "found his mortality satisfactory" (77).

In stories six and seven we get two rather sad portraits of young male misfits, at a loss in their families and the broader environment of school or age group. In "Aspiration" Junior C. Moss changes his name to Carl Moss and lies and deceives in order not to reveal his humble background – his family has moved in from the countryside. He wants to make friends, establish contacts, and belong with the others at school. He admires Phillip Woodrow who drives a gold MG, and, unable really to get close to him, he starts watching him all through the night. In a town haunted by a strangler, a young man prowling at night is soon taken in and questioned by the police, and Carl has a short period of "fame" at school as the strangler. When he later really attacks Phillip, he also goes away, never to be heard of again. It is obvious to everyone that he cannot be the strangler, and so what we have is really a story of stupidity and adolescent uncertainty. Because of the strangler and of everyone's propensity to start a rumor and to accuse even the most innocent who acts strangely, Junior Moss does not stand a chance in his attempts to deceive his surroundings and himself.

Another young man, although not as young as Junior Moss, is the chief character in the story "Bulwark" – Bucky Daniels. People remember that he was once accused of having molested a child, and being a fat and lazy good-for-nothing who earns a few dollars by mowing people's lawns, rumors easily point to him as the strangler. He is, however, only one of many. We have seen this in the stories we have presented, but at the opening of this story – or Chapter Seven – we have a beginning which is clearly the opening lines of a chapter of a novel, not of a short story. But even here the chapter functions as a short story if or when we see it as dependent on the other stories; i.e. as one story in a longer sequence of stories:

> Throughout the summer and fall and afterward too there continued to be an inexhaustible stock of rumors. They were based mostly on nothing: somebody's speculations or a sign misread or a flimsy piece of evidence blown up and distorted. By late summer there had been already at least half a dozen people named and for a time suspected of being the Strangler. In August, after the murder of Ernestine Bell, still another one was added to the list. (108)

The new suspect is Bucky Daniels, and what we get is a story about Bucky after the rumors started and till he finally breaks down, not because he is the killer, but because of his relationship to his former teacher, Angela Byrne. She talks friendly to Bucky, and he starts to visit her frequently; too often, in fact, because she also has old and senile Aunt Kate to take care of. Bucky needs all her support and comfort, and Angela thinks he has gifts, while most others think he is a moron. Then, when old Mrs. Gladys Stallworth who lives in the neighborhood is strangled to death, Bucky seems to be the obvious suspect. He is picked up by the police, questioned and set free, and waits anxiously for Angela to get back home. The situation gets out of hand, he attacks Aunt Kate, who survives the attack, and he is arrested. After weeks in jail, he is moved to a mental institution. And, as we know, we have also witnessed the last strangling, Mrs. Stallworth in September, although nothing in the text in any way indicates that Bucky is the Strangler. He is a loner and a loser, and there is the only three year old rumor of his having sexually assaulted an eight-year-old girl, so people quickly, easily, without a shred of evidence, point to him as the murderous villain who sexually assaults and strangles old women. Are people in Okaloosa worse than people elsewhere? Or is this the way we are? Every chapter, every new story, even with new people, a different focus, and shifting emphasis on individual or group behavior, seems to add to a complex picture of man's injustice toward man, elicited by fear and uncertainty, but executed willingly and destructively.

In Chapter 4 we met Sim Denny's son-in-law, Herman Coker, brooding, ill-tempered, angry, if not raging, all the time. In Chapter 8, "Rage," the rumor that we heard about in the Preface about the black person's hair is described as a rumor circulating among white people until it finds its way also to black ears. Herman has come to Okaloosa from Birmingham and has seen black riots much more violent than the racial unrest described in *Season of the Strangler* as a whole and, most particularly, in this chapter. But the story of Herman, even if it is linked also to the police-killing of Earl Banks, is the story of personal shortcomings, of hatred misdirected, and a violence finding wrong and useless outlets. Herman may have all the reasons in the world, being a black worker in a textile mill in a small town in the South dominated and owned and controlled by white people in the late 1960s, but his rage still seems to be largely private or personal. Herman loses his wife, Sim's daughter Maybelle, who runs away, he goes berserk and is put in jail for five years. Even if he in his violent rage may be modeled on Faulkner's 'Rider' from "Pantaloon in Black" in *Go Down, Moses*, there is nothing in the story to give him the pride and stature that Rider has, and "Rage" somehow seems to be one of the necessary but rather weak chapters. The book as a whole seeks to give a composite and reasonably varied picture of Okaloosa under the spell of the strangler.

To this picture of Okaloosa in 1969, with its racial unrest, its endless stock of rumors, its laboring under the fear of a strangler on the loose, shoe store owner Cecil Peck adds another fragment in the story "Break." We get a small glimpse of a marital situation where the husband is encouraged by the stranglings he hears about to consider this as an option for himself – or, rather, his wife Edna. This is one of the chapters that could easily function as an autonomous short story; a portrait of a shoe salesman who is fond of stroking the legs of his female customers, and who is told the truth about what he is and what he is worth, when his employee, Claude Manning, quits his job. Cecil changes after this, and he finds it more and more intolerable to live with his nagging wife and to take all the precautions she wants because of the strangler. Cecil dreams of the strangler, and the story reaches a dramatic climax when the returning images of stranglers and stranglings are linked to the neck of his wife, and he actually attacks her. Only their son's appearance saves her life. Cecil moves out, everyone knows he is not the strangler, but in the lonely life he now leads, he often hints that he has more than a good notion of who the strangler is.

The story of the lonely artist, painting in solitude and never showing his pictures to anyone any more, "Self-portrait," is clearly one of the stories in the sequence or one of the chapters of the novel that easily could have been developed into a novel of its own. For one thing it does in fact tell the story of a life, the life of Joel Trotwood, artist. As in the story about Dr. Carney, we here meet one of the aristocratic families in Okaloosa, even though there is little left of former glory. Joel has flunked out of everything, and has settled down in his mother's house where he paints in the attic and goes for long walks in the night. He is nearly forty when the stranglings begin, and is, as a night prowler, an obvious suspect. But the stranglings have a different effect. They change the balance of power in the relentless and lasting struggle between mother and son. The story more and more centers on this fight for supremacy, for the upper hand, for control and power. For a period from August, Joel seems to have gained control, but it slips away – and by what could be an ironic twist or simply something inevitable after all, a neighbor finds that "Joel had used a piece of the wire he kept to hang his pictures" (187).

Chapter 11, the story "Ashes," tells of a tragedy that took place after the last strangling, yet in a place we know from other stories of adultery and marital quarrel: the Cotton Street Hotel. Mrs. Stella Echols, who owns the hotel, is found dead in a fire that destroys most of the building. The police suspects foul play, but cannot find any evidence. Accordingly, the narrator takes over and has knowledge about Stella that even the collective memory and knowledge of Okaloosa could not match.

Yet the story is at the same time developed as if an investigation were going on, and so bits and pieces of information about the days leading up to the fire, fall in place and relate significantly to the knowledge of Stella's past that the narrator supplies. Stella is known to have had a love affair during World War II, and shortly before the fire she seems to have come to suspect that one of the guests was her old lover.

The love story, the story of Stella's short marriage, the rundown hotel and Stella's struggle to make a living in the changing world, is another incident and example of life in Okaloosa in the shadow of the strangler and the stranglings, although the story is only related to the summer of fear in the vaguest of ways since the season of the strangler is also the last summer of Stella's life.

And even if the strangler is on everybody's mind, and suspicion and rumors are everywhere, life goes on without much drama or change for most people. Things happen, people come and go, the world changes, and obviously most of what happened in Okaloosa in the summer of 1969 had little if anything to do with the strangler. Yet his presence is felt, even in stories so remote from the acts of the strangler and even from those rumored to be the strangler, that the "Season of the Strangler" can be seen only as a frame, a convenient tool to place stories and events in time and space. In "Familiar Spirit" the central character, Douglas, is having a love affair with a Lola Shanks, and is therefore out late at night and at a back door, so that he is brought in by the police. Also, growing somewhat tired of the relationship, he might be tempted to do Lola a little harm just to get rid of her. "Familiar Spirit" is a fine and even humorous story about the lazy and easygoing Douglas, who has come home from his so-called studies to live with his mother, Gloria, for a time. In the same house his grandfather, old Todd Quick, lives with his Civil War history and relics. Douglas comes home the winter before the killings start, and he leaves the day before Ernestine Bell is strangled, which we accordingly know is August 6, 1969. The story refers to a brawl at the high school, and in circumstantial ways it has race as a central topic. Gloria has a dialogue group and has decided to make it interracial; in other words, bring black people into the house where her father will get into an uncontrollable rage. Much of the story is about the Civil War, about Douglas' grandfather's stories about General Bragg and General Bedford Forrest and Sherman's march. Douglas' boredom and his fondness for his grandfather and quite a bit of impatience with his stupid mother and her "Dialogue Group" create a situation in which the old gentleman with his own eyes sees black people in the house, which makes him blow a bugle in the room just above the group in the living room. His mother is furious, but her father, Douglas' grandfather, falls down dead. He has seen what the world has come to, and even to live imaginatively in the stories of bravery, stoic endurance, white supremacy and the old institution of slavery, would do no good. Perhaps Douglas did the old man a favor, following his familiar spirit, which he also follows when he leaves Okaloosa shortly after.

"It was almost as if a spirit, having finished its evil season in the town, had gone back in just the same way it had come to whatever place it belonged" (228) are the final words of the brief Epilogue that rounds off the book. Between Prologue and Epilogue we have the twelve stories, the twelve chapters, a circular movement from beginning to ending. The story begins with full knowledge of how the stranglings ended, and it brings this knowledge to bear on all events that are singled out for narration in the course of the book. This gives the stories a certain uniformity, it gives the book its unity, but it also opens for a variety of stories and story telling techniques because the stranglings provide an established framework, a basis, in relation to which even stories only remotely related to the violent events can be told. By way of conclusion, I shall look at some of the unifying elements in the sequence of stories, but also, obviously, at some of the novelistic characteristics of the book as a whole.

In some stories, the stranglings are simply used to indicate when in time something happened. In "Loss", story number two, Myra Nettles remembers her becoming a brand-new-adulteress back "in May, about the time the stranglings started," but we soon experience that the stranglings bear violently on her illicit affair with Henry Gude. In the story about the struggle and final fall of Reverend Harold Gates, we get to know a lot about his problems in his church as well in his family, before the stranglings are mentioned. Here we get the only close and somewhat detailed description of a victim, the first one, the 78-year old widow Rosa Callahan. Otherwise the stranglings are all off-stage, not because decorum demands it, but rather as an indication of the relative unimportance of the killings themselves in the broader picture the stories and their overall effect. The strangling of Rosa Callahan is also used as the turning point in the life of the main character in the story "Sim Denny," since the black hair found under one of her fingernails is one of the factors behind Herman Coker's blind rage against Sim for his being an Uncle Tom.

In a number of stories the stranglings are barely mentioned, yet the stories even of well-to-do people show that the murders weigh heavily on people whom one would think safe and immune. Conflicts build up to a point where violence is used, as a rule an attempt to strangle someone. In other stories, death – by stroke or heart attack, but also suicide – comes as the end. The police shoot one innocent suspect, a deaf-mute black man, and the minister who pointed him out as the strangler, leaves town, as do many others to get away from its evil spell on them.

The most common pattern in the stories is to take the stranglings and the rumors – "an inexhaustible stock of rumors" – as a starting point, and then narrate a rather sad story about a pitiful person, a loser, a loner, who prowls the streets at night, for no apparent reason, who suddenly becomes another suspect. In chapter seven, the story "Bulwark," we get the most pitiful, dramatic, forceful and ironic version of such a character's plight. Young Bucky Daniels, who "was apparently not quite all there in the head" (109) has been seen in the neighborhood of the house where Ernestine Bell lived. He later seeks help from Angela Byrne, a school teacher who lives with her aunt Kate, but it all ends in assault, prison, and insane asylum. Almost funny in its wry irony is the story of Cecil Peck, shoe-store owner, who begins a new life after having been told what he is worth by a salesman in his store, and after a confrontation with his wife influenced by the strangler's evil acts. Although one of the weaker stories in the book, "Aspiration" uses the power and the threat of the strangler to give a dramatic and vivid portrait of a young man who desperately wants to be *seen* by others, even to the point where he insists that he *is* the strangler, attacks a young man he admires, and then disappears.

Relatively few characters appear in more than one story, so this unifying device is of little importance. Yet Myra Nettles from "Loss" reappears as a customer in Cecil Peck's shoe-store in the story "Break," and we have seen Sim Denney's son-in-law, Herman, become the central character in "Rage." There are also strong connections between the death of Earl Banks, the deaf-mute shot by the police, and the story about Jim Denney. But all characters live under the spell and threat of the strangler, and in numerous stories closure takes the form of violence, fighting, fleeing, or death. Time, place, and the strangler bind all stories together. One may ask how many intratextual links, how many unifying strategies, are required before we experience a short story collection as a sequence? There is no doubt that *Season of the Strangler* is a unified collection, almost to the point where it is more natural to discuss it as a novel than as a mere collection of stories. As I have tried to show, we profit in our reading and appreciation of the book if we see it as a hybrid form, and there is, of course, never any correlation between a book's adherence to abstract genre demands and the quality of the text.

A common unifying device in a story sequence is to use a recognizable personal narrator in all stories, so that the narrator somehow gets involved and relates significantly to characters and events. In *Season of the Strangler* the narration is authorial, omniscient, and from the outside. The narrator gives no indication that he represents the town or "us," and allows himself access to information that a personal narrator hardly could have. The narrative voice is in complete command and handles distance, perspective, and point of view with ease and elegance. Also, the narrator of the stories in *Season of the Strangler* and the implied author show compassion as well as understanding of a world where evil and violence and vices flourish, and a broad acceptance of the ways of the world, even the modern one, and its strange people. In small gaps in the text we see the better world of the past, and here and there the new or modern is criticized or scorned. Strange as it may seem, the final effect of *Season of the Strangler,* with its serial killer and all the trouble we see in his wake, is not a pessimistic book. It does not do much for the uplifting of people's hearts, but it shows that although darkness may be pervasive, it is not impenetrable, simply because this book is a serious work of art, a product of the human spirit.

WORKS CITED:

Bradford, M. E. "Madison Jones," *The History of Southern Literature*, Louis D. Rubin, ed., Baton Rouge, Louisiana State University Press, 1985, pp. 523-26.

Gretlund, Jan Nordby "Madison Jones's Last Southern Agrarians," *Frames of Southern Mind*. Odense University Press, 1998, pp. 45-56.

Ingram, Forrest L. *Representative Short Story Cycles of the Twentieth Century*. The Hague, Mouton, 1971.

Jones, Madison *Season of the Strangler*. New York, Charter Books, 1983.

Lundén, Rolf *The United Stories of America: Studies in the Short Story Composite*. Amsterdam, Rodopi, 1999.

Luscher, Robert "The Short Story Sequence: An Open Book," Lohafer and Clarey, eds., *Short Story Theory at a Crossroads*. Baton Rouge, Louisiana State University Press, 1989, pp. 148-67.

Mann, Susan Garland *The Short Story Cycle: A Genre Companion and Reference Guide*. New York, Greenwood Press, 1989.

COUNTRY INNOCENCE:

TO THE WINDS

Jan Nordby Gretlund

When Madison Jones was a boy, his father bought a farm near Nashville, and until he was grown he spent every summer there. He developed an emotional attachment to the area, which was so strong that when he had lived on the farm for almost a year (in 1949), Madison Jones seriously considered becoming a farmer. The area is Cheatham County, Tennessee, around the small town of Ashland City. It is a hilly county on the Cumberland River, and when Jones was growing up, life there was still in certain respects close to original frontier life. He once told me what the county means to him as a writer: "The familiar place offers inspiration and images to embody my ideas. Some images I remember from my childhood, and they retain a certain mystery for me. I could, of course, have seen fields of briars and buckbushes stretching to the horizon in other places. But I saw them in Tennessee, and for me they will always be associated with the country of my childhood" (Interview, January 1981). The remembered county of his youth has made all the difference in Jones's fiction, it was indispensable for the creation of all his novels, but proved most important for *The Innocent, A Buried Land,* and *To the Winds.*

To the Winds is an initiation story of what happened to a "middle-sized boy in the 1950s." Jones negates his self, invents a character, and finds the voice appropriate to that individual. Chester Moss is thirty years old when he tells his story, but the period of his life that haunts him covers his early years. We learn how he became a dreamer and a storyteller with an obsession that rivals that of Coleridge's mariner: "My best medicine," he says, "I've found out, is telling my story to somebody. So this time I'm telling it to you" (1). And through his memoir we learn what happened to a country boy and his family.

The facts of the story are expressed in Chester's voice so that they reflect his vision both then and now, and Chester's is a Huck-Finn voice. For Jones this is a new narrative technique, which offers him an opportunity to detail the process of a boy's changing psychology. In its account of "what-all-happened" to a family, his story goes beyond childhood joys and worries. It raises a question: to what extent was the Moss family to blame for its own downfall? It is a classic question: do we determine our own fate? The battle between heredity and environment, between memory and milieu, is acted out in this family's life. They seem caught in a web spun partly by their own deeds, or inaction, but beyond this they are primarily victims of their heritage.

The theme of a farming community superseded by an industrialized society is brought out in observations of clashes between farm children and children from the growing town near-by. Chester, the narrator, thinks of the others as "sons of new, big folks in town, the ones that were starting to run everything and that people like us couldn't touch, no matter what" (22). The story is told in an understated convincingly unaffected and word-economic style, which brings out the psychological conditions that make the events appear inevitable. Because their number has been reduced to the essential words, as in Mark Twain's style, and because they are presented in conjunction in compressed sentences, Jones's words seem to say more than they can. Twain's voice is heard in the tale of how the farm boys taught the outsiders from town a lesson. The five Moss brothers celebrate their triumph so much that Link Moss, their father, in his long johns, has to come out and tell them to shut up. In his Huck-Finn mental voice, Chester thinks: "I was glad when he did. I was more than just tired of it, it was too much. There was something wrong about it, the same way it had seemed to me when he [Dudley] kept raging around for the best part of a week about how those boys had treated him" (20). The words express the order and economy of great art. But the reader's interest is not focused on the style, which does not call attention to itself, for every detail is essential in relation to the novel as a whole. Instead the austerity of the form allows us to think about what the events will mean for the individual characters and to wonder how they will be shaped by the events. This is the fundamental tension in Jones's style, the tension he always tries to create in his fiction.

What the events mean for Dudley is that he is tarred and feathered by the boys from Riverton, which is a fictional town of twenty-five hundred people, located about thirty miles north of Nashville. The Moss farm is only three miles from Riverton, "though from the look of the countryside up there it might have been twenty miles." In all psychological ways the farm will prove to be even further removed. In his description of the farm Jones demonstrates his mastery at invoking a sense of place. The house is a log-house and has some rooms clumsily tacked on in the back. The family get their water from a well, use coal oil lamps, and are situated on a dirt road away from anybody else. They have some stock, a garden, and a smokehouse, and they live a way of life that has not changed essentially since the mid-nineteenth century.

With the scraps between boys from farm and town, the stage is set for a major clash between modern ways and traditional values. The Moss boys are furious with the outsiders who have invaded their native area, and we may safely assume, I think, that their rage reflects the author's anger. The poor farmers will prove no match for the pushy intruders, so traditional lives, minds, and relationships will disintegrate in the face of the so-called "world of progress." The conflict is between absolute change and farmers who refuse to accept that things are changing. Chester is deeply concerned about the family's reputation in the changing local society, and he is worried that his family will be swept aside as so much "trash." The failure, or refusal, of the Moss family to recognize and submit themselves to the imposed limits of their existence helps not a little to speed up the inevitable disintegration of their family. The novel details the final outrage against the ancient life of the farmer with the final days of the Moss family as an illustration. The real failure of the family is a lack of realism, as they will not admit to themselves that it is now impossible to survive by farming. Jones's plot is inexorable, as always, and this novel reads like an elegy for a way of living.

The family has been on "a downsloping field" for generations, also in a financial sense. Link Moss is the weak father who squanders his inheritance. The farm had around two hundred and fifty acres when Chester was born, but by the time he is ten, only ninety acres of poor land are left. Link feels he is caught by forces he cannot control, and there is at least one financial emergency in the Moss home every month.

Link is a man with a wandering mind, and he does not care much for hard work. In order to forget his situation he gets drunk, and hoping against hope itself, he gambles desperately. In imagined conversations with his long dead father, he pleads, "It ain't none of my fault." He obviously feels the presence of the past as an ever-present reproach, and faced with the memory of his father, he claims, "I never been nothing but just like you." He is not ignoring the past, like other Jones characters, but he is more haunted than sustained by it. In his memoir Chester considers whether his father can be blamed for his failures as a father and as a farmer.

Losing an acre of land is for a farmer like losing an acre of the family identity; and selling a piece of land is like selling a piece of one's self. It is a betrayal of the ancestors who once worked the same land and of the children who were to live off it in the future. There is a long history of selling off land in the Moss family. It is as if they have been designated victims for generations in a financial game, and their fates are so predictable that they could be characters in a Greek tragedy. The grown Chester sees that his father was not only weak, but also unlucky, to inherit the farm at the time that he did. He is just the last link in a chain of generations of desperation and hopelessness, "there wasn't a thing in the world waiting for him but the same old blundering path his daddy had followed to failure." The boy sees that his father's behavior may well have been caused by the hopelessness of the farming situation. In spite of his father's obvious flaws, Chester likes him. The two are alike; they are both dreamers and storytellers. Unlike Wendell Corbin of *Last Things,* Chester does not reject his family as "luckless morons." He identifies with every one of them and suffers with them in their bad luck. The boy's initiation is in finding out about his father's character and situation, as he is learning about the nature of his own situation in the adult world. Chester's emphasis in his tale is on the individuals within the family and their relations with the community. At the age of thirty Chester is realistic about his family and about what happened to them. But he tells their story again and again trying to determine what was caused by inherited traits and what was caused by the rapidly changing environment. Jones creates a country boy-narrator with existential thoughts of a universal magnitude; he keeps wondering whether it had all been predetermined, or had some of it been avoidable?

In the early parts of the novel Chester's story is told in a measured pace with much humor. The boys' attempt at branding their old cow in the manner of cowboys, as inspired by the picture show, rivals William Faulkner's "Spotted Horses" in its description of the pandemonium that breaks loose during their undertaking. The serious note is that the boys, who know enough about livestock to realize that their cow has "enough Jersey in her to give her plenty of meanness," readily nullify and manage to ignore hard-earned farmer's knowledge in order to imitate Hollywood's ideas of western cow-herding.

A second humorous story included in the novel has echoes of the Southern ante-bellum humorists. It demonstrates that humor is still the most fertile genre of Southern fiction. Jones tells us how the boys prevent their gullible father from swapping their good mules for a worn-out tractor. It is a hilarious tall story, complete with heroic boys, who force the mules to swallow whole jugs of white lightening, and limited grown-ups, who never realize that the mules are drunk. We learn that the farmer is as opinionated as the mules he wants to swap. Link Moss will remain faithful to his fixed idea, even when it has been proved a very bad one.

The most ambitious humorous pages in *To the Winds* are without doubt in chapter five, which has been published in the *Sewanee Review* as a short story. It is a bear story, not like Faulkner's, but in its tragicomedy and grotesqueness more like the bear stories of ante-bellum humor. As always it is the hard times that inspire the family to cook up a scheme to earn some money. They decide to start a zoo, stocked with local wildlife, including a bear cub. Two powerful maternal forces put a stop to this financial experiment. The mother bear decides to come and get her cub and destroys most of the farmhouse in the process, and Mrs. Omie Moss, with a face "the color of fatback," decides to save her family from their urge to self-destruct. Armed with a shotgun she kills all snakes and sets all other animals free.

The total confusion at the end of the zoo-story has its parallel in the everyday confusion on the farm. Link has his equal in the old rooster, which enjoys crowing, but has precious little to crow about. The boys all share in the fury of the wildcat; when they are crossed, they are inclined to act blindly in the anger of the moment. The three oldest boys have the brute strength characteristic of the bear, but lack its basic sense of direction. The noise, confusion, and destruction on the day the zoo closed, with "the snarling and baying and turning things upside-down," are simply the family's everyday writ large, and in this is the traditional humor. What makes the humorous sections fit into the basically tragic novel is that they illustrate one of its main themes. The clashes between the world of the farm and the encroaching modern world are brought out in the humorous sketches of cows on the farm vs. cows in the movies; necessary mules vs. a bad tractor; and farm animals vs. animals kept for display.

Link Moss is so happy to have his name on three signs, "Mosses Zoo," "See Mosses Wild Animals," and "See Mosses Dedly Snakes," that he spends money on cages and feeds the family chickens to his zoo animals, while he fails to set the tobacco and plant the corn. The only adult who always has her wits about her is the mother. Her common-sense reaction to her men's ludicrous zoo idea is typical for her. The counterpoint in this novel to their life of growing confusion and slow disintegration resides in Omie Moss's memory. She was born Omie Walls in Horn County about thirty miles from Riverton. She had a dramatic and romantic youth, complete with a secret lover, who was frail and died young, but not before Omie had become pregnant. After his death her life became emotionally impoverished, and the love child was still-born.

As the years have passed, Omie has become a victim of the structure of a traditional rural family. With eight children and much hard work her situation is not enviable. She is apparently more intelligent than her husband, but seems unable to influence his often rash decisions. She is a representative of a world that has now vanished. It was a world of community life that she was too young to experience the full flowering of, she only heard about it from her parents; but that world was "just as real to her as the one she remembered herself" (37). In this lost world of community values, people were always doing something together, for example "at church and square dances and corn huskings." They visited each other, and whole families would show up Saturday evenings, or Sundays, bringing homemade food. But nobody comes to visit with the Mosses anymore.

How it was in the past is communicated to the Moss children through Omie's stories and singing tales. In her mind the strong oral tradition serves as a stark contrast to the present of the 1950s: "Back then, she said, there were a plenty of folks around that beat all to pieces anything you could hear on a radio nowadays." In Clayton County people also used to help each other in times of trouble. According to Mrs. Moss, "Any worriment or grief in a family, sickness or childbirth or death, would draw in an hour or two more comfort and offers of help than you ever could have use for" (37-38). She mentions this because it is not the way it is any more. The rural parts of the county are now like the town, where everybody looks out for himself or herself only, and there is no sense of community. Old values have been replaced by moral relativism also in the country. When the youngest daughter of the Moss family becomes ill and nearly dies, nobody extends his or her sympathy and nobody offers help.

After the first few chapters the amusing episodes disappear from Chester's memoir. He remembers how his world shrunk and that the atmosphere in the home became ominous. The pace of the narrative quickens and the suspense grows. Once again we are made to think of Huck Finn's experiences. When he recalls the fatal summer in the life of the Moss family, Chester is sad in the manner of Huck: "I remember that time, that summer, as maybe the unhappiest time in my life, and the lonesomest" (109). He is sad because he knows that he is witnessing the estrangement of his brothers and with that, the end of the Moss farm as a family operation. His escape from that reality is like Huck's, with a friend, i.e. his brother Bucky, who is considered too dimwitted for modern society, Chester seeks comforting isolation in nature.

Some of the most poetic passages of *To the Winds* describe Chester's life with Bucky, *his* companion Jim, on the river. As in Mark Twain's best work, the great poetry in Jones's fiction resides in nature and in safe isolation from civilization:

> We'd mostly fish in the shade along the bank in the mouth of Stump Creek. But again, when the sun wasn't too high and hot, we'd paddle

out to mid-river and fish clear down on the bottom where the big cats would bite once in a while. I liked that best, though not for the fishing. I liked being far out from the banks that way, with slant sunlight lying like polish on the smooth water and no sounds but ones that barely got to us from a long way off. But just as much, I liked being out there with Bucky. He hardly ever talked and the expression on his face didn't express anything anymore than the river's face did. It was just there, taking the sun, not showing even a ripple. Off and on I'd spend a minute hoping it never would be any different for him." (110)

But it is going to be different, not only for Bucky, but also for Chester and everybody else in their family. Chester's recurring nightmare is that he will wake up and find not a soul in the house but himself. It is an ominous dream that slowly becomes a reality as the House of Moss encounters absolute Evil and, as a result, is emptied of anything and anyone of true value.

Though he has found himself "unable to believe with the absoluteness of the Christian," Jones has always been profoundly interested in ideas of innocence and evil. Evil is an ever-present characteristic of life in his fiction, and so is the violence that its presence often leads to. The fictional world of *To the Winds* is clearly a moral one. And the discovery of the existence of absolute and inexplicable Evil is one of the hard lessons in living also for the Moss boys. Chester, as the youngest of the brothers, loses his moral innocence when he is faced with the reality of innate human depravity. But first he has to become aware of it, accept its existence, and realize its absoluteness.

His story becomes a year-by-year chronicle of the misfortunes visited upon his family. In some instances it is clear that they contribute to their own bad luck, which does not mean that it is obvious what they could have done to avoid it. There is a decisive moment when Dorcas, the oldest daughter, becomes a victim of not knowing how much times have changed. She is not ready for a world where the new people, who work at the plants in town, "didn't care about a lot of things the old people cared about." Manners have in the town deteriorated to where "pretty soon you could whistle at a girl on the street and nobody but a few grayheads would turn and glare at you" (65). Instead of observing time-honored unwritten rules for the behavior of men toward women in the community, the new arrivals try to see "how much more they could get away with." In the case of Dorcas Moss, the son of rich outsiders gets away with all he wants, then ignores her, and she has to go away for an abortion. The new industrialists in Riverton would not even consider an alliance with this girl from a redneck family, and Dorcas is made a whore in the eyes of the community and, worse, in the opinion of her own brothers.

Omie and Link Moss do not stop Dorcas, they do not even try. Link does nothing because he is flattered that somebody rich takes an interest in his daughter, and Omie is passive, because she knows she could not stop her, and perhaps because she cannot imagine that a boy would take advantage of her trusting daughter. Dorcas contributes to her own misfortune by trying to get away from her roots by any means possible. She takes no pride in being a Moss, on the contrary, she is ashamed of her background. She breaks the family solidarity, and still hoping, demonstrates her loyalty to her new friend. Chester remembers this as the first "lasting shadow" cast over the family. For the first time the farmers are forced to realize that they are considered "poor trash," not only by the new people in the county, but also by the law. Link Moss talks about taking the boy to court, "But of course," Chester recalls, "he didn't know the first thing about lawing, and all he knew about lawyers was that they always got a bunch of money out of you. So, since he didn't have two thin dimes to rub together, as usual, what was he going to do? Sheriff Tipps kept getting brought into it, but everybody knew he wouldn't raise a hand against big folks like that" (74).

Clayton County has changed rapidly after WW II, but the rural families have no desire to change their ways to accommodate people with roots elsewhere, people who believe that new ways are better just because they are new. In this way *To the Winds* is an expression of an Agrarian way of thinking that many will find strangely outdated. Jones is concerned with the values that are native to an agrarian way of living, values residing in a family structure and togetherness now largely of the past. Even the failing farm is a home for the Moss children, a home in a now mostly forgotten sense. Chester is concerned that the "fancy folks" will look down upon his whole family, and he worries about what they will think of "the likes of us." As it turns out his worrying is fully justified. This is bad enough for the pride and confidence of the family, but what is worse, and does permanent damage to the children, is that they are forced to realize that age-old virtues, such as defending the family honor, telling the truth, and upholding the law, are no match for the "values" imposed on them by the new structure of society in their county.

One of the powerful families among the newcomers is, suggestively, named Sherman. Coop, the most intelligent of the Moss brothers, works for Sherman and has to submit to the businessman's "cold, steady, measuring look." In the portrait of Sherman there is an accusation against all the newly arrived industrialists in town: they lack respect for the humanity of the people already there. Dorcas breaks down when she faces the worst possible fate for a woman of her background, which is public shame. But she sees her own misfortune as a part of a familiar pattern, "It ain't never been nothing but shame for our family. Us poor as a snake, not even no 'lectric lights.... Sometimes I wish't I was dead. Be better'n being trash" (140-41). Chester also dislikes the "cool way" town people take his measure. Coop has informed him that the sheriff also considers them just trash and therefore thinks he can kick them around. So when Chester has to see the sheriff about his brother Dudley, who has been arrested on a trumped up charge, the narrator says he lacked the courage to enter the municipal building: "I would have, I think, except for the picture that came up in my mind. It was a picture of me ... with "poor" spelled out all over him from hair down to raggedy shoes. I looked down at my shoes and at my breeches, all dirty with cockle burrs stuck on them. Even my shirt sleeve had a tear.... I couldn't face those eyes" (132). The tragedy is that the children with all their horse sense and basic ideas of honor and justice are made to feel ashamed of who they are. The flaw in the Mosses themselves is that they seem unable to distinguish between what *is* shameful, such as Dorcas's sex life and Link's drunkenness and gambling, and what is only shameful because others consider it so, i.e. Bucky's life in the woods and the arrest of Dudley.

Although Chester worries about the family's position in the public eye, he is more concerned about how they will react within the family under the strain of outside pressure. In some cases the family makes the bed in which they must lie. There is the case of Uncle Clarence, who has not been in touch with his brother for thirty-five years, but now that he is wanted for murder comes to ask his family for help. At first, they all agree that being kin, they must hide him. But "daddy's brother" or not, there is a reward on their uncle's head, and one of the boys decides to turn him in. Dudley informs the sheriff of where Uncle Clarence is hiding on the Moss land. This splits the family for good. Dudley argues that the uncle "was fixing to get us in trouble. Wasn't no sense in it, him a murderer" (94). Coop, the boy with the Stoic values, and Eve, the youngest and most innocent, are as shocked as the narrator. They cannot forgive the betrayal of family loyalty and solidarity, but all they can do is watch, as the others, the father in particular, begin to discuss how to spend the reward money. Link even buys a refrigerator and a TV set, banking on the Judas money for his brother. The fact that Uncle Clarence dies from the effects of the sheriff's superfluous second shot makes it "real blood money."

As it turns out, Sheriff Tipps decides to keep the reward for himself. It is a degrading spectacle for the young members of the family to see the others go and beg for the money they thought they had earned by betraying their own. Especially, as they have to ask the sheriff who shot the already helpless uncle, out of pure "meanness." The sheriff is a man who demonstrates a savage brutality and primitive callousness that can only have an origin in innate evil. The demeaning spectacle of their father's daily inquiry about the reward: "Sheriff said When, yet?" breaks up the family circle forever. Coop leaves. His absence makes their loss obvious, for his departure leaves a big hole right in the middle of the family. He left because he saw most of his family getting behind the betrayer, "licking their chops about all that money they're looking to get. For killing Uncle Clarence" (102). This is not comic, not even tragi-comic; it is tragic in a classic Greek way. For the rest of their lives every member of the Moss family will have to live with the consequences and the knowledge of their shameful deed.

The betrayal is finally a part of a universal betrayal. The farm is taken away from the Moss family because of their debts. It is no longer possible to sustain a family by working the soil, and farmers are sacrificed to so-called progress. Coop sums it up in conversation with Chester: "A farm ain't anything anymore. Just scraping and straining ass to stay alive half-way. All it is. It ain't nothing... not nowadays" (103). – But who decided that a farmer's traditional way of life is now obsolete? At the time the Mosses are just one farming family out of hundreds going bankrupt in Clayton County, Tennessee, where farmers await bankruptcy, while trying not to go spiritually and emotionally bankrupt first.

From the portraits of the well-meaning parents, the tight-lipped mother and the bewildered father, to the creation of Bucky, the slightly "touched" brother, and Mabel, the self-absorbed sister, the characterizations of the farmers are masterful. But perhaps the best characterization is of Dudley, the young man who betrayed Uncle Clarence and became a tragic figure as a result of one mistake. It is a tribute to Jones's art that he is able to make his reader care about what happens to Dudley Moss. Like the others, he discovers that there is no law to turn to "for the likes of us." This becomes abundantly clear when the sheriff keeps the reward money and arrests Dudley, who suspects him of financial fraud. Dudley is charged with the possession of drugs and beaten so he cannot speak. The family sees the arrest as the last shred of respectability going down the public drain. But Dudley perseveres in his charges against the sheriff, is allowed to escape, and shot as a fugitive. In a cinematic scene it is Chester, who is about thirteen now, who brings the mortally wounded Dudley back to the farm: "In the backwash from the headlights I could see his open eyes. Open but not blinking anymore. The voice in my ear was Mama's, close to me now, her body pushing against me. Dud's blanket had slipped off, and his hand, all dark, was lying on it beside him. The dark on his hand, when I lifted it up to the light, was cool and slick and red instead of dark. Then Mama was in my place. She had his head, had it up against her. It seemed to me a long time before she made even one sound I could hear" (152-53). It is not hard to envision the pieta scene of mother and dying son. Every detail stands out graphically, and there is no sentimentality, and no hope offered. Religion has little influence on the lives of the Mosses, they stopped going to church a long time ago, and in their time of trouble they do not turn to religion for help. When they bury Dudley, it is to the accompaniment the unending muttering of old Mr. Beasley, who no longer notices his congregation when he preaches. His flow of Bible verses seems automatic, and he does not cease until he is interrupted and brought home. He personifies the presence of religion, but his words seem irrelevant for their experience, and in the Moss family he is unable to inspire hope.

The true betrayer of family life is a different kind of "religion." Throughout the novel it is represented by a small battery-operated TV that Link and to some extent his daughters are allowing to take over their mental lives. To the boys' desperate questions of how they can survive without working the farm as a farm, their father's only answer is to turn up the sound on his set. The TV offers a perfect flight from his sorry reality. His faith in his TV set rivals the idea of Flannery O'Connor characters, who firmly believe that "nobody with a good car needs to be justified." Link does not have to justify himself to anybody as long as the "TV pictures flicker like ghosts across the screen," and his reality is painlessly displaced by electronic images of a mock-reality. He cannot let go of the set, payments on the farm or none, for "without that TV to keep his head full of pictures, he'd have to think about things." He has given up, Coop has left, and it is left to Chester to express what is going out of their lives: "Once, halfway down a row, something made me stop her [the mule]. I think it was just the look of the dirt. I dropped the reins and down on my knees cupped some of it in my two hands. It was damp and fine from the good season, made for corn... even for corn put in too late. At first I didn't know why I'd started crying. Then I knew it was because, come fall, this dirt wasn't going to be ours anymore" (107).

Rejected by the town and actively pursued by the sheriff's people, the Moss family find themselves isolated and bankrupt even before the financial fact. It now appears to them that the money and the law in Riverton work together on stomping out their family, so that "the only difference between Sherman and Tipps was that Sherman had money instead of a badge" (179-80). Chester's hero in his memoir is his brother Coop, who takes stage center as the narrative with an ever increasing pace and intensity speeds toward the climactic ending and unavoidable tragedy. It is interesting that it is Coop who has to liberate the family from its evil spirit. After he left the farm, he acquired the ways of the town; innocent faith in the law is, however, not one of them. Senseless police brutality has cured him of that notion. Coop does what he has to do, as a poor man caught between family affection and duty to the law. He steps outside the law, because equality before the law is an ideal of the past. He is now convinced that Uncle Clarence was right about the law: "it wasn't anything but a way of hiding the real truth" (180). The hidden truth is that the man who represents the law in Riverton is a true representative from Hell. The presence of Evil has a finally more decisive role in what happens in *To the Winds* than the increasing social difference between poor farmers and monied intruders.

In his pursuit of money, to meet the payments on the farm, Coop becomes a murderer by accident. The hero of the novel becomes a tragically flawed hero. But even though he is in deep trouble himself, Coop is still able to worry about the others in the family and their survival. His time in town has taught him to recognize their enemy, but it is only when he reverts to his original way of a farm boy that he is able to revenge his family. It takes the old ways to slay the beast in mortal combat, and a farming tool dispatches the sheriff. The ever-cautious sheriff had been so long in town that he had forgotten that barns are full of potential weapons, so Tipps ends his life writhing on the tines of a hay fork.

Chester experiences "a dull satisfaction" that the evil spirit, who had haunted his family, has finally been laid to rest. But he realizes that Coop is now a double murderer, and that the farm now belongs to the bank. Like Huck Finn, he is a boy who is forced to grow up too quickly and sees too many dead people. Now that the story of his family was "the same as over with," he is forced accept some facts. The way they had thought, acted, and lived in the Moss family, down the generations, is now obsolete. Their world has vanished, and although the new world that has come to surround them seems insubstantial, the changes are real enough. As they all learned the hard way, the new world is a frightening place if you do not fit in. Chester concludes that what happened to them would not have happened if the Mosses had been smarter, not being "anybody" did the rest. The parents end up in a trailer on a bare lot with other trailers on the north side of town.

Omie works hard as always, now pumping at a gas station, Link spends his time drunk and watching TV, whereas Coop is on the run and probably out in the West. In many respects he seems to be repeating the life of Uncle Clarence, – maybe one day he will come to his brother Chester for help.

Madison Jones demonstrates in this novel that it is almost impossible for an individual to exist apart from a social framework and preserve one's innocence, but he also shows that every individual is ultimately responsible for his own actions. In *To the Winds* he has created a moral world and raised existential issues that transcend his own time and place.

THE INNOCENT STARE AT THE CIVIL WAR:

NASHVILLE 1864: THE DYING OF THE LIGHT

David Madden

All Madison Jones's fiction is about the Civil War. That claim derives from my conviction that in a profound and pervasive sense all fiction written by Southerners is about the Civil War. One may say of certain novels that do not ostensibly deal with the Civil War, therefore, that they are among the great Civil War novels: *Huckleberry Finn, Absalom, Absalom!* and even *All the King's Men.* That Madison Jones turned late in life to the Civil War in *Nashville 1864: The Dying of the Light* (1997) is not an expression of an acquired interest so much as it is a more direct expression of effects of the War (and Reconstruction) that underlie *all* his work. I am not talking about literal depictions of the war that we may find in isolated passages of Jones's fiction. *An Exile*, for instance, has few direct or implied references or allusions to the War, but the characters, the setting, and the cultural milieu are a creation of the effects of the War and Reconstruction. An even more expressive Civil War novel is *A Cry of Absence* because it deals head-on with complexities of the lingering effect of the War and Reconstruction as it exploded during the decade of the Civil War Centennial and the trauma and upheaval of the Civil Rights movement.

Given my premise about Southern writers in general and Jones in particular, Jones, by devoting an entire, though very short novel to the war, invites the question: what is the achievement of *Nashville 1864*, winner of the Michael Shaara Award, sponsored by the United States Civil War Center, and the T. S. Eliot award, as a late expression of Jones's vision and as a Civil War novel among other Southern contributions to the genre by William Faulkner, Allen Tate, Ellen Glasgow,

Caroline Gordon, Margaret Mitchell, Evelyn Scott, Robert Penn Warren, Andrew Lytle, and Mary Johnston?

The general story is very simple: thirty six years after the War, in 1900, Steven Moore writes a memoir of the two days when he, as a boy of twelve, searched for his soldier father during the battle of Nashville. Because many Civil War novels for young adults depict similar searches by children for family members, some readers have assumed that Jones's novel was written for young adults. Because the boy is accompanied by a young slave, one recalls the opening chapters of Faulkner's *The Unvanquished* (1938) which render the adventures of a young man and his young slave and give a similar impression of appealing to young adult readers – the characters and the action are simple and the style is clear. But *The Unvanquished* continues into adulthood and Faulkner develops a very complex vision of the War and Reconstruction. Whether Bayard Sartoris is writing or telling his story is left ambiguous. Allen Tate, however, in *The Fathers* (1938), makes the act of writing a memoir of the year before the war, also involving a slave, the primary vehicle for delineating a vision of antebellum life as it prefigures aspects of the Civil War and Reconstruction Southern mentality. As my own short novel, *Sharpshooter* (1996), evolved over fifteen years of rewriting, I was aware of its moving into and within the tradition of novels about adolescents who fight in or witness the war, searching for family members. The narrator, thirteen when he goes to war, begins to write his story ten years after the surrender. All four novels are short. The crucible in Faulkner's, Tate's, in my own novel, and in Jones's is the relationship between a young white boy and a slave. These similarities attracted me to Jones's novel.

Nashville 1864 falls into another category of Civil War novels, those that recreate but do not re-envision the war. For 140 years, Americans, especially Southerners, have been staring at the Civil War and Reconstruction – an innocent stare, because both Northerners and Southerners have, from the start, missed almost everything that happened back then and ever since. Out of that prolonged innocent stare, all fiction by Southerners, but none by Northerners, has been, directly or indirectly, profoundly and pervasively, about the legacy of the Civil War and, we should stress, as Shelby Foote does, Reconstruction. Even so, that innocent stare has achieved few visionary insights into the Civil War itself. The child's stare serves as an apt metaphor for the innocence that sees too little.

Paradoxically, it may be more difficult for Southern than Northern writers to produce artistically successful Civil War novels. They often strive so hard to recreate faithfully the Southern way of life, before, during, and after the War, and to recreate battles, that they neglect the art of fiction, which enables writers to render complex character relationships through a coherent conception that projects a vision. That is the problem I see in Madison Jones's *Nashville 1864*. His protagonist, as a boy and as an adult memoirist in 1900, seems to be fixated upon faithfully rendering battle details, depicting "benevolent" master-slave relationships, and attacking Northerners for destroying God's creation of a superior civilization in the New Eden of the South. I say "seems" because Jones's previous works (from 1957 on) and their artistry encourage a possible conclusion that unintentional ambiguity may be the source of the impression that the novel is neo-Confederate in attitude and performance.

The element of the novel that is most promising but neglected is the relationship between the white boy and his young slave, enhanced by the narrating voice of the boy as an adult thirty-five years later. I will examine the elements that dilute the impact of that relationship: the content and tone of the memoirist's and his grandson's commentary on slavery, Northern aggressors, and modern times; the fitful development of the relationship between the white boy and the slave boy; the rather perfunctory preoccupation with the details of battle; and the lapses in the art of fiction, especially in style.

Drawing upon a convention of the earliest novels, Jones presents a fictitious descendent, a grandson of our time, who finds the manuscript, feels a duty to get it published, and writes a foreword. "I had become a rather serious-minded fellow, a good deal less than pleased with what I saw happening in Nashville and elsewhere, and the reading of this memoir went straight to my heart.... But it was only recently, here in my old age, that I decided to seek publication for it. My hope is that it may affect others as it surely has affected me" (ix-x). That arrogant assumption produces the obsessions of neo-

Confederates – not that one may understandably expect others to be interested in the war, but that others may share the convictions and attitudes that sustained the Southern participants and that haunt their descendents. "We live in a time when it has become routine, at least in the most influential quarters, to view the Old South as a veritable nest of evils. This view was already there in its infancy even at the time when my grandfather wrote, and there is good reason to think that some part of his intention here was to counteract it. For me, at least, he quite successfully did so" (xi).

After the foreword by the present day grandson, the adult Steven in 1900 declares in the first paragraph of his memoir that his case is special because there was in his character, then and now, "what was already abundant in Southern people generally: an ideality that almost no facts in a case could mitigate" (1). My worry that Jones may share, to some degree, the views of both the grandson and his paternal grandfather, was aggravated by the eagerness with which the adult Steven knowingly launches into a digression defending slavery, while decrying its excesses, very early in his memoir: "Here I suddenly find myself digressing into the realm of polemics.... certain things cry out to be said in our defense." While granting that slavery was already dying out and should not be re-instituted, he indulges himself in the tired old arguments we hear to this day, such as this: "The intimacies common among us... were, though qualified, indeed family-like. Hence our feeling of betrayal when defections began to occur" (17). The prevalent response today is that maybe the slaves had an *ideality,* too – of freedom.

My apprehension derived from my impression that Jones does not seem to be preparing a context in which to take such arguments any other way than literally. I began to wonder what inspired him to create once again a character with whom readers are familiar to the point of tedium. The adult Steven's unnuanced hyperbole that "the institution of slavery was an inherited one, passed down from time immemorial to the first American settlers" is generally regarded these days as a contemptible defense, especially when we recall that millions of Americans said it was contemptible as early as 1820. Steven also trots out the divine sanction argument, blames the African and the New England slave traders, excoriates the abolitionists, quotes Grant's lack of interest in fighting to free the slaves, and concludes that "largely financial reasons and not slavery caused the war" (19).

Steven seems to argue that the Confederacy was justified on all grounds and that the maliciously destructive invasion of Northern armies only reaffirmed the justice of her cause. He tacks on the cynical argument that no field slave would trade places with a wage-slave in the sweatshops of the North. All that is so numbingly perfunctory that readers of all Jones's works will hesitate to conclude that he is offering this American citizen of 1900 as someone to care about. The early pages of the novel fly then like a Confederate flag and the effect is almost as offensive, for African Americans at any rate. While Jones clearly has not created a raving racist, he also is not creating a character whose capacity for rationalization is monstrous; the adult Steven is too one-dimensional to take on that kind of interest for a serious reader.

Jones's subtitle is "the dying of the light." But who is raging against the dying of the light and what light is dying? In the absence of any other source of "light," one is inclined to conclude that the adult Steven is raging against the dying of the light shed by the South's heroics in battle and by her glorious civilization, blessed by God. God gets Steven, the father, and an old lady who befriends them through tribulations, and when Steven kills a Yankee soldier, it is he who trumpets, God's "vengeance by my hand" (124). The very last words of the novel are those of the old lady, who cannot "believe God would ever forgive" the Yankees for destroying "civilization" – Southern, she means. "They might have been my father's words. Or my own words, even now, though thirty-five years have passed," Steven writes (129).

Faithful blacks, a cherished image throughout, are waiting at home for their masters to destroy the enemy. On the next to last page, Steven assures his reader that Pompey, the father of the slave boy, Dink, killed during Steven's search for his own father, never blamed him. It is Steven's perception that Pompey, the faithful slave now free, kept his "friendship with us through all the years till his death." Steven presumes to impute even feelings to the ex-slave: "his feelings were real. I feel sure he went down to his grave still yearning for that old vanished world." Unprompted by Steven, readers may pose the question: from where may forgiveness come for the slave owners and the fire eaters who inflamed them? – Expressed in the first twenty pages and reiterated at the very end, the rhetoric and tone of Steven's and his grandson's convictions pervade all the rest of the memorist's narrative.

Despite the slavery-justification polemics, the early stages of Jones's delineation of the relationship between the twelve-year old white boy Steven and the twelve-year old slave boy Dink led me to look for a possible contradictory line of thought, to be alert for the gradual creation of a context that would ironically reinterpret for readers today those antiquated but still destructive convictions.

The story begins when the Moore family receives a letter that the father is wounded. Sister Liza, sick, "lay there limp and wasted." Mother is failing, and might die if the father doesn't come home. One may wonder how compelling a reason that is to risk a child's life in the midst of battle to search for him. The first thirty pages are devoted to preparing for the search. The next sixty pages are devoted to the search, ending with the death of Dink, the slave boy, and the finding of the father. In the aftermath of forty pages, the boy takes the father home, with the aid of an old lady, and shoots a Yankee on the way.

I will now follow the relationship, in action, between the two boys, Steven and Dink. Steven, as adult narrator, says, "I, along with Dink, set out on my mission" (31). When they encounter a black Yankee soldier, Dink asks him, "You ain't never been a slave?" Steven tells us: "The word, in Dink's mouth here and now, was a kind of shock to me" (38). I hoped this moment might be the beginning of a series of minor but cumulative revelations that would transcend the white boy Steven's immersion as witness in battle as he searched for his father.

When Dink tells the black soldier, whom he calls "a Yankee nigger," that he is himself a Confederate, I thought the image of a black slave child as a self-proclaimed Confederate was another lunge at justification of slavery, but I expected there would be later on some ironic reversal. – Stereotypical descriptions of Dink and his behavior also seemed to be Jones's set up for reversal. Steven the grown man still describes Dink in danger as "standing beside me now, panting and white-eyed" (62). That description recalled the depiction of breathless, wall-eyed scared "darkies" in B movies of the 1930s. Dink is reluctant to go further into danger, but will follow his master, saying, "I ain't afeared if you ain't." He then says, "I'm a Con...." The broken word "confederate" is immediately juxtaposed to the boom of a cannon (40).

Then the adult Steven offers his readers the stereotypical and sentimental image of white and slave children sleeping together: "We slept on the ground inside" a soldier's tent, "wrapped in one blanket close together against the bitter cold" (49). But I expected that situation might prove to be one of several preparations for a change in their relationship that would undermine the proslavery polemics. – When they wake next morning, Steven announces that they must keep moving, but Dink, "rolling his eyes," observes that it is too cold. Steven recalls that "over the years I have a thousand times in memory profoundly regretted this, my forcing him to go along.... this was what it meant to be a slave. This fact... was the source of my discomfort with the word 'slave.'... So it was against his will I led him into dangers in no way his to face" (56-57). Surely, this passage would signal the possibility of Jones's intention to develop in some complex way, Steven's conduct, emotions, and thoughts about his relationship with Dink.

The passages richest in actual development of the relationship come in chapter seven. The boys see Yankee troops attacking. "Suddenly, 'Them's niggers!' Dink's pitched voice had said it" (74). As Dink watches "Yankee niggers" fighting his master's Confederates and getting slaughtered to free slaves like himself, a change comes over him. "The tone of his voice was strange, new to him. So was his expression, gloomy and sullen as I never had seen it before." And Steven notes that "Dink followed, but not up close anymore" (76). Continuing his search for his father, Steven becomes hesitant in his pace because, he says, "From the start it was clear that the grisly event back there by the railroad cut had shocked him deeply – as, in a way less acute, it had shocked me. But his lagging, his persistent and sullen silence as we went on, increasingly weighed upon me" (78).

This time, Dink only reluctantly accepts Steven's invitation to sleep next to him to keep warm. Sensing what is on Dink's mind, Steven declares, "'They were Yankees too, come to take our country away from us. We got to fight back.' The silence again, but this time it was brief. He said, 'They was niggers just like me'" (80). The most dramatic event in the story is a change in the secondary character, in Dink, not in the protagonist. I expected therefore that Jones would develop in the remaining fifty pages of this novel some internal conflict within Steven. But drifting off to sleep, Steven thinks only of his father, his mother, and his sick sister. Distant firing wakes him and Dink comes closer. Then Steven regains consciousness after an explosion and sees: "from under a slanting beam," Dink's "dim face" appear. – The title of my essay turns upon the passage that comes next: "His eyes were looking at me. 'Dink,' I said. His eyes looked... but did not look. It was some long time before I understood that this was a death stare I was facing" (82-83).

That dead stare is a charged image that embodies everything most powerful in the novel's potential – in character relationships, plot, style, theme, conception – but it is here that the book implodes, it is here that Jones misses a great opportunity, for the most expressive metaphor for the War, Reconstruction, and our legacy of the War *is* the innocent's stare, alive witnessing the war, in later life remembering the war, and in death still staring at the war, even as we Americans stare at it a hundred years after Steven wrote his memoir. The innocent stare at battle, at death, at the past, not in a positive, workable vision, but, for many Southerners, transfixed, is an ideal rotten at the core, transmuted into the Lost Cause. It is such a stare that Faulkner in *The Unvanquished* and Allen Tate in *The Fathers* asserted sixty-seven years ago and that I assert in my own novel, the stare of children. In Jones's novel this childhood stare, recalled in late middle age by Steven, is merely a floating metaphor, no more expressive than any other.

Steven is too weak to extract Dink's body from the debris: "I thought of Dink, and stopped. 'I've got to go back,' I said." But a young soldier urges him on, and Steven complies rather readily (89). Thereafter, he merely alludes to Dink, as the adult Steven conscientiously devotes himself to recalling details of battle, bemoaning the defeat of the Confederate army, and, ironically, on the same page where one of those allusions to Dink occurs, bemoaning the destruction of Southern civilization, but not at any depth the loss of Dink. – He refers to his "long nightmare" as beginning *after* Dink's death, at the sight of "a gory pile as high as my waist of severed arms and legs," suggesting dead Confederates are more "harrowing" than Dink's death (92). The effect on him of Confederate defeat in the battle "were the moments that remain most vivid in my memory" (95). The scene in which General Stephen Lee rallies his men, "Till this day… is alive in my imagination" (102). He comes to a cabin where a black woman and a black man befriend him, reminding him of the blacks at home, especially Dink's father Pompey. He sleeps, and "it was long but never much of a sleep. Dink kept coming back, and Pompey behind him, blaming me" (111). His hatred of the Yankee soldier he encounters on the road is more powerful than his brotherly love for Dink (117). Dink's attitude toward the enemy changed, but Steven's did not, not even with Dink's as example. Five pages from the end, he finds his father, but does not speak to him of Dink.

Jones attributes to Steven the boy only one more serious observation, twenty-four pages before the end: "suddenly, with a throb of bitter pain, Dink was in my mind. There was murmur of voices, speaking of Dink, and accusing eyes fixed on me," for deserting him, or his corpse. This is a mildly ironic reversal of the adult Steven's condemnation of slaves who desert their masters (105). But the force even of that line is diluted by adult Steven's declaration on the next to last page that Dink's father never blamed Steven for the boy's death, and that the father, in fact, remained a friend of the family until he "went down to his grave still yearning for that old vanished world" (129). On the final page, Dink is alive in Steven's memory only in reference to "remnants of the house where Dink had met his end." More important for Steven as a final memory is the spot where he had "unknowingly witnessed 'the great mistake'" that caused the Confederate defeat in the Battle of Nashville. Thus, Jones creates in Steven a character who recalls Dink and his death only incidentally and with no more emphasis or implication than he thinks of his father and his mother – rather idealized, one-dimensional characters who in no way compete with Dink for the reader's interest.

Having become keenly aware that the relationship that had been developing between young master and young slave in the search for the father had become, over half way through the novel, far more interesting and meaningful than the search itself, I was forced to conclude that Jones was not developing a dramatic internal conflict that was working its way outward into an external conflict. Steven and Dink stand in an old house, as if expecting some painful issue, but Jones does not, it later turns out, have a major developing issue between the boys themselves in mind. – Narrating his experiences with the young slave, Steven does not convey in the past, or in the present, any feelings about him that would even suggest a change of mind and heart about the slave himself or about slavery in general. Coming so early and expressed so fervently by Steven in later life, the master-slave family-tie ideality (or fantasy) reduces the relationship of Steven and Dink to the status of a mere illustration of that wishful claim, a claim that is presented, examined, but usually deconstructed by hundreds of Southern fiction and nonfiction writers.

Whether the convictions expressed by Steven's descendant in his foreword and Steven in his memoir reflect to some degree the author's own perspective remains for me ambiguous, but not, I feel inclined to conclude, in the positive sense of an author's deliberate ambiguity meant to encourage a range of possible insights. – The relationship between the white boy and the slave boy, even though it ends with the slave's death midway in the book, is intrinsically interesting, because while the narratively uninteresting search in battle for the father has a routine beginning, middle, and end, the boy's relationship with his slave playmate has a potential that, though only partially actualized, may haunt the reader more lastingly than it does Steven and his older self. We are left with a rather overwrought recreation of battle that fails to transcend the vacuous literalism of reenactments and a dogged mimicry of the kind of memoir a witness might write. Madison Jones stares at the War, his boy character stares at it, and the boy thirty-six years later stares at it, but the stare remains a fixed stare, unenlightened. The rage against the dying of the light is hollow and the light itself dies without illuminating.

As the boy Steven wanders into the battle zone and onto the battleground, I expected the adult Steven to try to recall the past in such as way as to enable the reader to experience the shock of battle *as the boy experiences it*, but although descriptions of stages of the single battle of Nashville that Steven witnesses take up most of the novel the author and his narrator are so enamored of battle details that they provide a full, knowledgeable recreation that undercuts our immediate experience of the lost boy's shock and confusion. Steven's depiction of the battles themselves has the air of a Civil War roundtabler's obsession with the facts, as if a full recreation is as important to him as the recovery and understanding in memory of the major events and issues in his own life. In pursuit of that recreation of heroic acts and glorious defeat, the narrator mixes indiscriminately specific events he witnessed as a boy with what he has learned over the years about the general setting of the battle.

Jones does not create a tension between the man's command of the facts and his memory of the boy's limited experience; the one seems merely to enhance the other; the effect, however, is that the adult Steven's compulsion to fill in the surrounding facts distracts us from the boy's immediate experience, dilutes its impact. Jones and his narrator, like many Southerners attracted to the War, seem to feel obligated or eager to render the battle fully in an attempt to enhance for his reader Steven's very limited and ignorant exposure to it. The effect is that the battle is not only vague and tedious, as is usually the case when the compulsion is to render every detail, but what is worse the boy's own unique experience is swamped for us by generalizations and facts he could not have made or known at the time: "The action was in fact a feint on the part of the Yankee army.... What Dink and I observed from our position on the hillside was not the main action" (67-68). Jones also attributes to the boy an unlikely perception of details and to Steven as a man an unlikely memory of such details (112). The boy's experience seems then to have had an effect on the man no deeper or greater than to motivate him to recreate the battle events. Everything is directly stated and, in the mode of nineteenth century rhetoric that Jones adopts for the narrator, overstated, and so the reader experiences almost no implications.

As an old fashioned narrative technique, Jones has Steven announce what's to come, mechanically, in general terms: "In April and May of '63 there were two events very damaging, and also disillusioning, to us" (16). "Two times, in '62 and again early in '63, Father came home.... that first time.... His second time..." (22). "The worst times, of course, were yet to come. The year of '64 was much harder than '63..." (26). "In the midst of this came unexpected news.... But this one had already happened…" (29). "But this came later in the day" (77). "The wonder, however, was something that came to me only in retrospect, from what I was later to learn" (101). The effect of this tendency is to undercut the illusion readers crave – of events happening *now*.

The action of the search is too simple. Neither Steven nor Dink ever really initiates an action along the way, although Steven, almost as the author's narrative afterthought, in the last six pages, shoots a Yankee to defend his father and the old lady who helps him. Chapter eight ends: "It is ironical that this, the memory of our soldiers constructing those works, should have left me feeling reassured when real sleep finally took me. For in fact, as I was to learn in aftertimes, I had been eye-witness to a most crucial error in the making" (88). The use of this device prevents the reader from sharing a major experience with the boy and also from experiencing with Steven as adult a deep insight about that missed experience. It is simply noted and left to dangle.

The most dramatic event remains the death of Dink. Steven does not initiate action of any magnitude, certainly not a line of action that produces external conflict the reader can follow with increasing interest; the action around Steven lacks imagined complications, and the rendering of battle actions is routine. Large episodes are rendered in much the same perfunctory way as such small episodes as this: an officer tells Steven and Dink to go to a house and eat. They go. They eat. They sleep. Up to page 31, Jones doles out routine summaries of routine daily life, nothing unusual, everything very basic, what we find in numerous other Civil War novels. Halfway, I wondered: what is being developed? In the absence of protagonist initiated action producing conflict, the reader expects an internal conflict, which I have argued is ambiguously posed but fitfully and finally inadequately developed. – Except for Dink, the characters are one-dimensional, even though we get the hero both as a boy and as memoirist narrator at age forty-eight. The object of the search, the father, presented early as a heroic image on a horse, is reduced to a stumbling blind man. The mother exists not much more than in this line: "I will never lose the vivid memory of my mother on that wagon seat with the lines in her hands, stiffly erect" (15). The passage goes on with a routine physical description of a woman the reader never really gets to know.

Adult Steven's direct references to the act of remembering and writing undercut for the reader the immediacy of the boy Steven's experiences. The context in which we respond to every word of Steven's memoir is that of self-conscious recall and writing. That could be a dimension of the experience that enriches our apprehension of it, but nowhere does Jones seem to be developing a pattern of implications, ironic or any other kind. Steven is still doing it eight pages from the end: "I need give no very detailed description of that long ride, continuing into the night, before we met with the brief but harrowing ordeal in store for us" (121). That experience cannot then be a "harrowing ordeal" for the reader. The most blatant example comes earlier, when Steven quotes a Yankee officer to make "my account as complete as possible" (96). The battle as a whole upstages the boy's experience of it.

From the beginning of the book and on the narrator mentions his memory at numerous points, calls attention to its imperfections, and in this way undercuts the effect of the experience being rendered, as in: "It is difficult for me to be even sequential, much less complete in my account of events following that shell's explosion" (99). Had the author involved the reader intimately in the boy's perceptions, the question of completeness would have seemed irrelevant, especially in a novel so brief. On a single page, Steven says, "I remember" three times, without significance (100). Time frames, such as Jones uses here, looking back from 1900 to 1864, usually serve to illuminate, but this one does not. There is no sense of rediscovery, new discovery, and revelation, or insight into self or community. The constant reminder by the adult Steven that he can or cannot remember, or only vaguely remembers this, that, and the other provides the reader with only superficial insight into the memory process and the frustrations of writing a memoir. Neither the experience itself nor the writing about it seems to have affected the narrator very deeply. In novels of complexly delineated irony, for instance, the facets of a narrator's failure to achieve revelation is a primary experience for the reader. The grandson's foreword also fails to add a perspective or attitude that might render the memoir more meaningful. We are left with a rather overwrought recreation that almost fails to transcend the vacuous literalism of reenactments.

The memorist's style also dilutes the effect of the relationship between the white boy and the slave boy. In his foreword, the grandson assures us that Steven's memoir is well-written and that factual accuracy, necessarily enhanced by imagination, is one of its virtues. Jones's own stylistic imagination seems quiescent in this recreation. The style is pretentious, pseudo-literary, full of formal phrases, in imitation of many memoirs, I suppose, but Sam Watkins's and General Grant's memoirs show how to avoid those stylistic trappings. Style, the life breath of a literary work, here undercuts every element it renders — especially the boy's relationship with the slave boy and battles.

Descriptions of extreme events are stilted. A cannon ball takes a man's head off, and "They fell silent… all, I guessed, with visions in their mind's eyes." "I suppose that, given the shock and terror my experience included, this is not surprising" (67). "I said it out of a throat drawn painfully tight" (70). "Then and for an unmeasurable time thereafter, with the cannon blasts above…." (71). "These registered only as stock events of the battle," an attitude that produces stock phrases in style (72). "Even when I saw that he was gone, distress remained like an object lodged too close against my heart" (84). "My confusion came back, increasing. In something like panic I strained at the knob, then knocked, and knocked again" (104). The stilted, formal quality in the quoted sentences infects the dialog as well, sometimes ringing false to this Tennessean's ear.

When a writer is not in control of point of view and style, even an astute reader and writer can get the style and the time of narration wrong, as Madison Smartt Bell does: "The language of the child-narrator is tone perfect for those times." It is not the child who narrates, in 1864, but the man, in 1900. Bell inadvertently touches, however, on the problem: the narrative might have been more effective had the boy at 18 or 19 written or orally told his story and dealt fully with Dink, as Bayard Sartoris dealt with Ringo, only with greater complexity, because Bayard's compulsion to tell a story sprang from several other characters, as well. Paradoxically, it is the innocent stare of the very young that sometimes provides a more meaningful view of the Antebellum, War, and Reconstruction eras as compared with adults who seem compelled to heap facts, out of a misdirected sense of obligation to authenticity, upon the heads of readers, diluting the impact of direct experience. The adult Steven brings to that past experience no fresh perspectives and derives from the act of memory and memoir writing no significant insights about either his personal experience or the national tragedy. To the extent that the art of fiction fails all else in a novel fails.

The innocent stare, fixed in his first novel *The Innocent* (1957), is reiterated in all Jones's work, especially, *Forest of the Night*, *A Buried Land*, *An Exile*, *A Cry of Absence*, and *Passage through Gehenna*. One has only to compare *Nashville 1864* with Jones's most ambitious, complex, and finest work, *A Cry of Absence,* to see that the basic Jones's art can serve him well. In *An Exile*, all the elements – character, conflict, theme, and techniques, point of view, style – cohere to create an intimacy with the protagonist that is almost unbearably intense and immediate.

Less obviously than Jesse Hill Ford, a Southern liberal who fought hard in life and in literature for the civil rights of blacks in Tennessee (but who ironically shot and killed a black soldier who trespassed on his estate), Jones has taken humanistic positions, especially in *A Cry of Absence*, on civil rights, never quite taking a liberal position, because his basic conception is of the limitations of human nature. Because *Nashville 1864* was written late in his life, one might expect to find either a departure from the consistent Aeschylean stance that M. E. Bradford posed for Jones's work to a critique of the South's position on slavery as expressed in the War or to an outright conservative apologia. My reading of the novel is that it lacks the one thing vital for the capstone of a distinguished career: a fresh perspective or vision of the war, whether liberal or conservative, that might enable us to reinterpret the body of Jones's work.

A RESPONSE TO DAVID MADDEN'S ESSAY

Madison Jones

Having carefully read David Madden's essay I am quite persuaded that he does not like my little book *Nashville 1864: The Dying of the Light*. He offers a plenty of reasons. Some of these are:

I did not write the book in the way he would have written it.
Except for Dink all my characters are one-dimensional.
My overwrought re-creation fails to transcend the vacuous literalism of reenactments. The action of the search is too simple: it is not a line of action that produces external conflict.
There is no significant internal conflict in Steven, the protagonist.
My style is pretentious, pseudo-literary, full of formal phrases, and my dialogue rings false.
Immediacy of experience is lacking. I produce no insights as to personal or other experience.
I sin by daring to put into my narrator's mouth words intended to mitigate the reader's perception of slavery in all its invariable and unrelenting horror.
Everything in the novel is vague, tedious, routine, vacuous, perfunctory, clichéd, worn out, etc.

And this is only a partial list of my sins and shortcomings. They go on adding up through fifteen pages until finally, alas, nothing at all is left standing. It is really remarkable that a not inconsiderable number of highly qualified readers and critics somehow failed to notice such a multiplicity of serious-to-fatal flaws. (Poor Jonathan Yardley, for instance, who in *The Washington Post* foolishly wrote: "It is, in all respects, a splendid piece of work.") But fail they did, almost to a man. Not, however, the fearless author of this massacre. He is there with sword and cudgel, meaning to kill and kill again, proceeding to dismember the corpse, and at last, still unwearied, he jumps up and down on the remains.

Many readers may wonder why. It may be said that the main reason is embodied in what he poses as the central critical issue: that of the slave boy Dink. But there could be an auxiliary reason. David Madden has also published a Civil War novel, of which he speaks warmly in his essay, and which by implication has all the virtues so eloquently lacking in mine. This could be a contributing factor.

A piece of criticism as egregious as this one is not worth serious rebuttal. But one thought does catch my interest. Let us say I had chosen to write my book in the manner David Madden describes as the proper one. It might go something like this: in the midst of this titanic battle to decide the fate of his country, in the midst of his desperate and uncertain personal mission, my twelve-year-old hero Steven, while staring into Dink's dead face, receives the shattering revelation that he, his family, his kin, and his country are guilty of all the unrelieved horror slavery has imposed. I suppose that then, given a little while to digest all this, Steven with my permission can forget about his family, who had it coming anyway, and get out of there with the intention of spending the rest of his guilt-ridden life doing social work among African-American ex-slaves and their descendants.

Maybe this summary of a conceivable Madden plot is a little of a stretch, but not too much. Think of all the fiction published over the last few decades in which we find a theme nearly identical with this one. Blind before, white Southerners now can see and feel appropriately guilty. The heroes of these stories do not even have to be in any way personally responsible for the evil, but they feel guilty just the same. Any excuse will do, it seems, for an act of penitence. I do not hesitate to declare that the cliché evident in the outlined plot far outmatches any attributed to my own book. Nor do my clichés, if they exist, have the unhappy effect of discrediting, or even demonizing, our ancestors.

I have already written more than I should have, and I am not about to embark on an undertaking to answer the enumerated multitude of misguided charges. The distortions so evident in David Madden's reading are mainly (for ego lurks in the background) caused by an affliction as pervasive in our current fiction as it is elsewhere. This affliction is Political Correctness, and practically speaking, David Madden's essay is a prime illustration of its working. Its immediate origin is a protective self-righteousness, resulting, when challenged, in easy indignation and blunted perception. In defense of its righteousness, unrestrained will asserts itself and in so doing obstructs real participation in the material *of* the text at hand. Thus liberated, the reader finds what he wants to find.

So it is, I perceive, with David Madden, whose outrage at my delinquency, ultimately my moral delinquency, subverts his judgment through every step of the way, e.g. his unquestioned conclusion that I agree in every respect with the opinions of my narrator, who wrote this memoir in the year 1900. Given my narrator's experience and the times in which he wrote, is it not probable that he would hold just these opinions? I may agree with them, but again I may not. It does not matter to David Madden. The question does not even occur to him. To him, I and my fictional creation are one and the same, equally deserving to be shot down.

Complaints about and ridicule of political correctness are widespread nowadays, but they seem to have little effect on the guilty parties. It appears that all of them, a multitude among the intellectually elite, consider that it is not them but others who are thus at fault. This frame of mind is, I suppose, in large part a product of democratization gone too far, equating not only people generally but also standards of judgment. Absence of standards, including moral standards, leads to alienation and guilt feelings, and the visible remedy is to seek the embrace of some cohesive group with inflexible standards, or attitudes, of its own. Their righteousness prevails, defended with a vigor that often betrays its self-assurance. Such, in my view, is the party of the Politically Correct. If I in my own way have sometimes been guilty of much the same failing, the fact makes this instance no less objectionable.

David Madden declares that he worries about my possibly being a neo-Confederate. Call it what he will, I am a conservative and have been all my life. I have never been on a guilt-trip, politically speaking, and I try to treat all men and even women with sweet charity.

SYMPATHY FOR THE DEVIL:

A READING OF *HEROD'S WIFE*

Richard Gray

Herod's Wife begins deceptively, as if it were a chamber piece, and perhaps a variation on Tolstoy's famous dictum about happy and unhappy families. A husband and wife, Hugh and Nora Helton, are lying in bed together after an extremely unsatisfactory sexual encounter. "It's crippling us," the woman complains bitterly. 'It' would seem to be the fact that Nora was once the wife of Hugh's brother Wilbur. After a turbulent affair, and Nora's divorce from Wilbur, Hugh and Nora were married. Instead of resolving problems, however, the remarriage has only left things in a kind of painful limbo. Or worse: "Married to your brother's wife. Incest, isn't it?" Nora observes sardonically. It is as if they are living in still worse sin than before, condemned to a form of damnation that seems to partake equally of the biblical and the gothic, the Old Testament and a tale by Edgar Allan Poe. Hugh, in particular, feels alienated from the brother he has betrayed. Worse still, he feels "excommunicated" from his church. For, like Nora as it turns out, Hugh has been raised as a Roman Catholic. Now, he feels estranged by his faithless conduct, not only from his faith, but also from his friend, the local priest, "a lonely young man" called Father John Riley, with whom he has previously shared time and confidences. Madison Jones has always been a master of generic switches, exploiting and mixing different narrative modes to pursue his novelistic aims; and already a tale that started out as if it were about domestic crisis is assuming a darker shape and deeper undertones.

As the narrative point of view switches from Hugh Helton to Father John Riley, with an ease and facility that is to become familiar as the story progresses, the reader is introduced, not only to the local priest, but also to the locality that he and the Heltons share. Lakepoint, as it is called, is a thoroughly modern place. Once, we learn, it was called

Lorreta, "after a woman dear to the old town's history. It had to do with Indians and lives she had saved from a raid." With time and change, however, had also come a change of name. The river that ran beside Lorreta was "swollen into a lake." As Hugh had earlier observed, gazing at the town from an upstairs window in his home, it was "like a flood... that overnight engulfed the town and, receding, left in its place a small metropolis of unfamiliar eager faces intent on business or merriment" (4). The reader familiar with Jones's work thinks, perhaps, of a much earlier novel, *A Buried Land* (1963), in which the flooding of the countryside by the Tennessee Valley Authority becomes coextensive with a general social act of forgetting and, more specifically, with the desire of the protagonist to bury his past, to consign it to oblivion. A similar resonance is registered here. Lakepoint is a place of "sleek store fronts and neon lights and marinas humming with the sound of motors along the lakefront." It is a place, Father Riley soon realizes when he is sent there by his church, where people are "impatient of ritual" and "openly in rebellion against the teachings of the church in such matters as divorce and birth control" (6-7). The inhabitants of Lakepoint, it seems, have suppressed their past and driven deeper matters of faith into some subterranean place, some strange, dark territory beneath the placid surfaces, the calm waters of everyday life. As a community, if they can be called such, they have experienced a separation from the beliefs and behavior of yesterday – and so, to a significant degree, from themselves – that is quite as complete, if not quite as dramatic, as the estrangement experienced by Hugh Helton.

As the narrative switches again, this time to Nora Helton, the reader soon learns that Hugh's wife has separated from the faith of her fathers in a more deliberate way. Raised as a Catholic in a lower-class suburb of Atlanta, Nora was in rebellion almost from the beginning of her life. Little acts of jealousy, spite and defiance, often directed against her younger sister, gradually escalated into outright resistance to the teachings of the church: "The Lord is my shepherd, but I am not a sheep," she once wrote in her school notebook, to the outrage of the head teacher, a priest, who discovered this among other blasphemies. Then, unexpectedly, Nora recalls, she made "a friend of sorts" of a mysterious stranger, a young man called Nick Meagher. He had once been a Catholic like her, he told her, and "had been to many cities and also other places she had never heard of." This secret friendship came to an abrupt end, when the young girl found a note "somehow there on her pillow." It was from Nick. "I have been away and have to go again," the note said. "But I will be back, to stay. Believe me" (15). So far, so naturalistic, although the reader possibly catches an echo of old, forgotten, far-off things and holy battles long ago in the first name of this strange young man. And the apparent naturalism of the narrative continues as we learn – while Nora rehearses further memories – that, after being attracted at college to a philosophy professor "whose rationalistic view of things she labored to make her own," she met and married Wilbur Helton, then gave birth to a daughter, Nora Jean, "too soon after the marriage."

One of the many pleasures of *Herod's Wife* comes from the ease and economy with which Jones sketches in the details of a wealth of characters. This is a short novel but it is also a richly textured one; and it is so partly because the narrative weaves its way, not just between different narrative viewpoints, but between discrete moments in time. The people in *Herod's Wife* may be lost in the delirium of the present, but they are not therefore immune to memory; and, as they remember, we begin to understand why they are where they are today. They, perhaps, can make little of it, but we can; as they play on what Faulkner once called the resonant strings of remembering, their past is there for us, as a source of understanding, even if its deeper resonances, remain unheard by and unknown to them. So, as Nora recollects, we discover that she soon became disappointed in and dissatisfied with Wilbur, not least because he was haunted "by a vague nostalgia that, as she was qualified to perceive, had its origins in the obnoxious Catholic religion he had discarded years ago." Ripe for the taking, when she and Wilbur returned to his hometown of Lakepoint, she soon fell into the arms of Hugh, a far more successful man than his brother. Hugh was drawn to Nora by, among other things, a "secret urge" that he "vaguely deplored in himself… to give his brother pain." Nora was drawn, in turn, by the wealth, the success and, in local terms, the power of Hugh. With marriage, she found herself "possessed of all she had hoped for" in terms of material comfort and security. Yet, true to a narrative in which the repressed always seems to be there, ready to have its revenge, she found that "a little edge of uneasiness remained" (19).

The tension, the unease that Hugh and Nora both feel in their separate ways is evidently shared with their neighbors. As the story opens out to incorporate local events, what is notable is the anxiety and incipient conflict that seem to typify the people of Lakepoint. Nora becomes involved in local politics, joining a group called Vistas, "whose business it was to trumpet and redress social abuses in the town and county." Fighting against what she perceives as "the tyranny of tradition," Nora takes her daughter Jean with her to one of the major events in the local campaign for mayor. This is a debate over a new abortion clinic that is about to open. The debate, between the candidate Nora supports, Ted Klein, "an urbane Jew of independent means," and the Reverend Stark, "a Church of Christ preacher pure and simple," gradually descends from jeering and tension into scuffling and then into fighting. "A cry of pain" terminates a crowd scene that seems to act as a social equivalent of the domestic strains we have already witnessed. *Herod's Wife* is a story in which something dangerous, something deadly is always threatening to swim up from below the equable surfaces of experience. All we witness for now is its symptoms: a vague unease, anxiety, and a cry of uncertain origin.

Father Riley, it turns out, is also involved in the turmoil. As the narrative returns to him, the reader discovers that he has spoken out against the clinic in a sermon, calling abortion "an act as brutal as Herod's murder, multiplied by thousands." Struggling to fight against what he perceives as "indifference certain to spread like disease through society at large," Father Riley joins in a protest outside the clinic. There, when the police try to make a way for some women to go through to the clinic, things again degenerate into violence. Father Riley is wounded, and some people in the crowd are arrested. Soon after the arrests, the rumor begins to circulate in the town that one of those taken into custody was "a nigger boy," "hurt enough so they had to halfway carry him off. Cop hit him with a stick." Rumor is one form that anxiety, the vague sense that the times are out of joint, takes in the claustrophobic environment of Lakepoint. And this rumor receives an added charge when a black boy named Quals, apparently the black boy in question, disappears. After the previous death of a black man in police custody – a death that, we learn, led to the resignation of the then police chief – people, especially black people, are suspicious, "muttering about police brutality." Father Riley thinks he may be able to help, to participate here too, as the tense politics of the locality take a racial inflection. He goes to see "the big man" in the black community, Cap Waters, in what turns out to be a fruitless attempt to calm things down. He then takes an anxious part in another public moment: when Cap, eager to stir things up, makes a public statement about Quals in front of the courthouse. "Our boy Quals is dead," Cap tells the crowd assembled there to hear him, and he adds: "Kilt by the police" (42).

This time, there is no violence and Father Riley escapes uninjured. Danger of a very different kind, however, much subtler and more sinister, is now threatening to engulf him. Nora is becoming obsessed with the father, as if all her accumulated hatred of the church, paternal authority, and our father who art in heaven had now gathered around him. The form her hatred assumes, in terms of action, is conspiratorial. "Have you ever heard anything about him," Nora asks her daughter Jean. "Anything not very nice. Anything ugly." When Jean confesses that she has not, Nora encourages her to dig for dirt. "Ask your friends," the mother instructs her daughter. "Anything about him and children, little girls. You know what I mean. Ugly things" (35). The mere presence of Father Riley at a potentially insurrectionary event, involving inflammatory speech making, quietly pleases Nora, because she knows that it is something his conservative parishioners will not understand or appreciate. In fact, she experiences what is called "a sort of double pleasure," as she sees events – and the words of Cap Waters, in particular – working to "achieve both her social and personal wishes": social change and upheaval and the degradation of the priest. The narrative, although predominantly still naturalistic, is weaving together a dense tapestry of the social and the personal, political anxiety, and domestic tension, by this stage. And the weave becomes ever more densely textured as Hugh tries, unsuccessfully, to dissuade his former friend, the father, from any further political involvement: an act that earns him the contempt of his wife and succeeds only in adding a further edge to his own unease. At night, after the abortive visit to Father Riley, Hugh is haunted by dreams of his old, discarded faith and the brother and the priestly friend from whom he is now estranged. Not only that, he is haunted by what is already becoming a dominant image in *Herod's Wife*. There is a window in the Roman Catholic chapel at which Hugh often gazed when he was younger and still had active faith. In that window is a portrait of "Christ in midair, a wonder, ascending with lordly outstretched arms to the blue of heaven above." The vision of that window stays with Hugh for a brief instant as he awakens from his dreams, opening his eyes to "the darkness of his bedroom" (47).

At this point, the narrative, never leisurely, begins to accelerate, shifting first to Wilbur Helton – whose hatred for Hugh, we find out, "eating away at his guts," is the one reason he does not leave town – and then to Cap Waters. Crisis seems to be in social terms, as, first, a police officer is killed trying to capture an arsonist – a series of mysterious arson attacks is another symptom of the anxiety, the latent violence plaguing the town – and then, to Cap's consternation, the Quals boy returns, very much alive. Cap wants Eddie Quals to leave town immediately, so that the campaign over police violence and his "death" can continue; and, when Quals shows reluctance, Cap in his frustration hits out at him, accidentally killing him. Again, violence has erupted suddenly, breaking without warning through the surface; and, again, it is quickly buried. This time, the submergence of a darker truth is literal as well as symbolic: Cap buries the body in the lake that has drowned out, too, so much of the past of the community. But the truth cannot be suppressed that easily or entirely. Before becoming a fugitive, an ironic victim of his own conspiracy, Cap is impelled to go to Father Riley to confess what he has done. The father offers his blessing – "I don't know anything else I can do for you," he tells Cap – and then, after Cap has fled, feels obliged to go to the police, to tell them what has happened. Rumors about the event are soon all over town; and, once more, however innocently, the priest is implicated (59).

As the pace of the narrative accelerates, so does its passionate yet mysterious purpose. The viewpoint shifts back to Nora. The news about the father, we are told, has "put the hint of a smile on her lips." What has happened, Nora suspects, has turned Father Riley in the eyes of the town into "a friend and confidant to the killer." "A gift from heaven, was her ironical thought;" "was not this brew quite strong enough to execute her purpose?" Just exactly what that purpose might be is now becoming clear (60). With clarity, though, comes a new depth and ambiguity. Nora thinks of priests and fathers, what she sees as their snares and deceptions. She thinks then of Lucifer, recalling "a certain moment years ago" when she first learned the derivation of Lucifer's name, "Bearer of light." "That was a luminous moment," she recalls; and now, "for the first time in a long, long while, she thought of 'him' again." As she recollects all this, in a gesture that is a regular and routine, yet somehow a chilling one, throughout the story, Nora turns to gaze at her own image in the mirror. There, in the reflection, "something" happens to her smile and her appearance, something that is worth quoting in full: "... a blurring that deeply shadowed her whole face, so that an altered image peered from out of a darkness at her. An instant only. It was but a trick of the light, a cloud passing across the slanted rays of the sun. She was not superstitious. A moment more and that altered image had gone quite out of her mind" (61). This is the first of several moments when the realistic surface of the narrative is ruptured, and something more mysterious, more full of portent erupts into sight. It is, in a way, a formal equivalent of those moments in the action when the fundamental darkness of things swims into view, breaking through the sleek appearances of domestic or social life. What the reader makes of such narrative moments suggests an analogy with the short story, "The Turn of the Screw," by Henry James. Famously, that story leaves different readings available, psychological or spiritual, naturalistic or gothic. So does *Herod's Wife*. We might, like Nora here, prefer to dismiss this as superstition, a relic of faith. We might want to see it in terms of Nora becoming a prey to her own obsessions and then, a victim of her Catholic upbringing, translating hatred into terms she has understood – even if she has rejected most of them – since she was a girl. Alternatively, we may wish to see this as a prelude to an act of possession, the human spirit being taken over by something genuinely diabolical. The beauty and subtlety of *Herod's Wife* is that it makes all these different readings possible, allowing them to coexist without conflict. However we read it, this is still a story about the revenge of the repressed. It is about how a human personality and a culture deny their origins, the circumstances of their past, and the condition of their spirit, at their peril – and how that denial in the end leads to devastation.

Nora now goes about her work – the devil's work, her own work, perhaps both – with a vengeance, planting rumors about Father Riley. Specifically, these rumors concern the abuse of a young girl called Mary McDougal whom Nora has seen with the priest. The father tries to counter the rumors, first by public denial and then with silence, but he finds himself impotent, still suspect. He is subjected to cold looks, suspicious glances, and the general withdrawal of his congregation; and, on one infamous occasion, he is surrounded, jeered at, and humiliated by a crowd of teenage boys. Nora now stokes the fire with lies. She tells Mrs. McDougal that she has actually seen Father Riley touching and kissing Mary; and she forces her daughter Jean to lie, to say that she has heard stories from people who have seen the priest involved in instances of abuse. She then persuades Mrs McDougal – who is, unsurprisingly, convinced by all this – to go to the police to swear out a warrant, "so it was all but accomplished," Nora tells herself (75).

The lies have done their work, and the priest finds himself the subject of a warrant. Looking at herself in the mirror, Nora again sees "an odd but somehow enhancing difference in the clear lines of her face." As the screw tightens, and the tension increases, fire breaks out again, once more the work of a mysterious arsonist. This time, it is the Roman Catholic church, where Father Riley is praying, that is set alight. The father is horribly burned and most of the building is destroyed. Returning to town just when the fire has taken hold, Hugh Helton visits the scene and is comforted by one thing. The church has "one still-standing segment of the wall, a rear corner including one of the windows." In that window is the image "he had vaguely hoped to see: the head though without the body now of Christ ascending to heaven." It is a small beacon of hope, possible redemption, amid the general devastation, what seems like the inevitable lurch of events into further violence and despair (81).

With the narrative perspective returning to Hugh here, then to his brother Wilbur, we are able to see Nora and her possible changes from another view: no longer her own but that of two men, one of whom was once married to her and the other of whom – despite the distance that has grown between them – still is. The uncertainty about just what, if anything, has happened to Nora remains, however. Looking at her while she sleeps, Hugh sees a difference in his wife about which he cannot be sure: "something in her expression, by a trick of the light, disturbed him in a way he could not explain," the narrative discloses. "It made him think of the blissful swoon that can follow intercourse" (83). The perspective supplied by Wilbur is more categorical but also more metaphorical. Suspecting that Nora has been up to something that has troubled Jean, Wilbur sees his former wife "in his mind's eye" as a diabolical figure, "sleek and cunning as a serpent." This may be insight or imagination, the truth of accurate vision or the truth of emotion – after all, Wilbur has every reason emotionally to see the woman who has betrayed and deserted him as evil, satanic. It is still for the reader to decide. This remains the case when the gaze of the story belongs once more to Nora.

Silence has grown between Nora and her daughter, we learn, evidently because Jean has become eaten up with guilt over her lying. Jean disappears from the house for a while, too long for Nora's comfort, and Nora goes in frantic search of her. Is the search prompted by motherly concern or by fear that the lying will be unmasked? Again it remains a tantalizing mystery; it is not clear and is left for the reader to decide. What is clear is that, once embarked on her search, Nora strays from familiar paths; and, in an episode that is at once utterly realistic and mythic, apocalyptic, becomes lost in a wilderness – cut and bruised by a nature that seems to be her enemy, that seems to be fighting against her. Eventually, she finds herself in a place of stones. "For one appalling moment," the narrative reveals, "she seemed to envision what had happened here, happened ages ago: a fiery blast, one titanic lightning strike, and all things turned to stone (91)." Cut and bleeding, Nora soon afterwards finds herself where she can see, in the distance, the town and the lake and the surrounding fields. And words rise up, take shape in her mouth: "Burn it. Burn it all to a cinder." It is a signal moment, issuing out of domestic crisis and prophecy, suggesting not only the identity of the mysterious arsonist but also the explosive nature of any impulse, any rebellious gesture that would deny the fundamental darkness of the human personality and the consequent need for anchorage, for tradition and faith. Nora has resisted, and even denied, what lies beneath; it has now taken possession of her, literally or psychologically or spiritually. A character in crisis, and in the active process of dissolution, she is also like Milton's fallen angel – the strangest, most compelling, and spellbinding figure in a story that casts her, nevertheless, as a force for evil.

Herod's Wife is not just the portrait of a woman possessed by her own demons; it is a series of scenes from a marriage – a marriage that seems to be in terminal decay. Hugh finds the behavior of Nora ever more perplexing and disturbing, continuing to wonder if she has taken up a lover. Along with a feeling of distance, there is also, on Hugh's part, genuine fear. Gazing at Nora while she sleeps, Hugh listens to her murmuring "something… impossible to translate," then hears her give out "a muffled cry." Suddenly, her body, springing to life it seems without her knowledge or volition, presses hard against him, and she cries out, as if between clenched teeth, "Fuck me. Fuck me Now!" Is this Nora speaking, or some voice that has taken her over? Is she talking to Hugh or to some strange demon lover? Is it the "little death," the swoon of orgasm that she wants, or some other kind of death? Neither Hugh nor the reader knows for sure (102).

The diabolism of *Herod's Wife* thrives in a condition of indeterminacy; confusion has made its masterpiece in the twisted personality of its central, female character and in the labyrinthine uncertainties of the narrative. Possessed for a moment by a violent impulse, then by an equally "violent recoil," Nora continues to act as if she were in a trance as, without a word of explanation, she rises from the bed, leaves the room, and goes out into the darkness of the night. Watching her leave the house – as if she were sleepwalking, like a character from one of the tales of Poe – Hugh thinks, for a moment, that he sees "a shape, a movement there against the backdrop of the woods." Or does he? It is, perhaps, "only deceptive light and too much staring." Peering into the dark, confused, perturbed, frightened, Hugh is no more capable of seeing things for sure than Nora was when she gazed at herself in the mirror. The shape may be a trick of the light, the shadow a result of staring for too long and too hard. Then again, it may be 'him,' old Nick, Lucifer, the devil.

The narrative now dips down from crisis to catastrophe. In the morning after this strange night when Nora had appeared possessed and departed, Hugh finds Jean still in bed and in a coma, having taken an entire bottle of her mother's sleeping pills. With the narrative shifting back to Nora, the reader next encounters her in a small, nearly empty restaurant. She had found Jean unconscious and perhaps dead, and then moved in a semi-comatose fashion through the woods and into town. Now, she feels "watched," although she is not sure by whom. *Herod's Wife* plays on watching and being watched, almost as much as *Sanctuary*, William Faulkner's vision of evil, does; and, like *Sanctuary*, it elides voyeurism, narcissism, and that acute self-consciousness that comes from feeling observed – looking at evil, in the image of oneself and others, feeling the discomfort, the potential guilt from suspecting that "somebody is watching me." So, feeling watched, Nora also watches; and she thinks she catches "a shape at the plate glass window" of the restaurant; "she knew who it was," the narrator confides, "could tell that it was 'him'." As usual, the 'him' remains unspecified and indeterminate, conditioned by our understanding of the reliability, the accuracy of vision of the observer (106).

For Nora, though, there is enough of a substantial presence there, or hint of a presence, to justify desperate pursuit. "A discernible movement, an obscurely beckoning motion" of the hand of the mysterious stranger – or is he a mysterious lover? – summons Nora to her feet. As she tries to follow this "spectral figure," he seems to be there then not there. Eventually, she loses 'him' or the hallucination of him. In the hospital, however, to which she drifts to find out if Jean is still alive, Nora again sees "someone" in the "unexpected gloom," "a figure beside her that moved close to her ear: 'Don't worry. I'll be with you'." The phantom image has now become a phantom voice, to both of which Nora offers a recognition that seems a cross between rapture and terror. Her throat constricting in a gesture of excitement and terror, her response is just one word: "You…." With that, 'he,' if he was ever there, is gone. The power and pathos of this episode, like the one where Nora finds herself lost in the wilderness, is that it forces us to share in Nora's visions or delusions even while it invites us to ponder over their delusory status: so that we awaken with her to Hugh telling her that she looks "pale as a ghost" – and that her daughter Jean is dead.

In the closing scenes of *Herod's Wife*, Nora Helton is, more than ever, at once a fearful and a tragic figure. Like so many of Jones's earlier protagonists, she has become the victim of her own overwhelming purpose, driven to destruction by the furies of her own obsession or possession. Like someone drowning, she appears to reach out for help, emotional rescue, to her estranged husband. "At least I only have you to love now," she tells Hugh desperately, plaintively, "Because I do love you." "I'll prove it to you," she implores. "You'll see." But she throws Hugh into further confusion by insisting Wilbur was not the father of Jean; the father, she tells him, was "someone you never knew," and so Wilbur does not need to be informed and comforted (111). Whether this is the truth or not, the reader never knows, like so much else in the story it remains a potent mystery. If the sole aim was to discourage Hugh from going to see Wilbur to break the news, it fails. And, in conversation with his brother, Hugh learns in turn about his wife's scheming: Wilbur has been to see Mrs. McDougal. "I remember her feelings about religion," Wilbur observes, searching for an explanation for Nora's behavior, and in particular her hatred for Father Riley, "But this... it's diabolical, or something." Once again, his observations have the truth of the literal, the metaphorical, or both. Whatever their truth, Hugh cannot sup or sleep with the diabolical. Despite her pleas, Hugh cannot contemplate taking Nora back now, even if she were able to return to him. She is steeped too far in evil, and the blood of others. And in the morning, after Hugh has rejected her – "Not now," he declares, "I'm sorry" – Nora is gone (114).

The final moments in the life of a woman given over to the "diabolical" are told by a series of witnesses, who then pass on what they have seen to her husband. Without draining these moments of their immediacy and terror, this adds to their mystery: we are, after all, only being told what others, with partial knowledge, have seen. A Mrs. Miller, Wilbur's secretary in his law office, is the first witness. She recalls how an "elegantly dressed woman" she did not know, with eyes "like the devil's own," tried to bribe or force her into handing over a letter that had arrived for her employer. The letter, which Mrs. Miller keeps a firm grip on despite being injured, turns out to be from Jean. It is a confession, a kind of suicide note. "I did it for Mama. What she told me to say. About the priest," Jean confesses in the letter, "she made me think it was true. It was wicked. I am so sorry. I love you" (117). Having failed to seize hold of what she evidently saw as evidence of her guilt, the "elegantly dressed woman" – who was, of course, Nora – appears to have gone straight to the restaurant where she had once seen a "spectral figure" through the window. The restaurant proprietor, a Mr. Krantz, is now the second witness to the bizarre behavior of Nora as, he recalls, she "sat staring at the big plate glass window that faced the street" as if waiting for a sign, ignoring everything around her – and then abruptly left. The third witness is then Ella Hobbs, Hugh's "black cleaning woman," who describes how Nora returned to the house and packed "blind to her presence," then departed with her suitcase as if embarked on a journey somewhere. As she departed, Ella recollects, there was "a kind of stink, like" to Nora, "somethin' ugly." The sulphur odor was, however, quickly supplanted by the smell of smoke: Nora, it seems, had set fire to the drapes in the house before leaving, a final act of arson, but this time the fire was quenched before the building was destroyed (118).

The final witness from whom Hugh and the reader hear is an anonymous one, the anonymity adding to the feeling that he, and we, are hearing the story from possibly unreliable sources – or, at least, from those who can only tell what they have seen as, with limited vision and knowledge, they gazed into the dark. This witness is the driver of a car who happened to see another car ahead of him moving erratically. Finally, it crashed through a guardrail, he explains; the car was wrecked and Nora, who was inside it, was killed. There are "two strange things," though, to the story the anonymous driver tells. The car, this witness recalls, swerved "for no apparent reason." Even stranger, only the "charred body" of Nora was discovered in the wreck, although the witness declares "with near certainty that he had seen, had kept seeing, two people in that car." There is "no evidence of the whereabouts of the second occupant;" so, once again, character and reader alike are left to decide, if they can, whether this other figure was there, or not there, a figure of fact or fantasy – real in some curious, perhaps inexplicable way, or a trick of the light, an hallucination. All is strange and indeterminate here.

What is not indeterminate or uncertain, however, is the moment of reconciliation, healing, and composure that follows and concludes the novel. Together again, the brothers Hugh and Wilbur, the two husbands of Nora, bury the ashes of Jean in the graveyard of the Roman Catholic church. The church is to be rebuilt, we learn; and, as Hugh looks around at what remains, something catches his eye. It is the "fragment of colored glass" in the surviving remnant of the building, with "the head and shoulders of Christ ascending above the aperture" (119). An appropriate moment of hope, a quiet signal of possible redemption, the image finds its narrative echo in the brief conversation the two brothers then have. Father Riley is dead, from the horrible burns he sustained when his church was burned down. "I'd hate to think the poor man's death didn't accomplish anything at all," Hugh reflects. "One thing, though," he adds, "It did give us a new start." "More than that, maybe," Wilbur responds, "A lot more." Hugh does not understand at first. Then the glance, the light in Wilbur's eye reveals his meaning. It also, as the narrative puts it, "brought 'her' to his mind's eye." "I see what you mean," Hugh declares quietly to the brother with whom he is now reconciled. 'Him' has become 'her' – whatever the gender, the diabolical has now been, at least for the moment, overcome. It is a partial victory, a muted one, considering the innocents – the priest, the young girl – who have been slaughtered but it is, nevertheless, a victory of sorts on which conversation and story end.

In a way, in terms of its narrativity, its rich narrative mix, *Herod's Wife* allows the wheel to come full circle. Just as, at the beginning, a story of domestic crisis slipped into issues of personal faith and doubt, and social and political tension, so, at the end, a tale of terror moves into the territory of the psychological thriller and then into tragedy, with a saving remnant finding something among the rubble, the devastation, to enable them to survive and go on. There are fundamental certainties of tone and tenor here, characteristic of Jones's work: a sense of the compelling, labyrinthine connections between the past and the present, an understanding of the darkness that hovers just beneath the surfaces of personal and social behavior, a belief in the necessity of anchorage, something to supply emotional and spiritual security to shore against the ruins of life. Jones has always been a writer aware of the dereliction that follows a loss of faith: faith, that is, in something other than the isolated, fragmented self. Without that faith, as his work discloses, the human animal strays disoriented and desperate, unregenerate and unredeemed, his body and spirit nothing more than a shape to fill a lack, his voice no more than a cry of absence.

At his best Jones has also always been a writer who accompanies a kind of spiritual certainty with narrative subtlety. As here: *Herod's Wife* is a triumph of storytelling indeterminacy, allowing the reader to respond to the story and its central characters on several planes, quite different although not necessarily in conflict. The power of this novel stems from the degree to which its every moment and image drive home the feeling, the conviction even, that, without an anchor, some means to fathom and perform their nature, human beings are nothing, or worse than nothing – they are, as Nora Helton shows, little short of diabolical. But its passion and its pathos arise from a steady narrative refusal to adhere to one narrative perspective or series of explanations, and its commitment to mystery, a sense of how enigmatic, obscure, or unintelligible things can be as we gaze into the dark. We are within and without a woman possessed here, simultaneously enchanted and repelled by her strange, even diabolical behavior. As a result, if *Herod's Wife* does not exactly arouse sympathy for the devil, it does certainly excite pity – as well as fear and wonder.

"OUT OF THE GARDEN, FOREVER":

INTERVIEWS WITH MADISON JONES

The conversations were mostly recorded at Madison Jones's home in Kuderna Acres, near Auburn, Alabama. The first session of Part I was taped on June 3, 1978, as *Passage through Gehenna* was being published; the second was done two and a half years later on January 12, 1981. Part II's sessions were taped two decades and four novels later, on April 18, 1999, in Chattanooga, Tennessee, and in Auburn on November 14, 2000. The final section on *Herod's Wife* is a telephone interview added on January 4, 2003.

PART I

Gretlund   May I call you a regional writer?

Jones   Certainly! It is pretty obvious to me that I *am* a regional writer. And there's nothing negative or even limiting about regionalism. I don't know of anyone who would consider Faulkner's regionalism a limitation in his creation of Yoknapatawpha County. My own regionalism is most obvious in *The Innocent*. A definite sense of place is very helpful as a guide for my vision. It helps me to know what is true. I don't always understand the full meaning of my images of place, but I always know when I am lying about them. They warn me when I am doing them violence, they let me know when I am dishonest in my writing.

Gretlund   How has your early life as a Southern country boy influenced your fiction?

Jones   I feel a strong attachment for the country of my childhood. Most people do in the South, probably more than people from other parts of the nation. Our sense of history has a lot to do with that, and for me as a writer this attachment to place has been indispensable. The familiar place offers inspiration and images to embody my ideas. Some images I remember from my childhood, and they retain a certain mystery for me. I could, of course, have seen fields of briars and buckbushes stretching to the horizon in other places. But I saw them in Tennessee, and for me they will always be associated with the country of my childhood. I hope that the mystery I feel in connection with the remembered images has been retained in my fiction.

Gretlund   Was there anything or anybody in your childhood that inspired you to become a novelist?

Jones   There were no writers or intellectuals in my family anywhere. They were mostly old-fashioned Presbyterians, and I'm afraid they considered writing a frivolous waste of time for a man. It wasn't considered serious work. I think they considered that it rather bordered on the effeminate. My family read the Bible and not too much else. Of course, it never occurred to them to read it as fiction or even as poetry. My grandfather, who was a very old man, born before the Civil War, lived with us when I was a boy. He read stories to me by the hour – from the Old Testament. That's the literature I knew best. So if there's a great author who had a decisive influence on me, I guess it is Moses.

Gretlund   Have you ever attended a tent revival or a faith healing meeting in Tennessee?

Jones   Yes, I've been to some of those meetings. I went to some when I was young. I haven't been to a faith-healing meeting in quite some time. But it hasn't been too long since I have been to one of those tent revivals, and they are still quite common. In middle Tennessee, in the country, it is still an Old Testament world, as I've tried to show in *Passage through Gehenna*. It is "Jesus, Jesus" all the time, but in a way the Old Testament has an almost equal status – in some cases even more influence. To Fundamentalists every word in the Bible is literally true and the real emphasis falls on the need for personal rectitude. Grace is, of course, insisted upon, but the big emphasis was always on rectitude. And, of course, I was trained that way.

Gretlund   What do you think of faith healers and their miracles?

Jones   They do produce these things, these faith healers. I don't know any explanation for them. Many of the illnesses are obviously psychosomatic, and you can count on that being the case. But then in other cases it seems to go beyond that. When somebody mends a broken bone, as they sometimes do, you wonder what is coming off. Salter in *Passage* is in a well-authenticated tradition, I guess you could say. You can still find plenty of these preachers not only in Tennessee, but also in Alabama, Arkansas, etc. Throughout the South, in fact. The rural Midwest, too, for that matter.

Gretlund   Does it seem grotesque to you that the backwoods of the South in our day and age are still peopled by Fundamentalists?

Jones   We probably have a good deal more than our share of unusual people in the South, even today. But I think there is a great deal of "grotesquery" in other places in this country. New York City seems to me to have more grotesque characters than the whole South does. We still have a lot of backcountry people, though a lot fewer than we did. There are still some enclaves around the South where the people would, by regular standards, be considered peculiar. But I never thought of them as "grotesque." It is a word

I learned when I started reading about Southern fiction in books by Northern critics.

Gretlund How do you select specific material for your fiction?

Jones In a way I am always walking around with my material. Usually, I *am* my material, for unconsciously the selection of material is determined by the problems and discords of my own life at the time. Serious fiction is in a way autobiographical, but, of course, you can't really see that in the finished novel, if it is any good. *The Innocent* is close to my own experience. I began with my own background, but I ended with something entirely different. The setting, the horse, the moonshiner, and traits of the protagonist are borrowings from my early life in Tennessee. But in the novel these elements end up as fictional facts. Step by step they change physically and in psychological effect. It is the idea behind the writing that transforms the autobiographical material so it becomes part of the artistic reality of the novel.

Gretlund Why did you call your first novel *The Innocent*?

Jones I can't remember when I first thought of that title. But at first I saw Duncan Welsh as a social victim. Then I brought in McCool, the moonshiner, and the title took on a different meaning for me. I realized that my protagonist is really a victim of a flaw in himself. He rejects life as it is with Evil as a prime fact, and he tries to return to the innocence of Eden. But he finds that Satan is there now, and Duncan is destroyed. The flaw in him is that he wouldn't accept the existence of Evil and that man has been forced out of the Garden, forever. But this change in the meaning of the title only dawned on me as I was writing. The story came to life and talked back to me.

Gretlund   Your second novel, *Forest of the Night*, is my favorite. Why did you choose to take us back to the frontier life of the early 1800s?

Jones   Well, I was a good deal younger then than I am now, and a bit more ready to believe people would listen to wisdom, or what I thought was wisdom. Here was an exemplum of the idea of American innocence encountering the wilderness; he, the hero, was going to bring light into its dark. You might say there were ideological commitments behind the novel, it is a sort of philosophical fiction. The story is largely imagined. There is a little about the Harpe brothers on record, but very little. We know what kind of men they were and a few things they did, but we don't even know with certainty what their end was. But I hope this much is clear: the virgin forest has become a forest of the night for the enlightened hero and the confrontation issues in the near extinction of his real humanity. It is the fatality of badly misreading the nature of things.

Gretlund   Is there a connection between *The Innocent* and *Forest of the Night*?

Jones   Although I wasn't fully conscious of it, I created Jonathan Cannon of *Forest* in the image of my first hero. But, as I said, the novel is also about the Harpe brothers, the bloodthirsty outlaws who lived near the Natchez Trace at the time. After *The Innocent* I could see what was in the subject of this murderous pair, for me, fictionally. My imagination was excited by the traditional accounts of them. It was an advantage for me that so little is known with any certainty about them. I saw the Harpes as innocents who return to the Garden to serve the new master there. But I had a hard time with the brothers; they weren't human, they were just monstrous freaks. I couldn't credit them with any intellectual stature. I finally decided to keep the Harpes in the background, as a reminder of the evil potential of man. What really interested me was how the brothers had come to be what they were. So, I brought in my innocent hero. He is a disciple of Rousseau, Jefferson, and Paine. And his background has prepared him to see Evil only as a product of factors external to human nature. In the rest of the novel I illustrate the making of "a Harpe." Jonathan comes to see his fellow men only in their brutal aspect. He is finally identified with Wiley Harpe. I hope the novel illuminates the moral steps by which he loses his humanity. In this way you can read *Forest* as continuing a theme from *The Innocent*.

Gretlund   What do you think of *A Buried Land* today, after almost twenty years?

Jones   In a way it is the dimmest in my mind of all my novels. I am unhappy with Percy Youngblood, the main character. He is just too cold, and too callous. But at that time in the early 1960s, I was angry at the Tennessee Valley Authority, angry at what they were doing when they flooded large areas of Tennessee, and northern Alabama. They destroyed a lot of good farms, entire communities, and much rare wildlife. I wanted to write a novel about that destruction, but also about disintegrating lives, minds, and relationships as a result of the physical destruction, which, of course, was meant to stand for much more than the immediate destruction. Percy works for the TVA and he destroys his relations with his family and the community. He also lets a girl be killed by an abortionist to insure his own happiness.

Gretlund   Do you think in retrospect that *A Buried Land* was too much of an attempt at being topical?

Jones   No, not really. The novel is primarily about a spiritual bankruptcy, and not so much about the TVA. As I indicated earlier, writing is a form of self-discovery, and my subject is therefore always basically myself. This is my true topic, and I must be directed by it to keep my integrity as a writer. I have to ignore questions about reader interest in my fiction. I may sweat a bit if nobody will buy my books, but when I write, sales are irrelevant – I don't worry about them. It would be something else if I wrote "entertainments." Then I would have to consider what the public will swallow.

Gretlund   Your novel *An Exile* has been a popular success. I saw the film version "I Walk the Line" with Gregory Peck and I think it is well done. Has this Hollywood success influenced your writing?

Jones   I am not consciously writing for the movies. When I wrote *An Exile*, it didn't even cross my mind. But since that book was made into a movie, that possibility has naturally occurred to me while writing other books. But it has never been any influence. I tend to write in visual scenes; that's just the nature of my imagination. It is not because of any design like "when I do this, it will be suitable for the movies." Of course, I would like for them to make a movie out of *Passage through Gehenna*. But a wish like this has never had any part in my thinking about how I was going to handle a scene. I am sensitive to scenes and to visual things – that's why there are lots of "film shots" in my fiction.

Gretlund   Your novels tend to be grim and pessimistic. They deal with "man's failure to submit himself to the limits of the human condition," as you have phrased it. Have you ever expressed your view of mankind in more comic tones?

Jones   I wrote a picaresque novel about fifteen years ago. It was never published except for two sections. Humor doesn't seem to be my strong point, but that novel was intended to be entirely comic. One of the sections that was published is farce, whorehouse farce. There is a woman who has a jealous husband, so she puts the psychiatrist on him to remove the jealousy. Whereupon she proceeds with her whoring. It ends up that she seduces the psychiatrist. I think it is quite a funny novel, but my humor didn't go over in New York. Like lots of other things about me don't go over in New York.

At this point at least one of the large episodes is out of date. It was more topical, you know, based on particular events. There is a part on civil rights. You can imagine why that part wouldn't be published. I called the whole novel "Tales of Dixie." I had a picaresque hero. He meets a young man, a novelist, who has been hired by a Northern newspaper to come down and report on the civil rights trouble in Mississippi. It is partly making fun of the Northern idea of what was going on. But that episode, at least, is dead now. At the time I'm sure it made a lot of publishers mad. Now the trouble with it is that it is out of date.

Gretlund   In your fifth novel *A Cry of Absence*, you write about the bitterest period of the civil rights struggle in the South. Why did you publish a novel about civil rights as late as 1971, and during the Vietnam War?

Jones   As I see it, the history taught to young people all over the country and in the South presents everything from a Yankee point of view. Young people down here are taught to feel guilty about our past. This is sad and probably dangerous. You can hardly ever hear "Dixie" played in public places anymore, or couldn't for a good while. If we were to believe Yankee historians, all Southern resistance to the civil rights changes of the 1950s and 1960s was based on racist or economic motives. Nothing could be more wrong, and that is one of the reasons – though only one – why I wrote *A Cry of Absence*. I consider it my best novel.

A main factor behind our resistance was our impulse to hold on to our identity, to preserve our Southernness. Racial segregation was seen, at least in part, as one of our last links with our past, as maybe the one really fleshly link surviving. This is not to defend an inhumane system, but to put a strong reaction into its proper perspective. In *Absence* I try to give an objective statement of this problem in the setting of a small Southern town in the 1950s. It is a story about the old conflict between family affection and duty to the law.... But of course this whole statement indicates only one aspect of what I was trying to do in the book.

Gretlund   I read *Passage through Gehenna* as a return to the dark vision of *Forest of the Night*. What gave you the idea to write *Passage*?

Jones   I read a French novel by Laclos called *Les Liaisons dangereuses*; it is late eighteenth-century. It is about two ambitious seducers – not only out to seduce, but to sow malignity with those seductions. Mostly those of the woman, who is about as evil a person as you can find anywhere outside of Shakespeare. That is where *Passage* ultimately came from. That's what started me down the slide.

The novel has a history I couldn't even describe to you. It was so different when it started out: it was about a boy who had a religious conflict with his father – and the book just wouldn't go. And then I wrote this piece about Salter, the country preacher, and thought about it a while, and then I rejected it. And I still had the woman, Lily, but she was doing something else then. I sent the book to Monroe Spears when I had first written it. It was originally in first person. He didn't suggest that I change it, but he speculated about the idea. I ultimately decided to change it to third person. I brought some of the characters over from my unpublished picaresque novel. And in this manner it went through four or five different versions.

Gretlund   What is the true character of Lily Nunn?

Jones   People in Hallsboro think this and that about Lily – they can't agree whether she is ugly or handsome. But the sexual magnetism is clearly there. Her name is, of course, meant to suggest the flower. But her name also recalls Lilith, the wife Adam is supposed to have had before Eve. In legend Lilith is said to have been of the devil's brood. And she preys on children, murders them. In my novel her origin is obscure; her father is named North, which in the context may, I hope, hint at satanic connections. You know the devil comes from the North. That is not Southern ideology – traditionally the devil comes from the North. I think of Lily as a witch, deliberately doing the devil's work.

Gretlund   The discovery of the existence of Evil by an innocent young man has been the theme of your novels since *The Innocent*, and it is also the theme of *Passage through Gehenna*. Why do you return to the theme?

Jones   I don't know if I am becoming more optimistic or not. But at least I like to think that *Passage,* if you can call that progress, doesn't leave you with nowhere to go; as I think my earliest novels sort of did. I think of it as a turning to a more complete version of the theme. One that puts the emphasis on grace and sacrifice, as compared with the boneheaded determination to be perfect that Jud Rivers started out with. With his original attitude he couldn't do anything but try to stare the devil down, which can't be done. The devil is simply stronger in a head-to-head encounter. But learning to love is part of the theme of *Passage*. Something Jud didn't really know about to start with. At the end presumably he has the means to make himself a whole person. I hope it emerges that Jud is at least capable of love when he asks why somebody else should

	have had to go through Gehenna, or hell, for him that he might learn to love. I guess that happens all the time.
Gretlund	Why is there so much violence in *Passage*?
Jones	The violence is off stage. *Passage* is half as violent as the work of Aeschylus or somebody like that. The novel is not as violent as a typical Shakespeare play. I have more violence in *Forest of the Night*. Violence happens. It happened in the rural world that I used to know, and it seems to me characteristic of life.
Gretlund	Who are some of the writers you have learned from over the years?
Jones	I learned a lot from the Agrarians, and Fugitives, at Vanderbilt; especially from Donald Davidson. He confirmed my belief in the lasting value of Southern culture. Another major influence on me was Andrew Lytle. He guided me when I specialized in creative writing at the University of Florida at Gainesville. And, of course, I admire William Faulkner. He was the big man, the man of genius. He could animate so many kinds of things and bring them in, really integrally, to the whole being of a book.
	Faulkner wasn't afraid of relaxing at times in his books. It is maybe a fault that I can't stand, when I perceive one, a loose moment in my own books. I work very hard to reduce all unnecessary elements – words, events – between the climactic parts. In *Passage* it worried me that Hannah's death comes so quickly after the abortion. But there just wasn't any way around it. I always try to build things as much as possible. But I'm satisfied that I couldn't, if I had waited a long time to decide what to do, have made any more preparation. I knew it was right what happened. I simply wished at the time that I had a way to hold it back, to get more of a sense of time passing, so that the event

could ripen. But there just wasn't any way to do it and still keep the novel moving. The tension is always a primary consideration for me.

Gretlund Flannery O'Connor spoke very highly of your novels in several of her letters collected in *The Habit of Being*. How well did you know her?

Jones I knew her over a period of about seven years. It began when she wrote me a kind letter about *The Innocent* – an act entirely typical of her. She was such a good writer. And she was awfully courteous and hospitable to me and Shailah. We went to see her once in a while at Andalusia, near Milledgeville. She gave us a lot of ducks and geese and so on. From the time of that first letter I went to see her, off and on, until she died. She was a gracious, witty, and pleasant person. I appreciated the way she was trying to help me get more notice as a writer.

    I remember how certain critics used to consider her fiction cold and without feeling. Most of them have changed their opinion now, but if anybody needs further testimony of Flannery O'Connor's warm feeling for her fellow man, he will find it displayed generously in her private letters. She is surely the best writer the South has turned out for twenty-five years. Her writing is clear, straight, unpretentious, and full of humor. She had an integrity and courage that impress me and inspire me. Flannery had a dark view of the human condition, but she also had self-knowledge, humility, and real human compassion. Unfortunately, I lost some of the best letters she wrote me.

Gretlund What do you think of Truman Capote, Norman Mailer, and Tom Wolfe's non-fiction novels?

Jones For me a novelist is a man who is at liberty to shape the material he chooses from real life – exactly as he wants to.

The way I see it, he must make the facts speak in his voice, so that they reflect his personal vision. In nonfiction novels the facts are supposed to speak for themselves. Capote and Mailer are not responsible, it seems, and the vision is left to the reader's predisposition. If a writer has no vision to communicate, he can't choose his facts according to it, and the account, the story, will fail to come really alive. This doesn't mean that a traditional novelist is free to distort facts, on the contrary. But he must bring a vision to his facts so they will be able to speak to him.

My book *Season of the Strangler* has a sort of journalistic origin, in the way of Dreiser's *An American Tragedy*. There are twelve stories all related to the central matter of a local strangler – as a symbolic figure – so the whole has somewhat the effect of a novel. The stories are portraits of people who, in a non-literal sense, and for personal reasons, strangle their own lives.

PART II

Interview with Madison Jones, the Reed House, Chattanooga, Tennessee, Sunday, April 18, 1999. Including a follow-up conversation in Auburn, November 14, 2000.

Gretlund   When we talked about your novels back in the 1980s, *Season of the Strangler* was just being published. It is one of your best books, but it never got the attention it deserves.

Jones   I think the stories were difficult, for one thing. I sent the book to Robert Penn Warren, and he wrote me back: "No doubt these are powerful stories, but I'm not sure I know what they mean, or what the whole thing means. But it takes a lot of reading." I think that maybe most people do not like to do a lot of reading. I mean heavy reading. I think maybe it is pretty thick soup. When you speak of reading

Henry James, you speak of heavy reading. It is closely knit, rendering more than most people want to bother with. Maybe my book has more description, more details than people generally want to deal with; that may be the case. I had not thought about it until Warren said that.

Gretlund   Is *Season of the Strangler* more densely textured than *A Cry of Absence*?

Jones   I wrote *Strangler* in the rather flat voice of a detached narrator, whereas in *A Cry of Absence* the voice, voices, in this case, reflected the qualities of my participating characters and were more precisely fitted to individuals. In *Strangler* the narrator's voice, a single voice, is constant all the way through. A lot of people seemed not even to notice that there was a fictional narrator telling the stories. Probably I should have developed him more.

Gretlund   After *Season of the Strangler* it took you seven years to complete *Last Things* (1989). Was there a particular reason why you took your time after *Season of the Strangler*?

Jones   In fact it was almost that long between *A Cry of Absence* (1971) and *Passage through Gehenna* (1978). – *Passage* is the book of all my books that caused me the most trouble. I would start it, throw part of it away, work and work on the first part again. I thought I never was going to get it right. And then after I got it finished to my satisfaction, I had a time getting it published. The New York publishers didn't go for it, though it seemed for a while that Farrar, Straus, Giroux was going to take it. I finally sent it to LSU Press. It became the first LSU "original novel." But years were consumed in the process.

Gretlund   How important was the father-son relationship for you in the writing of *Last Things*?

Jones   Are you thinking about my own father and me? – My father was nothing like that! He was nothing like anybody in any particular book I have written. He was a very honorable, upright man – and stern; although he had some humor and lightness, too. But he was stern about principles.

Gretlund   Was he a religious man?

Jones   Yes. – Yes, very much so. He was intelligent, but he did not have the breadth of mind or the kind of education that gave him much tolerance of different ways of thinking. I have his name, which was my great-grandfather's, and I have a son named Madison Percy Jones. Wendell Corbin of *Last Things* never did have communion with anybody, including his father, who was hardly worth communing with. But after all Wendell went through, he found at last a communion with what he was and with what his father was. It is a kind of a moral or spiritual regeneration to be able finally to communicate, if not with a whole community, at least with somebody who is difficult to love.

Gretlund   I had the impression that we had read an account of Wendell's slow moral disintegration, and that he comes to a bad end.

Jones   At the end I intended that he'd be on the way to a regeneration. I think he is subject to legal action at the end of the book, but at the same time he's got his foot on the right path again, morally and spiritually. – I don't know if anybody spotted it, but I did something in *Last Things* that I had not done in any other book, in suggesting ghostly experiences. For instance, there is a preacher in the book, a fundamentalist hell-fire type, and he comes to visit Wendell at one point in this old dark house, upstairs. I tried to write the scene so that you cannot tell whether it is really the person in the flesh or not. I tried to write it with that sort of ambiguity. This was meant to bring a supernatural element into the book, which I hoped would give it a spiritual dimension. Also, in the part where he goes upstairs and is thrown out the high window, it is really like a possession. I tried to create that effect. When he is lying under the window on the ground, semi-conscious, the young black man named Cat Bird is talking to the car-dealer, who is described in various reptilian terms. They are talking on another-world plane. The effect, I hope, is a bit like some passages in Hawthorne where we overhear spectral voices talking abstractly from somewhere. The car-dealer's name is Jason Farrow, which suggests pigs. He is the satanic force that has been in control of Wendell. But he breaks with Farrow near the end of the book.

Gretlund   What is the meaning of the title of *Last Things?*

Jones   I intended a theological connection. Last things are death, heaven, and hell; the last things to be considered in a life.

Gretlund   Were you satisfied with the reception of *Last Things?*

Jones   No! [laughing] It did not get enough press notice. Only a few, very few, seemed as though they saw what I was trying to do. But I never have had really satisfactory responses on a large scale. I have had lots of good reviews that I was delighted with, reviewers that I thought really understood the book and liked it, and so forth, but just never enough of them. If your book is going to prosper, you have to have the reviews hit the streets pretty close together, and a lot of them. I have never had that happen. You need something in *Time,* something in *Newsweek,* something in the *New York Times,* and *Chicago Tribune;* the reviews have got to be all around.

Gretlund   It seems obvious that *To the Winds* (1996) means more to you than any other novel.

Jones   It was based on the farm near Ashland City [Tennessee]. After my father sold the farm, a family that had worked for us moved to a cabin over across the Cumberland River in the hills there, high above the river.

Gretlund   Why did your father sell the farm?

Jones   For one thing he was needing the money, I think, *and* I was no longer up there. My brother was concerned with the farm he lived on, the one where my father's home was, raising cattle. It had got to be more than my father wanted to fool with, and I think he was beginning to have business troubles about that time. I was thirty-three when he sold it. – The family that inspired the novel had eight children. In my book they are pretty changed from what they were really like. The father was not the kind of irresponsible fellow that the character in the book is. He was very responsible, very religious, a man I admired. In the course of the book the family is destroyed, both as a family and as a representative community. Those kinds of hill folks ceased to exist. They all went away, scattered all over the world, and lived in trailers instead of on farms.

Gretlund   The clashes between the hill folks and the town people are memorable in *To the Winds*.

Jones   You are thinking about the chapter where the daughter gets seduced by this fancy boy. It follows a scene where the young hill folks play jokes on the university boys and give them some peppering with a shotgun, – birdshot! And then finally the older boy gets tarred and feathered by the university boys. – The conflict is with the "modern" element now dominant.

Gretlund   Does the seduction of the girl become symbolic of how everybody in the hill community is "seduced" and exploited by the new people who move in?

Jones   I hope so. I don't know about "everybody," but certainly the poor who are relatively defenseless are subject to a flashy exterior, as this young man illustrates. Not the older generation, not the parents, but the girls are excited by this... although I don't know but what that sort of thing has gone on back through history [laughing].

Gretlund   The clash between the farmers and the adult town-people, including the law, seems to be more alarming.

Jones   The urge for big money is corrupting, and the sheriff has fallen to it. His individual corruption is not necessarily everywhere, but it is common enough to where it is something to be looked out for, I think, in all such small communities. The family on the farm was subject to it because of their relative helplessness and ignorance. It was no longer the kind of world that could accommodate them.

Gretlund   Isn't this what makes it a tragic story? It is clear that they will lose everything, including the family unity.

Jones   It is the conflict within the family that begins tearing it up. The older brother wants to turn in Uncle Clarence, who has come back home, escaped from prison. They need money so badly that the older brother feels that he is in a way justified in betraying the uncle: otherwise they will lose the farm. So he is not entirely a rascal for so doing, even though his younger brother "Coop," who turns out to be almost the protagonist of the book, finally comes to hate his older brother as a traitor to the family. The two conflicts seem to mesh there.

Gretlund   Is it the throwing to the winds of the old culture that makes the book special to you?

Jones   If you remember chapter four, it is almost like a folk narrative, it is the mother's history. She came from the last intact hill culture. The narrator describes her youth and her background, what it was like among the hill people. And the woman tries to maintain those values in her family. But her husband turns out to be pretty worthless, although he is well intentioned. He doesn't have much of a chance. So the mother is of the last generation that tries to maintain the original values of the hill people. She fades away, too, of course.

Gretlund   It is obvious that you have seen this life and lived it in Tennessee.

Jones   Yes, in a lot of ways. Like that cabin that they lived in, which they expanded very considerably, built onto. I knew that cabin when a man lived there alone. We wanted shakes, wood shingles, to put on a roof. When we took the smokehouse and made a little outdoor den, bedroom, out of it, we wanted wood shakes. People used to cut those with axes, and this old man still made them. He lived up in that cabin in the woods, and we got those shakes when I was maybe fifteen or sixteen. He was, I suppose, as far back as it went, history that still survived: somebody was still making shakes that way. – I well remember that cabin. And then later one of the boys from the family bought it and the little property around it. He lived up there alone for a while, but then when my daddy sold the farm, the young man's family, or what was left of it, came to live there. Through them I got to know the place well. I used it, the imagery of it all, in *To the Winds*. It was almost as if I had lived there, especially because I knew them so well.

Gretlund In spite of all the experiences and private emotions you invested in the book, its sales are not impressive.

Jones I was not surprised really, because I have had that experience too many times. But I thought that it had a chance. I was hoping that the kind of humor that is a part of the novel might have general appeal; its first eighty pages or so are episodes that are only connected by happening to the members of the family. These present an aspect of what that life was like. I thought that a lot of people who appreciate the old Southwest humor would like it very much. Some did, but one reviewer liked the book only *after* that part was over! I had hoped that I would get readers who would like both that and the sort of detective story that follows – which I thought was an exciting story.

Gretlund Your change of the mood in mid-course from humor to suspense may have irritated some readers.

Jones As soon as the uncle comes in, when they discover Uncle Clarence, it changes everything, because they are harboring a much wanted criminal. The change doesn't seem to me to jerk you around, it just falls into their life, the way accidents do all the time and all of a sudden poison everything. I did not feel it give a wrench to the book. Suddenly they were outlaws, for harboring an outlaw, and in a sense that is symbolic of what they almost had become anyway. "Outlaws" – not so much as criminals, but as no longer living *within* the law. They couldn't imagine, for instance, not being able to bury on the place. Suddenly, here is the law saying: you can't bury this dead boy here! You have got to do it in accordance with the legal code. They didn't know anything about that; they just thought it was natural that when somebody died in your family you buried him close by.

Gretlund   With "Familiar Spirit," the final story of *Season of the Strangler,* which is a Civil War story, you seem to open up a new topic in your fiction.

Jones   Yes, that's right. Although I had written another version of it a long time before. I published it, I think, in *Delta Review* about thirty years ago. It was a magazine that only ran briefly, a few issues, I think, then conked out. So I had written that story essentially, though I rewrote if for *Season of the Strangler.*

Gretlund   After a lifetime of complex fiction on complex issues, you write a plain and simple Civil War novel, and it becomes your perhaps-greatest critical and popular success. Did the praise for *Nashville 1864: The Dying of the Light* (1997) surprise you?

Jones   Yes, but do not overstate the success, because it got almost no notice in the North. In great part surely because it was published by a small Southern publisher, that was one thing. In fact, a member of the committee in Chicago that awarded me the T. S. Eliot prize, partly for *Nashville 1864,* said that he saw the book and thought it must be just something I had wanted to get rid of and had published with a small publisher. And I am sure lots of people said, "Oh, why review this book, there are ten more from Random House, Harper, and wherever." So it was almost completely ignored in the North, except for those journals that review them all, like *Kirkus, Publishers Weekly,* etc. But nothing in New York, or Chicago, or any place like that.

Gretlund   A change for the better was Jonathan Yardley's review in "Book World" of the *Washington Post.* I remember that he did not like *Season of the Strangler.*

Jones   Washington is not really the North, and the novel got reviewed by a Virginian. I have heard him described a number of times as one of the best two or three book reviewers in the country. I think that's probably true. But he reviews a lot of books, and occasionally he just doesn't like something, and he didn't like *Season of the Strangler.* – But *Nashville 1864* could have used a lot more reviews than it got in the South! For instance in the Atlanta paper, which off and on has given me good reviews. They never did review it. This was just after the appearance of the issue on me of the *Chattahoochee Review,* an Atlanta journal that was wholly devoted to my work. The fact made no difference to Atlanta newspaper reviewers. But now that *Nashville 1864* is in Penguin, it has a chance to meet up with readers in, presumably, other parts of the country.

Gretlund   How did it come to be picked up by Penguin?

Jones   I guess it just had the good fortune for somebody to read it who knew about good books [laughing].

Gretlund   What is successful in the novel is the combination of the topic and the style. You always write in a superb style, but here the simple everyday realism of your style walks hand in hand with the classic account of days in the lives of two boys.

Jones   I have gotten a lot of praise from people, not just my good close friends, who referred among other things to the style, as Yardley certainly did. As a matter of fact Fred Chappell told me that the book "really knocked them dead." – Anyway, they all mentioned my style here, which was a surprise to me because I was just writing a simple story and hadn't thought about the matter. Incidentally, in the process of writing I never give a thought to style, but only to the best way to say a thing. Many people think of style as being the way such as John Updike writes, or William Styron, with hopped up language, rich and often esoteric images, and so forth. In my case here, the essential simplicity of my subject dictated the way I wrote about it. I couldn't have written it differently. In fact it was easy writing for me; I wrote faster than I had ever written before. It had used to be that if I got a good solid, permanent page, 350 words or so in a day's work, I was satisfied. I hardly ever got much more, but in this case I could often get two or three finished pages. I don't often revise later. Except for *Passage through Gehenna,* I have rarely done more than minor revisions on any of my books.

Gretlund We are talking about style and pretending to be innocent of the book's provocative contents. But the novel is a deliberate provocation on your part, isn't it?

Jones Only to a small degree. Are you talking about the memoirist's, the fictional author's, opinions? Yes, I knew that some things I had him say were going to provoke, at least in the present climate of thought. You and my wife held the view that I should delete some of the things I have my memoirist say about life in the Old South. I put the question to another friend, David Bovenizer, who is an editor and a great collector of memoirs, some from his own Virginia family. He thought my handling of the matter perfectly characteristic and convincing, typical of the memoir form. This pleased, and continues to please me, even though it certainly has cost me by giving offense to the politically correct. I admit to pleasure in taking licks at the established view of the Old South. Whether I did too much in the book might be reasonably debated. Nevertheless, it should somewhat balance the opposite view, which holds it impermissible to speak of anything except the horrors of slavery and the wickedness of those who owned slaves. As an absolute statement this is just not true, and I was anxious to say so. If, literally speaking, that is an intrusion on my part, it is too bad. I think it enriched the book.

Gretlund *Nashville 1864* is about two boys and the War, but it is also about the idea of slavery becoming clear to one of them. Isn't this what makes it more than a boys' book?

Jones Yes, Steven comes to understand the racial situation, but that is part of his growing up, and surely that was so for most people who grew up in a slave-holding family. William Faulkner makes the same point. I didn't borrow it from him, but it is in *The Unvanquished*. He talks about how Bayard Sartoris sleeps beside his black friend Ringo, and so forth, when they are boys, but at a certain age suddenly the difference between them becomes manifest and relationships change. That is what happened to Steven, it is just a part of this historical material. It wasn't meant to show the horrors of slavery, but simply the consciousness of the situation that comes at a certain point in life.

Gretlund The novel isn't really about the Battle of Nashville, is it?

Jones It is about the destruction of a way of life. I try to depict that life as best I can in the early stages of the book and in the comments of the memoirist. So it is about the wiping out of a world, and Steven's coming to consciousness about his difference from Dink, his black friend, is just a part of the consciousness of that world. I think of it overall as a rendition of a society that has vanished from the face of the earth. The War is mainly a vehicle. – I appreciated Fred Chappell's review of the book in which he ends by saying that I show the reason why Southerners' memories are so full of regret at the loss of this world, with its faults and its virtues and everything else, but still a world that seizes the imagination and certainly produced many lovely things.

PART III

The final section of the interview is on Jones's novel *Herod's Wife,* which was published in 2003. The telephone interview was added on January 4, 2003.

Gretlund — Why are the people in *Herod's Wife* so burdened by anxiety? Has the Lakepoint community become estranged from itself?

Jones — The loss by displacement of community in the real sense of the word is most openly symbolized by the change in the name of the town, from Loretta to Lakepoint. Before, presumably, there was a workable moral coherence. But this was drowned out and replaced by a population with no common past or *values* fully deserving of the name. This, as I see it, is generally typical of our time. Without a past, including a religious inheritance, choices are ill-defined, producing anxiety, confusion, and ultimately distrust.

Gretlund — Is there a deliberate parallel to the estrangement of the Heltons, a parallel between community conflict and domestic strain?

Jones — A parallel exists, I hope, between the community at large and the marriage of Hugh and Nora Helton. A ghost of the past haunts Hugh and so, with bitterness, his wife. It should be remembered that the word 'religion' has the root meaning of 're-binding.'

Gretlund — The 'new abortion clinic' and violent disagreement about it in Lakepoint are brought up, and you show racial tension in town. Cap Waters and young Qualls come to life but quickly disappear out of the novel. Were you tempted to dwell on abortion and racial issues?

Jones	The several instances of radical disagreement in the town (racial, religious, and otherwise) are there for the purpose of illustrating the general moral incoherence. Further development of any one of them individually would have defeated my over-all purpose in *Herod's Wife*.

Gretlund	Shouldn't we feel some compassion and pity for Nora Helton? Don't you share her doubts about Christian faith? Is she a victim of basic human curiosity about the sinful and forbidden, or is she simply evil?

Jones	Abstractly speaking, given the prevailing moral and spiritual climate, there is room for some compassion and pity for Nora. Bishop Wells puts it succinctly: "'Nothing' is the word. Our Word." But Nora's total acceptance of the bishop's despairing assertion, whether or not it inspires in the reader a sympathy for her, is an open invitation to the sprit of evil. For evil's personification, Satan, is after all a nihilist. Take him for real as a person or not, his destructive aura whatever its provenance is a presence in our world. And Nora is obsessed, or possessed, by this presence.

Gretlund	Are you considering writing new fiction at this time?

Jones	I am thinking about going back to my abandoned humorous novel "Tales of Dixie."

A MADISON JONES BIBLIOGRAPHY

Jan Nordby Gretlund and *Thomas Ærvold Bjerre*

BOOKS

The Innocent. New York: Harcourt, Brace, 1957. Novel. Br. ed. London: Secker & Warburg, 1957. New York: Popular Library, 1957, and 1971. Southern Classics Series: Nashville: J. S. Sanders & Company, 1993.

History of the Tennessee State Dental Association. Compiled by Thomas Davidson Dow. Nashville, Tenn.: Tenn. Dental Association, 1958. History.

Forest of the Night. New York: Harcourt, Brace, 1960. Novel. Br. ed. London: Eyre & Spottiswoode, 1961. New York: Popular Library, 1971.

A Buried Land. New York: Viking, 1963. Novel. Br. ed. London: Bodley Head, 1963. New York: Popular Library, 1971. Sag Harbor, N.Y.: Second Chance Press, 1987.

An Exile. New York: Viking, 1967. Novel. Br. ed. London: André Deutsch,1970. Republished as: *I Walk the Line.* New York: Popular Library, 1970. Br. paperback: Harmondsworth, Penguin, 1971. Dutch ed.: Wereld-Bibliotheek, 1972. Japanese ed. Kadokawa Shoten, 1972. Savannah, GA.: Frederic C. Beil, 1990; Illustrations by Dean Bornstein.

A Cry of Absence. New York: Crown, 1971. Novel. Br. ed. London: André Deutsch, 1972. New York: Pocket Books, 1972. Dutch ed.: Oniebook, 1978. Baton Rouge: Louisiana State University Press, 1989.

Passage through Gehenna. Baton Rouge & London: Louisiana State University Press, 1978. Novel.

Season of the Strangler. New York: Doubleday, 1982. Short Story Cycle. New York: Charter Books, 1983.

Last Things. Baton Rouge & London: Louisiana State University Press, 1989. Novel.

To the Winds. Atlanta, GA.: Longstreet Press, 1996. Novel.

Nashville 1864: The Dying of the Light. Nashville: J. S. Sanders & Company, 1997. Novel. New York: Penguin, 1999.

Herod's Wife. Tuscaloosa: The University of Alabama Press, 2003. Novel.

Short Fiction

"Dog Days." *Perspective* (Spring 1952): 78-94.

"The Homecoming." *Perspective* (Spring 1952): 135-148. Rpt. in *Best American Short Stories, 1953,* eds. Martha Foley & Joyce F. Hartman. Boston: Houghton, 1953, pp. 189-206.

"The Fugitives." *Sewanee Review* 62/2 (April-June, 1954): 271-291. Rpt. in *Craft and Vision,* ed. Andrew Lytle. New York: Delacorte Press, 1972. Also rpt. in *Stories of the Modern South,* eds. Benjamin Forkner & Patrick Samway S.J. New York: Bantam, 1978, pp. 165-182.

"The Cave." *Perspective* (Winter 1955): 187-196.

"Prologue." *Sewanee Review* 64/4 (Oct.-Dec. 1956): 615-631. From *The Innocent.*

"The New World." *Sewanee Review* 68/1 (Jan.-Mar. 1960): 100-117. From *Forest of the Night.*

"The Watery Grave." *Sewanee Review* 71/2 (Apr.-June 1963): 179-200. From *A Buried Land.*

An Exile. Sewanee Review 75/1 (Jan.-Mar.1967): 25-158. First publication of the novel.

"Home Is Where the Heart Is." *The Arlington Quarterly* 1 (Spring 1968): 12-69.

"A Modern Case." *Delta Review* 6 (July-Aug. 1969): 42-52, 72-75.

"The Family That Prays Together, Stays Together." *The Chattahoochee Review* 3/2 (Winter 1983): 1-35.

"A Beginning." *The Chattahoochee Review* 5/3 (Spring 1985): 84-98. Rpt. in *Homewords: A Book of Tennessee Writers*, ed. Douglas Paschall. Knoxville, TN. Tennessee Arts Commission and University of Tennessee Press, 1986, pp. 83-89. Became most of chp. 3 in *Last Things*.

"Zoo." *The Sewanee Review* 100/3 (Summer 1992): 347-365. Became chp. 5 of *To the Winds*.

"Rage." *That's What I Like (About the South) And Other New Southern Stories for the Nineties*, eds. George Garrett and Paul Ruffin. Columbia: University of South Carolina Press, 1993, pp. 192-209. From *Season of the Strangler*.

"Nashville 1864: The Dying of the Light." *The Chattahoochee Review* 17/3 (Spring 1997): 4-23. Story; from chps. 6, 7 and 8 of the novel.

"From *Nashville 1864: The Dying of the Light*." *Literary Nashville*, ed. Patrick Allen. Athens, GA.: Hill Street Press, 1999, pp. 273-285. From chps. 1 & 2 of *Nashville 1864*.

"Sim Denny." *The Cry of an Occasion: Fiction from the Fellowship of Southern Writers*, ed. Richard Bausch. Baton Rouge: Louisiana State University Press, 2001, pp. 82-94. From *Season of the Strangler*.

Essays and Reviews

"Recent Southern Fiction: A Panel Discussion." With Katherine Anne Porter, Flannery O'Connor, Caroline Gordon, and Louis D. Rubin. *Bulletin of Wesleyan College* [Macon, GA.] 41 (Jan. 1961): 1-6.

"The Novels of Robert Penn Warren." *South-Atlantic Quarterly* 72/4 (Autumn 1963): 488-498.

"*Do, Lord, Remember Me* by George Garrett." *Mississippi Quarterly* 19/2 (Spring 1966): 101.

"*North toward Home* by Willie Morris." *New York Times Book Review* (Oct. 22, 1967): 5.

"*The Liberation of Lord Byron Jones* by Jesse Hill Ford." *Mississippi Quarterly* 20/1 (Winter 1967): 61-64.

"*Dark Hills to Westward* by Harry M. Caudill." *New York Times Book Review* (July 13, 1969): 38.

"A Look at 'Mister McGregor'." *Mississippi Quarterly* 23/4 (Fall 1970): 363-370.

"*The Southern Tradition at Bay* by Richard Weaver." *Southern Humanities Review* 4/1 (Winter 1970): 92-93.

"*One Time, One Place* by Eudora Welty." *New York Times Book Review* (Nov. 21, 1971): 60, 62, 64.

"*South to a Very Old Place* by Albert Murray." *Book World, Washington Post* (Dec. 26, 1971): 11.

"*The Children of Pride* by Robert Manson Myers." *New York Times Book Review* (May 7, 1972): Pt. 2, p.1.

"*The Snare* by Elizabeth Spencer." *New York Times Book Review* (Dec. 17, 1972): 6.

"A Novel on the Situation of the Southern Jew: *The Covenant* by Paige Mitchell." *Book World, Washington Post* (May 1, 1973): B 4.

"Craft as Mirror." *Sewanee Review* 82/1 (Winter 1974): 179-189.

"Frederik Manfred: Parallels with Homer." *New York Times* (Feb. 16, 1975): VII 6.

"Fiction and Career: An Interview." *Ohio Valley Writers Project*. Murray State University Oral History Program, 1975.

"The Writer's Sense of Place." *South Dakota Review* 13/3 (Autumn 1975): 56-57.

"Variations on a Hawthorne Theme." *Studies in Short Fiction* 15 (Summer 1978): 277-283.

"Curtains for the Southern Renaissance." *Southern World* (March-April, 1979): 32-33.

"Cause for Wonder." *Flannery O'Connor Bulletin* 8 (Autumn 1979): 18-19.

"The Impulse to Fiction." *Southern Humanities Review* 14/3 (Summer 1980): 211-220.

"On *I'll Take My Stand*." *Mississippi Quarterly* 33/4 (Fall 1980): 455.

"Robert Penn Warren as Novelist." *A Southern Renascence Man: Views of Robert Penn Warren*, ed. Walter Edgar. Baton Rouge: Louisiana State University Press, 1984: 39-57.

"A Good Man's Predicament." *Southern Review* 20/4 (Fall 1984): 836-841. Reprinted in *"A Good Man Is Hard to Find": Flannery O'Connor.* Women Writers: Texts and Contexts, ed. Frederick Asals, New Brunswick, New Jersey, Rutgers University Press, 1993: 119-126.

"Andrew Lytle, Mentor." *The Chattahoochee Review* 8/4 (Summer 1988): 100-101.

"The Writer's Sense of Place." With Wallace Stegner, Rudolfo A. Anaya, Ross MacDonald, Thomas E. Sanders, and Robert Roripaugh. *South Dakota Review* 26/4 (Winter 1988): 93-120.

"Madison Jones." *Contemporary Authors: Autobiography Series*, vol 11., ed. Mark Zadrozny. Detroit: Gale Research (1990): 171-187.

"Foreword." *Literary Nashville*, ed. Patrick Allen. Athens, GA.: Hill Street Press, 1999, pp. vii-x.

"O'Connor and Current Fiction." *Flannery O'Connor: In Celebration of Genius*, ed. Sarah Gordon. Athens, GA.: Hill Street Press, 2000, pp. 57-64.

Reviews, Criticism & Biography

Anonymous. "South in Ferment." *Time* 69/8 (Feb. 25, 1957): 102.

Anonymous. "Madison Jones." *Contemporary Authors* 13/14, eds. James M. Ethridge & Barbara Kopala. Detroit: Gale Research (1965): 237.

Anonymous. "Books about the South." *Southern Living* 13 (Sept. 1978): 147. With a letter by Madison Jones.

Anonymous. "Jones, Madison (Percy, Jr.) 1925-," *Contemporary Authors* 7, New Revision Series, ed. Ann Evory. Detroit: Gale Research (1983): 252-257.

Anonymous. *"Nashville 1864: The Dying of the Light."* A review. *The Virginia Quarterly Review* 74/1 (Winter 1998): 22-28.

Bell, Madison Smartt. "Mister Jones: A Memoir." *The Chattahoochee Review* 17/1 (Fall 1996): 6-12.

Benson, Robert. "All Flinders Now." *Sewanee Review* 105/4 (Oct.-Dec., 1997): cxxii-cxxv. Review of *Nashville 1864: The Dying of the Light*.

Bickford, Alan Kent. *Innocents in Gehenna: Calvinism in the Novels of Madison Jones*. Ann Arbor, Mich.: University Microfilms, 1985.

Binding, Paul. "Madison Jones." *Separate Country: A Literary Journey through the American South*. New York & London, Paddington Press, 1979, pp. 57-68. Rev. ed.: Jackson: University Press of Mississippi, 1988, pp. 43-53.

Boozer, William. "*Season of the Strangler* by Madison Jones." *Nashville Banner* (April 11, 1982).

Bovenizer, David A. "*Nashville 1864: The Dying of the Light*: A Review." *Chronicles Magazine* (January 1998) p. 27.

Bradford, M. E. "Madison Jones." *Contemporary Novelists*, ed. Janus Vinson, 2nd ed. London: St. James Press, 1976, pp. 737-739.

Bradford, M. E. "Madison Jones." *The History of Southern Literature*, eds. Louis D. Rubin, Jr. et al. Baton Rouge: Louisiana State University Press, 1985, pp. 523-526.

Bradford, M.E. "Novel Is an Extended Parable." *The Dallas Morning News* (July 23, 1978). Review of *Passage through Gehenna*.

Brooker, Jewel Spears. "The Desolate Houses of Madison Jones's *A Cry of Absence*." *The Chattahoochee Review* 17/1 (Fall 1996): 82-89.

Brown, Ashley. "Experience in the West: Madison Jones's Immersion in History." *The Chattahoochee Review* 17/1 (Fall 1996): 67-73.

Brown, Jerry Elijah. "Madison Jones: *Passage through Gehenna*." *Southern Humanities Review* 13/4 (Fall 1979): 356-357.

Brown, Larry. "Chattanooga Nights." *The Chattahoochee Review* 17/1 (Fall 1996): 33-37. Rpt. in *Billy Ray's Farm*, by Larry Brown. Chapel Hill, N.C.: Algonquin Books of Chapel Hill, 2001, pp. 29-38.

Campbell, Don G. "Feeling the Backlash of Brutal Murders." *Los Angeles Times* (June 30, 1982): 10. Review of *Season of the Strangler*.

Cantinella, Joseph, "*A Cry of Absence* by Madison Jones." *Saturday Review* 54 (July 10, 1971): 28.

Caton, Bill. "Madison Jones." *Fighting Words: Words on Writing from 12 of the Heart of Dixie's Best Contemporary Authors*. Montgomery, Alabama: Black Belt, 1995, pp. 72-79.

Chappell, Fred. "Southern Psyche." *The News and Observer* (Raleigh N.C.), August 31, 1997, sec. G. Review of *Nashville 1864*.

Childers, Joanne McEvilley. "Madison Jones—Place/Person: The Effect of His Early Years on His Work." *The Chattahoochee Review* 17/1 (Fall 1996): 13-17.

Christopher, Gena. "Madison Jones Delivers Another Punchy Story." *Anniston Star* (Alabama) September 7, 2003. Review of *Herod's Wife*.

Cohen, Sandy. "Images of Allegory: Madison Jones's *Passage through Gehenna*." *South Atlantic Review* 53/1 (Jan. 1988): 67-81.

Cohen, Sandy. "Madison Jones." *Dictionary of Literary Biography* 152 (1989): 92-98.

Cohen, Sandy. "*Nashville 1864: The Dying of the Light*." A review. *Southern Humanities Review* 33/1 (Winter 1999): 107-109.

Cook, David. "*Nashville 1864: The Dying of the Light*." A review. *Southern Living* 32/7 (July 1997): 52.

Curley, Thomas. "The Tree of Knowledge of Good and Evil." *Commonweal* 65 (March 22, 1957): 642. Review of *The Innocent*.

Current-Garcia, Eugene. "*Forest of the Night* by Madison Jones." *Mississippi Quarterly* 13 (Winter 1960): 149-151.

Day, Daphne. Review of *Last Things*. *Southern Humanities Review* 25 (Spring, 1991): 194-196.

Finkle, Davis. Review of *Last Things*. *New York Times Book Review* (September 24, 1989): sec. 7, p. 48.

Garrett, George. "Good Medicine: Some Personal Notes on the Art and Life of Madison Jones." *The Chattahoochee Review* 17/1 (Fall 1996): 18-22.

Gretlund, Jan Nordby. "Madison Percy Jones." *First Printings of American Authors: Contributions toward Descriptive Checklists*, vol. 4. Detroit: Gale Research (1979): 231-232.

Gretlund, Jan Nordby. "Madison Jones: *Passage through Gehenna*." *South Carolina Review* 12/1 (Fall 1979): 70-71.

Gretlund, Jan Nordby. "Madison Jones: A Bibliography." *Bulletin of Bibliography* 39/3 (September 1982): 117-120.

Gretlund, Jan Nordby. "Madison Jones: An Interview." *Contemporary Authors* 7, New Revision Series, ed. Ann Evory. Detroit: Gale Research (1983): 252-257.

Gretlund, Jan Nordby. "Madison Jones: *Season of the Strangler*." *The Georgia Review* 37/1 (Spring 1983): 219-221.

Gretlund, Jan Nordby. "Novelists of the Third Phase of the Renaissance: Walker Percy, Madison Jones and Barry Hannah." Aspects du Sud Aujourd'hui. *Revue Francaise D'Etudes Americaines* 23 (Fevrier 1985): 13-24.

Gretlund, Jan Nordby. "The Last Agrarian: Madison Jones's Achievement." *The Southern Review* 22/3 (Summer, 1986): 478-488.

Gretlund, Jan Nordby. "Right Hand of the Devil." *South Carolina Review* 23 (Spring, 1991): 188-190. Review of *Last Things*.

Gretlund, Jan Nordby. "The Mosses of an Old Tree: Madison Jones's *To the Winds*." *The Chattahoochee Review* 17/1 (Fall 1996): 103-115.

Gretlund, Jan Nordby. "Traditional Life Falls by the Wayside in Madison Jones' Newest Novel." *The State*. Columbia, S.C. (July 7, 1996): F4. Review of *To the Winds*.

Gretlund, Jan Nordby. "Madison Jones's Last Southern Agrarians." *Frames of Southern Mind: Reflections on the Stoic, Bi-Racial & Existential South*. Odense University Press, 1998, pp. 45-56.

Gretlund, Jan Nordby. "Silencing the Voice of the Past in Southern Fiction," *Frames of Southern Mind: Reflections on the Stoic, Bi-Racial & Existential South*. Odense University Press, 1998, pp. 145-156. With a discussion of *Nashville 1864*.

Griffin, Carl H. and Alan Jackson. "Somewhere Outside of Auburn, Alabama: A Conversation with Madison Jones." *The Chattahoochee Review* 17/1 (Fall 1996): 116-139.

Hall, Wilson. "A Memory of Madison Jones: Teacher." *The Chattahoochee Review* 17/1 (Fall 1996): 27-32.

Hiers, John T. "Buried Graveyards: Warren's *Flood* and Jones's *A Buried Land*." *Essays in Literature* 2/1 (Spring 1975): 97-104.

Higgins, Fitzgerald. "*Season of the Strangler* by Madison Jones." *Grand Rapids Press* (Jan. 17, 1982): 15F.

Hoffman, William. "The Tempter Is always with Us." *The Chattahoochee Review* 17/1 (Fall 1996): 74-81

Jack, W.T. "Return to the Past." *New York Times Book Review* (Sept. 3, 1967): 22. Review of *An Exile*.

Jeffrey, David K. "Madison (Percy) Jones (1925-)." *Contemporary Fiction Writers of the South: A Bio-Bibliographical Sourcebook*, eds. Joseph M. Flora and Robert Bain. Westport, CT: Greenwood, 1993, pp. 261-266

Jeffrey, David K. and Donald R. Noble. "Madison Jones: An Interview." *The Southern Quarterly* 21/3 (Spring, 1983): 15-26.

Kirkpatrick, Smith. "*A Buried Land* by Madison Jones." *Sewanee Review* 71 (Fall 1963): 652-654.

Landess, Thomas H. "Preface." *The Innocent*. Nashville: J. S. Sanders & Company, 1993, pp. v-xii.

Leber, Michele. "*Nashville 1864: The Dying of the Light*." A review. *The Booklist* (Chicago) 93/18 (May 15, 1997): 1563.

Long, Grady M. "Shattering Climax." *Chattanooga Times* (Sept. 24, 1967): 24. Review of *An Exile*.

Loyd, Dennis. "Contemporary Writers." *Literature of Tennessee*, ed. Ray Willbanks. Macon, GA.: Mercer University Press, 1984, pp. 183-200.

Meeker, Richard K. "The Youngest Generation of Southern Fiction Writers." *Southern Writers: Appraisals in Our Time*, ed. R.C. Simonini. University Press of Virginia, 1964, pp. 168-170.

Michael, Marion C. "Madison Jones." *A Bibliographical Guide to the Study of Southern Literature*, ed. Louis D. Rubin. Baton Rouge, Louisiana State University Press, 1969, pp. 232-233.

Michael, Marion C. "Madison Percy Jones." *Southern Writers: A Biographical Dictionary*, eds. Robert Bain, Joseph M. Flora & Louis D. Rubin. Baton Rouge & London, Louisiana State University Press, 1979, pp. 256-257.

Mizener, Arthur. "Some Kinds of Modern Novel." *Sewanee Review* 69/1 (1961): 154-164.

Montgomery, Marion. "How to Get Here from There: A Tribute to Madison Jones on Our Passage through Gehenna." *The Chattahoochee Review*, 17/1 (Fall 1996): 43-51.

Murray, Michele. "Southern Guilt." *Commonweal* 77 (Aug. 9, 1963): 486-487. Review of *A Buried Land*.

Noble, Donald R. "'The World Would Be better off with a Sterner Conscience': A Talk with Madison Jones." *Society for Fine Arts Review* 4/2 (Summer 1982): 14-15.

O'Connor, Flannery. *The Habit of Being: Letters*, ed. Sally Fitzgerald. New York, Farrar, Straus & Giroux, 1979. *Passim*.

O'Rourke, William. "Madison Jones: *Passage through Gehenna*." *American Book Review* 2 (Oct. 1979): 24.

O'Rourke, William. "Clark Blaise and Madison Jones." *Signs of the Literary Times: Essays, Reviews, Profiles, 1970-1992*. Albany: State University of New York Press, 1993, pp. 109-111. Essay on *Passage through Gehenna*.

Parrill, William. "Jones Is Worth Keeping up with." *Nashville Tennessean* (Aug. 27, 1967): 12D. Review of *An Exile*.

Payne, David. "Notes From an Alabama Underground." *Washington Post: Book World* (Oct. 15, 1989): 4, 11. Review of *Last Things*.

Pearre, Howell. "Southern Novel Maintains Tradition." *Nashville Banner* (Aug. 25, 1967): 28. Review of *An Exile*.

Pierce, Ovid. "Perpetuating Stock Images about the South." *New York Times Book Review* (July 4, 1971): 7, 10. Review of *A Cry of Absence*.

Reeves, Garland. "The Struggles of Daily Life Are Jones' Latest Targets." *Birmingham News* (Sept.24, 1989). Review of *Last Things*.

Reisman, Rosemary M. Canfield, and Suzanne Booker-Canfield. "Madison Jones." *Contemporary Southern Men Fiction Writers: An Annotated Bibliography*. Lanham, Md.: Scarecrow, 1998, pp. 237-247.

Rice, William. *National Forum* 70 (Spring, 1990): 47. Review of *Last Things*.

Richardson, Kathleen. "Shades of Scarlett." *Des Moines Sunday Register* (March 14, 1982): 4C. Review of *Season of the Strangler*.

Rieben, Cynthia J. "*Nashville 1864: The Dying of the Light.*" A review. *School Library Journal* (New York) 44/1 (Jan. 1998): 136-138.

Riley, Carolyn. "Jones, Madison 1925-." *Contemporary Literary Criticism* 4, ed. Carolyn Riley. Detroit: Gale Research (1973): 262-263.

Rose, Charles. "Madison Jones and the Unleashed Will. A Review of *Season of the Strangler.*" *Southern Review* 18/3 (Summer 1982): 678-681.

Rubin, Jr., Louis D. "The Difficulties of Being a Southern Writer Today: Or, Getting Out from Under William Faulkner." *Journal of Southern History* 29 (1963): 486-494. Rpt. in *The Curious Death of the Novel: Essays in American Literature*. Baton Rouge: Louisiana State University Press, 1967, pp. 282-293.

Samway, Patrick H. Review of *Season of the Strangler*. *America* (May 29, 1982): 426.

Simpson, Lewis P. "A Good Writer's Predicament." *The Chattahoochee Review* 17/1 (Fall 1996): 57-66.

Simpson, Lewis P. "Southern Fiction." *Harvard Guide to Contemporary American Writing*, ed. Daniel Hoffman. Cambridge, Mass.: The Belknap Press, 1979, p. 185.

Slavick, William H. Review of *Passage through Gehenna*. *Commonweal* 108 (April 10, 1981): 221-222.

Smith, Lee. "On Madison Jones." *The Chattahoochee Review* 17/1 (Fall 1996): 90.

Spears, Monroe K. "A New Classic." *Sewanee Review* 80 (Winter 1972): 168-172.

Spears, Monroe K. "Madison's Humor." *The Chattahoochee Review* 17/1 (Fall 1996): 23-26.

Starr, William W. "*Season of the Strangler*: A Tale of a Town's People." *The State* (Columbia S.C.) (March 7, 1982).

Steinberg, Sybil. Review of *Last Things*. *Publishers Weekly* 236 (July 14, 1989): 59.

Steinberg, Sybil. Review of *To the Winds*. *Publishers Weekly* 243 (April 15, 1996): 50-51.

Steinberg, Sybil. Review of *Nashville 1864*. *Publishers Weekly* 244 (April 14, 1997): 56.

Stroud, Oxford. "Master of Psychological Drama Achieves Chilling Goal." *Atlanta Journal-Constitution* (March 7, 1982): H10. Review of *Season of the Strangler*.

Sullivan, Walter. "The Continuing Renascence: Southern Fiction in the Fifties." *South: Modern Southern Literature in Its Cultural Setting*, eds. Louis D. Rubin & Robert D. Jacobs. Westport, Conn., Greenwood Press, 1961, pp. 380-381.

Sullivan, Walter. "The New Faustus: The Southern Renascence and the Joycean Aesthetic." *Southern Fiction Today: Renascence and Beyond*, ed. George Core. University of Georgia Press, 1969, pp. 1-5. Rpt. in *Death by Melancholy: Essays on Modern Southern Fiction*, Baton Rouge, Louisiana State University Press, 1972, pp. 97-102.

Sullivan, Walter. A *Requiem for the Renascence. The State of Fiction in the Modern South*, University of Georgia Press, 1976, pp. xxiii-xxiv.

Sweat, Joseph. "Crises of Faith." *Nashville Scene*. November 20-26, 2003, p. 59. Review of *Herod's Wife*.

Troy, Judy. "Madison Jones." *The Chattahoochee Review* 17/1 (Fall 1996): 38-42.

Vauthier, Simone. "Gratuitous Hypothesis: A Reading of Madison Jones' *The Innocent*." *Recherches Anglaises et Americaines* 7 (1974): 191-219.

Walsh, William. "Unsung Writer Deserves Fame for *Last Things*." *The Atlanta Journal and the Atlanta Constitution* (Dec. 31, 1989): N8. Review of *Last Things*.

Walsh, William. "An Interview With Madison Jones." *Southern Humanities Review* 23/1 (Winter 1989): 39-51. Rpt. in *Speak So I Shall Know Thee: Interviews with Southern Writers*, ed. William Walsh. Jefferson, N.C.: McFarland & Co., 1990, pp. 146-156.

Walsh, William. "Madison Jones: Rising to the Level of ART." *The Chattahoochee Review* 17/1 (Fall 1996): 52-56.

Warren, Robert Penn. "A First Novel." *Sewanee Review* 65 (Spring 1957): 347-352. Review of *The Innocent*.

Watkins, Floyd C. *The Death of Art: Black and White in the Recent Southern Novel.* University of Georgia Press, 1970, pp. 45-46.

Wetzel, Donald. "Tale of a Dark Frontier." *New York Herald Tribune Book Review* (March 13, 1960): 10. Review of *Forest of the Night.*

Whittemore, Reed. "*A Cry of Absence* by Madison Jones." *New Republic* 164 (June 26, 1971): 29-30.

Winchell, Mark Royden. "Winesburg South." *The Sewanee Review* 91 (Winter 1983): xvi-xviii. Review of *Season of the Strangler.*

Wyllie, John Cook. "Guilt-Ridden Dixie," *Saturday Review* 40 (Feb. 23, 1957): 18. Review of *The Innocent.*

Yardley, Jonathan. Review of *A Cry of Absence. Partisan Review* 40/2 (Spring, 1973): 291-292.

Yardley, Jonathan. "Summer of Suspicion." *Washington Post Book World* (Jan. 27, 1982): B1, B-11. Review of *Season of the Strangler.*

Yardley, Jonathan. "Children's Confederacy: A Southern Boy Confronts the Civil War." *Washington Post* (May 28, 1997): C2. Review of *Nashville 1864.*

Young, Thomas Daniel. *Tennessee Writers.* Knoxville, University of Tennessee Press, 1981, p. 107.

Young, Thomas Daniel. "The Lady Ageth but Is Not Stoop'd: Agrarianism in Contemporary Southern Fiction." *Selected Essays, 1965-1985.* Baton Rouge: Louisiana State University Press, 1990, pp. 153-174. Essay on *A Buried Land.*

CONTRIBUTORS

Thomas Ærvold Bjerre is a graduate of the Center for American Studies, University of Southern Denmark, where he currently teaches American Literature. He is hoping to publish his thesis "Male Mississippi: Reading Masculinity and Violence in the Works of Barry Hannah, Larry Brown, and Lewis Nordan." He reviews American literature for Danish newspapers and has published essays on Barry Hannah and an interview with Lewis Nordan, both in the *Mississippi Quarterly*.

Jewel Spears Brooker is professor of comparative literature at Eckerd College in St. Petersburg, Florida. She is the author of *Mastery and Escape: T.S. Eliot and the Dialectic of Modernism* (1994) and co-author of *Reading the Waste Land: Modernism and the Limits of Interpretation* (1990). She has edited several books, including the MLA *Approaches to Teaching Eliot* and written numerous essays on modern literature. Her current projects include an edition of the letters between Katherine Anne Porter and Cleanth and Tinkum Brooks.

George Garrett, poet, novelist, essayist, dramatist, critic, translator, and scriptwriter, is the author of twenty-five books and editor of nineteen others. He is Henry Hoyns Professor of Creative Writing at the University of Virginia. He has received the T.S. Eliot Award of the Ingersoll Foundation and the Pen/Malamud Award for short fiction. He collected some of his new and old poems in *Days of Our Lives Lie in Fragments* (1998). He is widely known for his cycle of historical novels *Death of the Fox, The Succession,* and *Entered from the Sun* (Doubleday 1990). He collected some of his essays and reviews in *The Sorrows of Fat City* (1991), and his latest novels are *The King of Babylon Shall not Come Against You* (1996) and *Double Vision* (2004).

Richard Gray is professor in the Department of Literature at the University of Essex. He is the author of *The Literature of Memory: Mod-*

ern Writers of the American South; Writing the South: Ideas of an American Region (which won the C. Hugh Holman Award); *American Poetry of the Twentieth Century; The Life of William Faulkner: A Critical Biography;* and *Southern Aberrations: Writers of the American South and the Problems of Regionalism.* He has edited two anthologies of American poetry, two editions of the poetry of Edgar Allan Poe, a collection of original essays on American fiction, and a collection of essays on Robert Penn Warren. He has just completed editing a *Companion to the Literature and Culture of the American South* and writing *A History of American Literature.* A regular reviewer for various newspapers and journals, including the *Times Literary Supplement*, and formerly editor of the *Journal of American Studies*, he is the first specialist in American literature to be elected a Fellow of the British Academy.

Jan Nordby Gretlund is a lecturer in American Literature at the University of Southern Denmark at Odense. He is literary editor of the EAAS *Southern Studies Forum Newsletter.* He is the author of *Eudora Welty's Aesthetics of Place* and of *Frames of Southern Mind: Reflections on the Stoic, Bi-Racial & Existential South* (Odense, 1998). He has co-edited (with Tony Badger & Walter Edgar) *Southern Landscapes,* and (with Karl-Heinz Westarp) *Realist of Distances: Flannery O'Connor Revisited; Walker Percy: Novelist and Philosopher;* and *The Late Novels of Eudora Welty* (1998), and he has edited *The Southern State of Mind* (South Carolina, 1999) and "A Southern Issue" of *American Studies in Scandinavia* (33/2- 2001). He is co-editing a collection of essays on *Flannery O'Connor's Radical Reality.*

Madison Jones grew up in rural Tennessee, served in Korea, and has degrees from Vanderbilt and University of Florida. He has taught at University of Miami, Ohio, the University of Tennessee, and from 1956 at Auburn University, from 1968 as Professor of English and *Alumni* writer-in-residence and is at present Auburn University Writer-in-Residence, Emeritus. He was inducted into the Fellowship of Southern Writers in 1989. He is the author of eleven novels *The Innocent* (paper, Sanders 1993), *Forest of the Night* (1960), *A Buried Land* (1963), *An Exile* (made into the film *I Walk the Line*), *A Cry of Absence* (paper, LSUP

1995), *Passage through Gehenna* (1978), *Season of the Strangler* (1982), *Last Things* (1989), *To the Winds* (Longstreet 1996), and *Nashville 1864: The Dying of the Light* (paper, Penguin 1998) winner of the T.S. Eliot Award for Creative Writing. His new novel *Herod's Wife* appeared in 2003.

Lewis A. Lawson is professor emeritus of English at the University of Maryland, where he taught from 1963. With a strong interest in modern Southern literature he has written essays on Southern writers, particularly on William Faulkner, William Styron, Flannery O'Connor, and Walker Percy. With Melvin J. Friedman he edited *The Added Dimension: The Art and Mind of Flannery O'Connor* (1966). He is the author of *Another Generation: Southern Fiction Since World War II* (U.P. Mississippi, 1984), his *Wheeler's Last Raid,* a Civil War history, was published in 1986. With Victor A. Kramer he has edited *Conversations with Walker Percy* and *More Conversations with Walker Percy* (1985 & 1993). He published his first series of essays on Walker Percy, *Following Percy,* in 1988 and the second series as *Still Following Percy* in 1996. He is publishing *A Gorgon's Mask: The Mother in Thomas Mann's Fiction* in 2005.

David Madden is the Donald and Velvia Crumbley Professor of Creative Writing at Louisiana State University, where he was writer-in-residence 1968-92. He is the founder of The United States Civil War Center, which he directed 1992-99. He has written and edited numerous critical studies and scholarly books on the art of writing and a host of textbooks for creative writing and literature courses. He has written two short-story collections and eight novels including *Cassandra Singing* (1969); *Bijou* (1974); *The Suicide's Wife* (1978), perhaps his best-known novel; *The New Orleans of Possibilities* (stories, 1982); and *Sharpshooter*(1996). He has edited *Beyond the Battlefield: The Ordinary Life and Extraordinary Times of the Civil War Soldier* (2000). He is working on a novel set in London during the 1666 plague and fire.

Hans H. Skei is professor of comparative literature at the University of Oslo in Norway. He has published articles on a number of Southern writers, among them Shelby Foote, Mary Chesnut, Eudora Welty, and Flannery O'Connor. He is the author of *William Faulkner: The*

Short Story Career (1981) and *Willam Faulkner: The Novelist as Short Story Writer* (1984). He is also the author of *Reading Faulkner's Best Short Stories* (1999). He has translated Faulkner's Snopes trilogy into Norwegian and was the editor of the *Yearbook of Norwegian Literary Scholarship* 1989-2002. He is the editor of *William Faulkner's Short Fiction: An International Symposium* (1997), and he is on the editorial board of *The Faulkner Journal*.

INDEX

Alabama 16, 74, 93-109, 160
Andersen, Hans Christian 27
Anderson, Sherwood
   Winesburg, Ohio 16, 98
Arkansas 160
Atreus, House of 74
Auburn University 8

Bell, Madison Smartt 7, 138
Bible, the 26, 40, 42, 43, 45, 65, 74, 79, 83, 85, 90, 159
Bjerre, Thomas Ærvold 184-96, 197
Botticelli, Alessandro "Birth of Venus" 46
Bovenizer, David 180
Bradbury, John M. 11
Bradford, M. E. 64, 139
Brooker, Jewel Spears 14, 71-92, 197
Brown, Ashley 7, 64, 67
Brown, Larry 7
Brown vs. Board of Education 75, 89

Capote, Truman 169-70
Chattahoochee Review, The 64, 179
Chappell, Fred 179, 181
Chicago Tribune 173
Civil War 16, 20-21, 26, 71, 73, 76-77, 81-82, 88, 99, 105-106, 125-39, 178-81

Clinton, William Jefferson 69
Coleridge, Samuel Taylor
   "The Rime of the Ancient Mariner" 110
Confederacy, The 20, 74-75, 77
Conrad, Joseph 85
Contemporary Authors: Autobiography Series 61, 63, 65
Core, George 64
Creed, Barbara 59 n2, n5

Davidson, Donald 8, 9, 29, 63, 168
Delta Review 178
Dickey, James
   Deliverance 13
Dickinson, Emily
   "One need not be a Chamber" 83
Dostoevsky, Fedor Mikhailovich 86
Dowd, Maureen 69
Dreiser, Theodore
   An American Tragedy 170

Eliot, T. S. 7, 24, 178

Faulkner, William 7, 69, 77, 125, 145, 158, 168
   Absalom, Absalom! 125
   "A Rose for Emily" 73

Go Down, Moses 16, 47, 103
Sanctuary 153
"Spotted Horses" 114
The Sound and the Fury 73
The Unvanquished 126, 132, 138, 181
Foote, Shelby 126
Ford, Jesse Hill 139
Frankenheimer, John 7, 13
Freud, Sigmund
   "Interpretation of Dreams" 35
   "Leonardo da Vinci" 38, 46, 48-49
   "The Uncanny" 32-60
   "Three Essays" 47
   "Universal Tendency" 39
Fugitives, The 69, 168

Garland, Judy 62
Garrett, George 7, 11, 61-70, 197
Girard, René 75, 88-89
   Violence and the Sacred 71-73
   The Scapegoat 71, 76, 89-90
Glasgow, Ellen 125
   Barren Ground 44
Gordon, Caroline 126
Grant, Ulysses S.
   Personal Memoirs 138
Gray, Richard 22, 143-57, 197-98
Gray, Zane 25
Gretlund, Jan Nordby 7-23, 110-24, 158-83, 184-96, 198
Grimm Brothers 27

Harpe Brothers 11, 66, 162-63
Hawthorne, Nathaniel 173

Hemingway, Ernest
   Francis Macomber 16
Henry II 85
History of Southern Literature 64
Hoffman, William 7

Ingram, Forrest L.
   Representative Short Story Cycles 95
Ingersoll Foundation 24

James, Henry 170-71
   "The Turn of the Screw" 149
Jefferson, Thomas 9, 66, 163
Johnston, Mary 126
Jones, Madison 24-31, 140-42, 158-183, 198-99
Family background: 24-31, 110, 159, 161, 169, 172, 174
Ideas:
   Abortion 22, 168, 182-83
   Agrarianism 7, 8-9, 19, 23, 29, 31, 110-24, 168
   Civil Rights 12, 14-15, 16, 71-92, 125, 139
   Drugs 18
   Evil 15, 18, 19, 22, 31, 66-67, 106, 117, 120, 147-57, 161, 167, 173, 183
   Family, the 71-92, 110-24, 175-77
   Nihilism 183
   Political Correctness 19-20, 141-42
   Poverty 110-24
   Race 20-22, 71-92, 97, 99-101,

103, 107, 128-34, 140-42, 146-48, 166, 180-81, 182-83
Religion   121-22, 143-57, 159-60, 172, 182, 183
Religious Fundamentalism   15, 18, 21-22, 24, 159-60
Slavery   20-21, 128-34, 141-42, 180-81
Southern Past, the   17, 20, 21, 71-92, 125-39, 144, 165-66, 176, 180-81
Violence   168
Works:
   A Buried Land   11-12, 15, 65, 93, 110, 139, 144, 163-64
   A Cry of Absence   13-15, 63-64, 65, 71-92, 93, 125, 139, 165-66, 171
   An Exile   7, 13, 63, 65, 125, 139, 164
      I Walk the Line (film)   13, 63, 164
   Forest of the Night   11, 15, 61-70, 139, 162-63, 166, 168
   Herod's Wife   21-22, 143-57, 158, 182-83
   Last Things   17-18, 113, 171-73
   Nashville 1864   16-17, 19-21, 64, 71, 125-39, 140-42, 178-81
   Passage through Gehenna   15, 17, 65, 139, 158, 160, 164, 166-69, 171, 180
   Season of the Strangler   15-16, 93-109, 170-71, 178, 179
      "Familiar Spirit"   178
   "Tales of Dixie"   12-13, 164-65,
166, 183
The Innocent   9-10, 17, 29-31, 32-60, 63, 65, 71, 110, 139, 158-59, 161-63, 169
"The Red Bird"   8
To the Winds   13, 19, 110-24, 174-77
Style and technique   17, 19, 22-23, 73, 93-95, 107-108, 111, 114, 134-39, 140-42, 156-57, 168-69, 169-70, 170-71, 172-73, 177, 179-80, 183

Kirkus Reviews   178
Kristeva, Julia   59 n2

Laclos, Pierre Choderlos de
   Les Liaisons dangereuses   166
Lawson, Lewis A.   10, 32-60, 199
Lewinsky, Monica   69
Library Journal   62
Louisiana State University
   Press   171
Lundén, Rolf
   United Stories of America   95-96
Luscher, Robert   95
Lytle, Andrew   8, 9, 29, 63, 64, 126, 168

Madden, David   7, 20, 125-39, 140-42, 199
   Sharpshooter   126, 132
Mailer, Norman   169-70
Mann, Susan Garland
   The Short Story Cycle   95
Marlowe, Christopher   25

Mèrimèe, Prosper
   Carmen   13
Miami University, OH   8
Mississippi   12, 165
Mitchell, Margaret   126
Mizener, Arthur   64
Molière   69
Montgomery, Marion   7

Natchez Trace, The   11, 162
Newsweek   173
New York Times Book Review   63, 69, 173
Nietzsche, Friedrich Wilhelm   17

O'Connor, Flannery   7, 12, 15, 63, 64, 122
   The Habit of Being   169
Oresteia, The   74

Paine, Thomas   163
Peck, Gregory   13, 63, 164
Percy, Walker   64
Perspective   8
Poe, Edgar Allan   18, 143, 152
Publishers Weekly   178

Ransom, John Crowe   9
Rousseau, Jean Jacques   9, 163
Rover Boys, The   25
Rubin, Louis D., Jr.   64

Sartre, Jean Paul
   Being and Nothingness   91
Scott, Evelyn   126
Sewanee Review   8, 64, 114

Shakespeare, William   168
Simpson, Lewis P.   7
Skei, Hans H.   17, 93-109, 199-200
Smith, Lee   7
Spears, Monroe K.   7, 13, 63, 64, 166
Spencer, Elizabeth   64
Styron, William   7, 180
Sullivan, Walter   63, 64-65

Tarzan   25
Tate, Allen   9, 63, 125
   The Fathers   126, 132
Taylor, Peter   64
Tennessee   15, 34, 66, 74, 159, 170, 174, 176
   Cheatham County   8, 110
   Sycamore Creek   27
   Tennessee Valley Authority   11, 144, 163
   Tennessee Walking Horse   25, 28
Thomas à Becket   85
Thomas, Dylan
   "Fern Hill"   78
Time Magazine   62, 173
Tolstoy, Lev Nikolaevich   143
Twain, Mark
   Huck Finn   19, 111, 116-117, 123
   Huckleberry Finn   125

University of Florida   8, 29, 168
University of Tennessee   8
Updike, John   63, 180

Vanderbilt University   8, 29, 168
Vauthier, Simone   32, 43
Vietnam War   165
Virginia Quarterly Review   65

Wagner, Richard   17
Warren, Robert Penn   7, 9, 10, 170-71
   All the King's Men   125

Watkins, Sam
   Company Aytch   138
Welty, Eudora   64
   The Golden Apples   16
Wizard of Oz   62
Wolfe, Tom   69, 169-70
Wordsworth, William   26

Yardley, Jonathan   178-79

ACKNOWLEDGEMENTS

Publication was made possible by grants from the Humanities Publication Council of the University of Southern Denmark and The Danish Research Council for the Humanities.

For research time and support the editor is grateful to the Center for American Studies and the Center for English, University of Southern Denmark; the English Department and The Library, University of South Carolina Beaufort; and the Institute for Southern Studies, University of South Carolina. The editor thanks Lila N. Meeks, David E. Nye, Curt Richter, and Karl-Heinz Westarp for their help and friendship.

The essays by Jewel Spears Brooker and Jan Nordby Gretlund have appeared in shorter version in *The Chattahoochee Review* vol. 17/1 (Fall 1996), a special issue on Madison Jones.

The first part of Jan Nordby Gretlund's interview with Madison Jones appeared in *Contemporary Authors* vol. 7, New Revision Series, 1983.

"A Madison Jones Bibliography" has its point of departure in Jan Nordby Gretlund's "Madison Jones: A Bibliography," *Bulletin of Bibliography* vol. 39/3 (Sep. 1982).

Cover photograph of Madison Jones © Curt Richter Photography. Used with permission.